Articulating Change
in the "Last Unknown"

Studies in the Ethnographic Imagination

John Comaroff, Pierre Bourdieu, and Maurice Bloch, *Series Editors*

ARTICULATING
CHANGE
in the
"LAST
UNKNOWN"

FREDERICK K. ERRINGTON
DEBORAH B. GEWERTZ

1995

Westview Press
Boulder • San Francisco • Oxford

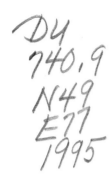

Copyright © 1995 by Westview Press, Inc.

Published in 1995 in the United States of America by Westview Press, Inc., 5500 Central Avenue, Boulder, Colorado 80301-2877, and in the United Kingdom by Westview Press, 12 Hid's Copse Road, Cumnor Hill, Oxford OX2 9JJ

Library of Congress Cataloging-in-Publication Data
Errington, Frederick Karl.
   Articulating change in the "last unknown" / Frederick K. Errington
and Deborah B. Gewertz.
      p.   cm.
   Chiefly a collection of previously published material.
   Includes bibliographical references (p.   ).
   ISBN 0-8133-2453-X.—ISBN 0-8133-2454-8 (pbk.)
   1. East New Britain Province (Papua New Guinea)   I. Gewertz,
Deborah B., 1948–   . II. Title.
DU740.9.N49E77   1995
995.8'5—dc20   94-45532
                                                                                                          CIP

Printed and bound in the United States of America

The paper used in this publication meets the requirements of the American National Standard for Permanence of Paper for Printed Library Materials Z39.48-1984.

10   9   8   7   6   5   4   3   2   1

To Wilson Tovalaun

Contents

Illustrations

Maps

Photographs

Preface and Acknowledgments

We each feel privileged to have been able to do long-term fieldwork in two separate parts of Papua New Guinea: in the East Sepik Province among the Chambri and their neighbors and, as the basis for this book, in the East New Britain Province among the Karavarans and other Duke of York Islanders. Some time ago, Fred joined Deborah in the work she had begun in 1974 in the Sepik, and more recently, Deborah joined Fred in the work he had begun in 1968, and continued in 1972, in the Duke of York Islands. Through this collaboration, we have been able to develop some firsthand (though still, of course, limited) sense of Papua New Guinea's great cultural diversity. Indeed, Karavar proved very different from Chambri in many respects, not the least of which was a significantly distinct colonial history. But in one important respect the two places were the same. In both, people were remarkably generous to us. They took us in and taught us about their worlds. However, since this book is primarily about Karavar, we begin it by directing our thanks to many friends and teachers there. There is one, moreover, to whom we wish at the outset to express our particular gratitude: Wilson Tovalaun, our friend and collaborator and one of the most civil, patient, intelligent men we have known.

Fred had long wished to return to Karavar after his 1972 research there, especially to see Wilson (who had never been much of a correspondent). Initially he was caught up in other research, but eventually his return was delayed by the East New Britain provincial government.

In 1983, we were denied research visas because Fred, it seemed, was deemed a political threat: For years Karavarans had been flouting government directives, and it was feared Fred's visit might fuel their resistance. Karavarans had, in fact, previously used Fred's presence as justification for recalcitrance—including nonpayment of taxes—claiming that he had advised them to do this or that. Although the Karavarans had frequently discussed their interests and aspirations with Fred and he had often told them what he thought, many of their claims about his advice had been shaped more by their ongoing strategies than by what he had actually said. In any case, the provincial government had decided that Karavarans could be more readily controlled if Fred was kept away. We were unable to alter this decision.

By 1991, circumstances had changed and our renewed request to visit Karavar was granted. After all, Karavarans had the previous year begun to pay taxes. Fred, now (somewhat!) more advanced in years, especially looked forward to returning to the place where he had begun his career as a young anthropologist: Both he and the discipline itself had greatly changed since 1968. And Deborah felt that she had worked in the Sepik long enough and very much wanted an ethnographic contrast. Moreover, we both were interested for political reasons in working among people who had for so long been obdurate in asserting their identity and worth when dealing with colonial and postcolonial powers.

As we stated in a grant proposal, we wanted to study the long-term uses and effects that an indigenous shell money might have had in contributing to this obduracy. (See Chapter 2, in particular.) What we had not anticipated was that our visit to Papua New Guinea would coincide with the countrywide gearing up for national parliamentary elections. In part, through the effects these national elections were having on local life, we found ourselves bringing our concern with history and identity to bear on a number of specific events—contexts—that were proving compelling to local people. These contexts struck us as rhetorically thick, as ones in which local people, frequently with passion, sought to define themselves and their interests, often with respect to national political leaders and issues. Indeed, with the exception of the first chapter, which provides a general background for the long-term Karavaran struggles to achieve identity and worth, each of the chapters is about one such context and its historical grounding.

*   *   *

Prior to our joint field research on Karavar Island in 1991, Fred made two trips to the Duke of York Islands. In 1968, in collaboration with Shelly Errington, he spent a year on Karavar Island under a grant from the National Institute of Mental Health; in 1972, he spent four months on Karavar, sponsored by a Crary Summer Fellowship from Amherst College. He expresses gratitude to each of these institutions. We are also grateful to the granting agencies that supported our four months on Karavar in 1991. Fred received a grant-in-aid from the American Council of Learned Societies and a faculty research fellowship from Mount Holyoke College. Deborah received a faculty research grant from Amherst College. These grants also enabled us to engage in two months of historical research in Papua New Guinea and Australia. We thank our Papua New Guinea colleagues at the National Archives and University of Papua New Guinea for their assistance. To Joe Nom of the university's New Guinea collection and to Tom Barker, Marta Rohatynskyj, and Karolus Walagat, formerly of the East New Britain provincial government, we send a special thanks. In Australia, we worked primarily at the Mitchell Library in Sydney and at the National Archives in Canberra. Librarians at both of these institutions were very helpful. In addition, we thank our friends and colleagues at the Research School of Pacific Studies at the Australian National University—particularly Jim Fox and Michael Young—for facilitating our stay in Canberra by appointing us visiting fellows. And we wish to thank friends and colleagues for advising us and for reading and commenting on parts of this book: Alan Babb, John Barker, Aletta Biersack, Don Brenneis, Paula Brown, James Carrier, Ed Casey, Dorothy and David Counts, Jan Dizard, Jesse Dizard, Jane Fajans, Robert Foster, Kris Fossum, Jerome Himmelstein, Janet Gyatso, Dan Jorgensen, Amy Kaplan, Henry Landi, Monty Lindstrom, Kellie Masterson, Ron May, Nancy McDowell, Mark Mosko, Jane Nadel-Klein, Donald Pitkin, Anton Ploeg, Jim Roscoe, Peter Sack, and Margaret Willson. We once again thank Carolyn Errington for her close reading of the entire manuscript and her many editorial suggestions.

Finally, we want our readers to know that in this book, as in all of our writings, the order in which our names appear as authors should not belie the equality of our collaboration.

Frederick K. Errington
Deborah B. Gewertz

Introduction

Neither Shattered Eden nor Inflexible Tradition — A Hundred Years of Entanglement in East New Britain

THE CHAPTERS IN this book concern the social and cultural changes that have occurred among people living on (or near) the small Pacific island of Karavar during the century after Europeans arrived on their shores. (See Maps 1 and 2.) These changes have led Karavarans to wonder about—and to assert—their identity and worth within contemporary Papua New Guinea. Read collectively, the chapters illuminate our topic in a way they cannot when read singly. Together they elucidate the complex problem of Karavarans' increasing preoccupation with who they were as one of the many linguistic and cultural groups that composed a developing country striving to create national coherence. (By some estimates, Papua New Guinea's 1993 population of 4.3 million was divided into over 700 such groups.)

By compiling this cluster of inquiries into how this preoccupation has played out in various social contexts within a rather small place, we have endeavored to make good use of the particular strengths of anthropology. We hope to make *grounded* sense of how these people have actually lived with and engaged in some of the rather large and widely compelling issues of our time (cf. Rebel 1989), issues pertaining to ethnic diversity and the development of national unity.[1] We wish, in other words, to present a historical and ethnographic analysis that, both in its fine grain and in its scope, does some justice to the complexity and significance of change in a colonial and postcolonial world. We intend this collection to convey, thus, diverse aspects of the continually changing circumstances whereby people—often differing in their inter-

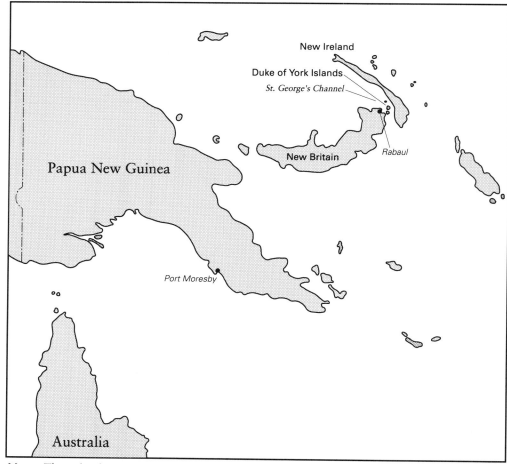

Map 1 The Duke of York Islands within Papua New Guinea

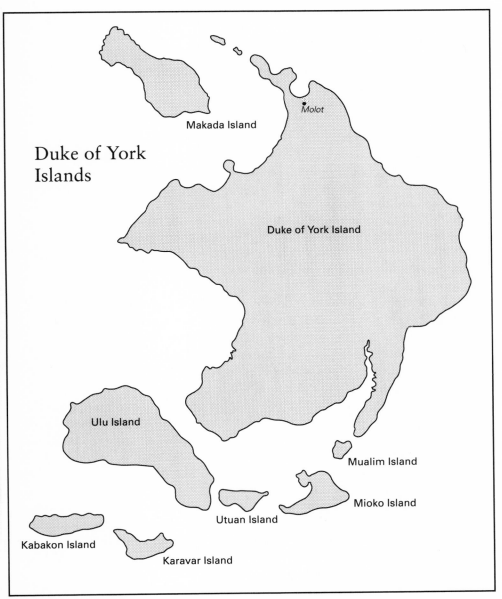

Map 2 The Duke of York Islands

ests and resources—have asserted, affirmed, contested, and ignored claims about who they were (and were not) and who they wished to be.[2]

MISPERCEPTIONS OF CHANGE:
TWO PREVAILING WESTERN MODELS

In writing this book, we have tried to address the general student as well as the professional anthropologist. For example, it might be useful in teaching an anthropological perspective in American classrooms, where we have frequently encountered misperceptions about the processes of change. Each chapter conveys a perspective that simultaneously makes both "others" and "ourselves" more understandable—more readily comparable—as culturally constructed, historically contingent, and mutually determinative. In addition, all of the chapters are designed to counter two rather widely held (and complexly related) Western models that importantly contribute to misperceptions about the kinds of changes that happened to and were precipitated by people such as Karavarans as the result of long and extensive European contact.

Indeed, one purpose of the book is to portray the course of social and cultural change among Karavarans and their neighbors as to confound—to complicate—certain Western conventional wisdom concerning how these apparently remote people got to be as they were and what they wanted to be in the future. We do this in the interests of both empirical accuracy and political efficacy. We complicate in order to elucidate because we want students (and others) not only to get the story relatively right but also to recognize the consequences of getting it wrong. Simplified explanations—certainly those of the sort we wish to counter here—often misrepresent the capacities and interests of such people to shape their own lives even under adverse circumstances. Such misrepresentations make it easier for "us" (those of the "first world") to disregard local ("third" and "fourth" world) aspirations, including those that focus on establishing identity and worth. These misrepresentations also make it easier for us to discount the consequences of our own actions so as to evade our own historically, as well as currently, engendered responsibilities.[3]

We do not trace the historical origins or the determinants of the contemporary models we wish to complicate; it is, however, important to realize that they and (as we shall see in the concluding chapter) the practical applications derived from them have long been available in Western tradition as *possible* explanations of change. The first model, for example, might be applied to, or seen as implicit in, understanding the fall of Adam and Eve from Paradise as well as the consequences of the settlement of the New World. Perhaps its most presently influential manifestation, and the manifestation we particularly wish to confront, underlies the plot of the recent popular film *The Gods Must Be Crazy* (Uys 1980). In this film, members of a small and isolated African group of hunter-gatherers became disoriented to the point of losing their social viability and cultural integrity when a (mere) Coca Cola bottle—an item of which they had been unaware—fell from an airplane into their midst. According to this model, which might be called the myth of the fragile Eden, change among "remote" peoples is undesirable and occurs all too easily; it is thereby likely to be demoralizing, catastrophic, and virtually inevitable.[4]

The second model has also long been available within Western thought as an explanation of change. Still broadly used (at least outside anthropology) to account for human diversity, it was initially applied by scientists in the nineteenth century to explain the relationship between "us" and many contemporary non-Westerners: "We" were seen as having progressed and "they" as having remained "frozen in time," as essentially static renditions of our former and simpler selves. This model has also been employed to account for underdevelopment. In literature ranging from Peace Corps documents to influential writings by former U.S. assistant secretary of state W. W. Rostow, (1971), "primitives" have been depicted as clinging to their backward and superstitious ways unless compelled or strongly encouraged to embrace the beneficial social and technological forces of modernity. Quite blatantly—and again, in the form we most wish to confront—this model was used by an Italian tourist depicted in the recent film *Cannibal Tours* (O'Rourke 1987) to argue about the nature of change that had to come to Papua New Guinea if "vegetating" locals were to progress. He asserted that well-dressed tourists could play important roles by inspiring locals to engage in hard work so as to emulate them. According to this model, which might be called the myth of the inflexible tradition, change among "remote" peoples is desirable but difficult to effect unless great and transforming pressure is applied; it is thereby likely to be either all or nothing.

Thus, in the expectations of many of our students (and others), on the one hand, the changes experienced by Karavarans over the past hundred years might well have left them shattered following the tragic, immediate, and essentially unavoidable devastation of their beautiful and vulnerable traditions; on the other hand, such changes might either have had little effect, with the Karavarans remaining obdurately backward, or they might have had great effect, with the Karavarans catapulted into (a better) modernity. But neither outcome has, in fact, been the case. Moreover, although the impulses that prompt each expectation might be quite different, the political consequences are probably similar in that people like Karavarans are denied equality with ourselves. In the case of either expectation, Karavarans are regarded as largely incapable of determining and pursing their own interests and thus as having little positive effect on the world. This, in turn, means that they are almost necessarily, if not appropriately, caught up in processes largely of "our" determination. Consequently—and this is an important political consequence of getting it wrong—we are led to believe there is little we can or should do except perhaps continue to inspire them (with our nice clothes) or transform them into our image or otherwise pursue our own objectives without taking theirs into account.

It is crucial, therefore, to counter these two models of change (the fragile Eden and the inflexible tradition) if we are to get things relatively right: if we are to make any accurate sense of the changes that have led Karavarans to be concerned about their identity and worth within the nation of Papua New Guinea; if we are to know how politically to appraise local struggles concerning identity and worth—to appraise, for example, whose interests they were likely to have served; and, moreover, if we are to gain any understanding of the large issues their situation reflects, that is, ethnic identity and the development of national unity. Making accurate sense of the changes so as to get things relatively right is only possible within a historically grounded ethnography of systemic interaction, one that takes into account, as does each of the chapters here, the changing relationship among the Karavarans and their neighbors—both indigenous and European.[5]

Getting things relatively right means, thus, recognizing that the interactions of the world are often much more complex than either of the previously described models of change. First, the Western presence was not unidimensional and uniform in its consequences (cf. Ortner 1984; Comaroff 1989). As our chapters make clear, the Europeans who arrived on Karavaran shores (and elsewhere in Papua New Guinea) included different kinds of people—missionaries, traders, planters, government officials, anthropologists—with different kinds of interests and different kinds of effects. Moreover, Karavarans and their neighbors were not passive in their encounters with these intruders. Often resilient in the face of their intruders' expectations, if not demands, Karavarans have long engaged Europeans in acts of resistance, differentiation, and sometimes, qualified emulation. Far from experiencing devastating collapse or all-or-nothing change, Karavarans have often shrewdly and forcefully negotiated with Europeans in various ways at various times during the past century. As active agents in the construction of their history,

Karavarans have carried out negotiations that significantly affected the system in which the interaction with Europeans was taking place. In other words, this colonial (and postcolonial) history—the history that has provided the context for recent and ongoing struggles over identity and worth in the emerging nation of Papua New Guinea—must be understood as mutually constructed.

It would, however, also be misleadingly romantic not to recognize that this history has had as its axis a crucially important power differential. The colonists came with the might and the intent to conquer—to convert, to extract, to order—and their wishes did assume a far greater significance in the lives of Karavarans than Karavaran wishes in theirs. We return here to our concern with the political importance of getting it right. To put it bluntly, we think the privileged of the "first" world blameworthy if they do not, at the very least, commit themselves to thinking through systemic interconnections: They must commit themselves to understanding the political relationships that have effected and informed our very complex, culturally constructed, historically contingent, and mutually determinative world so as to avoid reproducing past power differentials.[6]

We mean our book to facilitate this endeavor and think our focus on Papua New Guinea particularly germane.[7] This is so in part because many of our students (and others) would find it comfortable to think of their models of the fragile Eden and the inflexible tradition as especially applicable to this "last unknown."[8] (For instance, recent tourist literature about the country used the phrase "virtually untouched by Western ways"; we object to this not because we think that Papua New Guineans had already become thoroughly Western but because such language denies that Papua New Guineans existed as negotiators within a world system where the West and Western tourists played significant roles.) In addition, the story about Papua New Guinea we tell in our chapters contributes to this endeavor not only because the circumstances there confound simplistic models of change but also because these circumstances involved changes of a particularly informative sort.

HISTORICAL BACKGROUND

Although Karavarans have had among the longest colonial histories of Papua New Guinea peoples, their significant encounters with the European presence occurred relatively recently, in the late nineteenth century. This presence precipitated changes that were sometimes dramatic, frequently intense, and often indelible. That they occurred within a relatively brief time also means that crucial processes concerning colonial and (of course) postcolonial changes could be remembered and related to investigators with considerable clarity. (Indeed, in some parts of the country where "first contact" occurred later, these processes were described to recent investigators by eyewitnesses.) Moreover, these signal changes have also occurred in a context of great cultural pluralism. Thus, the peculiarities of this postcontact history—its brevity, intensity, and pluralistic context—facilitate insight into the processes that have both generated a new nation and continued to sustain contention among its culturally diverse members about their roles and current worth within that nation.

From the perspective of many of the 365 people living on Karavar in 1991,[9] these signal changes began in 1875 with a "first contact" with the Reverend George Brown and his Fijian missionary assistants, who had rounded the Duke of York Islands in his ship, the *John Wesley,* in search of an appropriate location for a Methodist mission station.[10] Sailing up St. George's Channel, past these islands fringed by coral reefs and white sand beaches, he must have been within sight of Karavar, the southernmost of this group, an island about a mile long and less than a half-mile wide (see Maps 1 and 2). Although Karavar and some of its most immediate neighbors had attractive harbors, Brown chose to land and settle at Molot. It was located on a fine harbor as well as on the largest and most heavily populated of the islands. Brown's choice to begin his missionary efforts in the Duke of York Islands was a strategic one: From his newly constructed mission station at Molot, he could bring the Word not only to the people in these relatively small places but also to those on the much larger islands of New Ireland and New Britain, which flanked the Duke of York group on either side of St. George's Channel. In particular, he was interested in pursuing mission work among the Tolai of the adjacent Gazelle Peninsula of New Britain. Indeed, he soon shifted his primary focus from the Duke of York Islanders to these more populous but culturally similar Tolai neighbors. (Both, for instance, spoke closely related [Austronesian] languages.)

Brown's was, however, only one of the European enterprises then operating in the area. In fact, ships from all over Europe, though primarily from England and Germany, had for some time been visiting this region regularly in search of trochus, tortoiseshell, and indigenously produced copra. Trading continued to expand, and with it, increasing numbers of European became residents. Thus by the early 1880s, missionaries were not the only exogenous presence in the Duke of York Islands. Two European trading companies, for example, operated from the island of Mioko—each of which employed, in addition to locals, Europeans, Malays, and Filipinos. After some wrangling among colonial powers, formal German control was soon established throughout the area of what became known as New Guinea. Karavar was briefly the headquarters of the initial colonial administration with over twenty Germans living there in 1884. (In 1884 New Guinea was a protectorate of the German New Guinea Company and then in 1886 it became a German colony.) Under colonial rule, European enterprises expanded rapidly. Coconut plantations, in particular, came to dominate the coastal landscape.

Karavarans and their Duke of York neighbors (as well as those on New Britain and New Ireland) lost considerable land in this period through trickery, extortion, or confiscation. In one case, Karavarans told us, land they controlled on the neighboring island of Ulu was sold by a casual visitor from New Ireland whom the European buyers happened to find sitting on the beach; the sale then was declared binding by the colonial regime. In another instance, they said, the eventual loss of the adjacent island of Kambakon—a small island only a few hundred yards from Karavar—began with a ridiculously small infraction: A Fijian missionary (one of Brown's original contingent), already occupying an area of Kambakon as the beneficiary of Karavaran generosity, demanded additional land after a Karavaran killed his dog. From the Karavaran perspective, the killing of the dog was justified, since it had been stealing food. Moreover, the death of the dog was not a matter of great concern, and the Karavaran who had killed the dog had offered to pay compensation for its death. The missionary, however, insisted that his claim was on behalf of the church and, with threats of heavy European reprisals, got his way.

These Karavaran stories provide an instructive complement to a story told by the Reverend R. H. Rickard in 1882. Recently arrived in the Duke of York Islands from Australia, he found the locals contentious and obstinate, lacking the Christian spirit of generosity. He wrote home:

> Again, the principle here is as the proverbial Irishman said, "Nothing for nothing." They will not even give you a small shell or a nut without something in return. One day this week a chief [probably simply a local leader] came from a distant village to see the new missionary and his wife. He looked at us well then told us, through an interpreter, that he "liked us," that he even had "great regard" for us: then in evidence of this he threw us a betel nut [often exchanged and consumed in mutual sociability], which I took up. He came back a few minutes afterwards and said he was surprised we had not given him a little tobacco in return for the nut. This was his "regard"—"a bite for a bigger fish" (1882: n.p.).

In dismissing the overture of the "chief" without reciprocating, Rickard apparently interpreted what was probably (at least in part) a rather insistent offer that sociability be established among potential equals as if it were *only* an aggressive demand for personal profit (tobacco had become a currency [Brown 1972: 297]). Certainly, he felt that the chief was unduly self-interested and did not adequately recognize the importance of supporting the church in its civilizing presence.

To be sure, these accounts of unsatisfactory transactions do differ in ontological status. The Karavaran accounts were standardized recollections gathered by anthropologists years after the events; the European one was a contemporary account written largely to raise funds for continued Protestant missionizing efforts. (The comparison Rickard made between the presumably Catholic Irish and the largely pagan Duke of York Islanders is interesting in this latter respect: Perhaps both groups were regarded as comparably backward and iniquitous.) Nonetheless, the stories reveal—or can at least be regarded as parables of—important intersecting themes characterizing many interactions between Europeans and locals within the entire colonial period. It was by such interactions that Europeans often created abiding resentment among locals and locals often created chronic frustration among Europeans. Many local people (including, probably, the chief whose betel nut was not repaid) frequently felt ill used and regarded Europeans (or their agents) as denying them worth by repudiating their claims of reciprocity. Many Europeans, either misinterpreting or rejecting claims by locals for reciprocity, frequently regarded them as uncooperative and obstructionist—as simply in the way or as making inappropriate demands. In short, although the Europeans whom Karavarans and their neighbors encountered were not uniform in either their interests or in their dealings with locals, most asserted their own superiority; most Karavarans, in their turn, asserted their right to achieve equivalence, looking for ways to win the respect of Europeans or even place them in their debt.

In this regard, Karavaran recollections of the phases and aspects of the colonial period often contained a mixture of still-raw grievances (such as those concerning loss of land) and proud assertions of worth. For example, many resented the fact that they received so little pay for hard labor on, for instance, plantations, but they also said with pride that their own shell currency had always been superior to European currency. They maintained that shell money (which shared many of the formal characteristics of money in that it was imperishable, divisible into uniform units of small value, and employed in a wide variety of transactions ranging from subsistence to ritual) not only once dominated the colonial economy because the Germans were forced to trade in it but remained preferable to European money: Shell money was used both to transact and to create enduring relations of reciprocity; it was substantial, or "heavy," and European money was flimsy, or "light."

Karavarans also had come to mention with some pride that the Germans located their first administrative headquarters in the region on their island. Indeed, Karavarans could readily point out house foundations (including that of a saloon littered with shards of German beer bottles), the area where the flagpole stood, and even the remains of a tree on which a native from New Britain had been executed by hanging. Many continued to bemoan the subsequent move of the German administration to the New Britain towns of Kokopo and then Rabaul, attributing to this move their current economic and political peripherality relative to the closely related Tolai. Referring in moments of braggadocio to the events now interpreted as denoting early eminence, many Karavarans have come to say that because they gave "birth" to the German administration (and, as Duke of York Islanders, to Methodism) they were as trawler to the (attached and trailing) Tolai dinghy and therefore should lead the Tolai rather than the other way around.

The events of World War I, consisting in this area of only a brief scrimmage, had little apparent effect on the Karavarans and their neighbors except to precipitate an abrupt change of colonial regime. After the war, Australia, the most proximate of the Allies, oversaw the Territory of New Guinea for the League of Nations. (It was already administering the adjacent Territory of Papua).[11] The events of World War II were, in contrast, traumatic: Karavarans, as well as the other Duke of York Islanders and many Tolai, felt they had little control over their circumstances. During the Japanese occupation, they were subject to heavy Allied bombing, to serious food shortages, and to direct and frequently very harsh military discipline (including torture and execution). Yet Karavarans described resisting when they could. For instance, they risked their lives in order to hide or otherwise help downed Allied aviators.

Although greatly relieved when the war was over, Karavarans (like many other Papua New Guineans) greeted the return of the Australian administration with misgivings, wondering whether prewar conditions would simply be resumed. They thought, at the very least, that the privations they had experienced and the service they (and other Papua New Guineans less under direct Japanese control) had offered the Allies should result in fundamental transformations of prior colonial inequalities. Many wished the Australian administration to be replaced by a U.S. one. After all, U.S. soldiers had appeared far more generous and racially tolerant than their Australian counterparts. (Fred was initially welcomed to Karavar because he might inaugurate a U.S. presence.)

The Australian administration did return, and although important continuities in regime persisted, there were some significant changes. As administrators of what had become a UN trusteeship during a postwar period in which empires were being dismantled and colonies gaining independence, the Australians had become much more self-conscious about their responsibilities to natives. They focused more directly on native welfare, especially economic and educational developments, so as to prepare Papua New Guineans for eventual independence.

For the Karavarans, this postwar commitment meant an increase in the degree and frequency of colonial penetration. Karavarans and their neighbors became additionally regulated by a system containing levels of organization, established procedures, and official records. Patrolled, documented, exhorted and occasionally fined and jailed, Karavarans described themselves as responding with confusion, truculence, evasion, wry amusement, and, periodically, excitement and optimism for the future.

One man told, for example, of offering a patrol officer visiting Karavar a few eggs. The patrol officer rejected them, calling them a bribe. After all, the donor had refused to buy the license that, for reasons he and other Karavarans found baffling, was deemed by the Australians as necessary for him to operate his small local store. The man said that he was not, in fact, operating a store. Its shelves were empty, as the patrol officer would see if he cared to inspect. Describing the event with amusement, the man said that he had emptied the store of its goods before the officer's visit; he had offered the eggs in the hopes that it might prompt the officer to make a fool of himself by angrily inspecting an empty building. Still, this same man, whose store was at the best of times not well stocked, very much hoped to get European assistance (perhaps, as we shall see, secret knowledge) so as to achieve business success and prosperity on a European level. Indeed, the administration's commitment to "development" during the postwar colonial period was widely greeted with high expectations.

However, subsequent to independence in 1975, many of the expectations Karavarans had held concerning the possibilities of economic development had waned. Too many stores had failed, too many government development schemes (from oil-palm to fisheries projects) had fizzled. A worldwide recession affected the price of coconuts, which were still the major source of local income; the recession also affected the chances of working elsewhere in Papua New Guinea in construction jobs created by foreign exploitation of mining and timber resources. Moreover, from the Karavaran perspective, the relatively few positions of influence and affluence in government and business were likely to be monopolized by other Papua New Guineans—Tolai in particular.

In this latter regard, Karavarans (and other Papua New Guinea villagers peripheral to the centers of power) were increasingly aware that a class system, reproduced through differential access to education and through kinship connections, was operating. (We use here the concept of class primarily in what Larmour [1992: 96] called its "weaker," or sociological, sense, that is, to denote the existence of groups for which significant resources are unequally accessible.) The colonial class and caste system had, in significant part, been replaced by an indigenous one in which equivalence remained elusive. As another of the peripheral peoples within New Britain (a Baining) put it when speaking about the powerful Tolai, "They are just like Europeans; they'll occasionally offer us food but never condescend to eat with us." But in Papua New Guinea, as elsewhere, class differences might partially conform to cultural distinctions and might also cut across them, leading the wealthy and powerful to unite across ethnicities in support of the privileges of class. And it was in this environment of sometimes conforming and sometimes conflicting ethnic and class relationships that a national unity, perhaps once naively assumed by many Europeans and Papua New Guineans to be a natural product of independence, had become problematic and contested in its construction. It was in this unfolding context of change that Karavarans were continuing to wonder about and to assert their role and worth in contemporary Papua New Guinea.

CHAPTERS IN THIS BOOK

As we have already indicated, each of the chapters in this book concerns the ongoing changes that have occurred on Karavar since European contact, changes that were far from simple. They did not indicate the shattering of an Eden or the persistence or complete replacement of an inflexible tradition. These changes stemmed from a process of mutual engagement whereby people who differed in their interests and resources contended about who they were and would become.

We open with the chapter "Resistance Through Emulation: On Patrols, Reports, and 'Cults' in Colonial New Britain" because it describes some of the most basic practices of colonial interaction as they affected Karavaran life. Periodically patrolled and disciplined by government officials attempting both to control and (eventually) to "develop" them—to shape their identities into those of dutiful workers and prospective citizens—Karavarans were indeed affected. But they did not capitulate.

Implicated briefly in this field of change were anthropologists living on Karavar (Fred and his first wife, Shelly Errington). They became drawn in when they were reported by a local colonial newspaper as supporting Karavaran recalcitrance in the face of the administration's directives. Disciplined by the administration and threatened with expulsion from the territory, these anthropologists learned rather abruptly about some aspects of colonial coercion. However, the administration was less successful in controlling the Karavarans. By ostensibly adopting many of the values of Europeans while at the same time defying many of their directives, Karavarans managed to turn European standards against their colonial masters. In other words, through highly qualified emulation of Europeans, they sought to achieve the full equality that was being denied them by Europeans while at the same time maintaining their own worth.

In the second chapter, "Dueling Currencies in East New Britain: The Construction of Shell Money as National Cultural Property," we go back in colonial history to the German administration in order to explain a contemporary attempt to transform Papua New Guineans by convincing many of these culturally diverse residents to give up a measure of their distinctiveness in order to become subsumed within a unified nation. More specifically, we examine an effort by a well-educated Tolai to convince Papua New Guineans in general that certain traditions distinctive to Tolai and Duke of York Islanders should represent the nation as a whole, that these traditions should be defined as national cultural property.

In particular, this Tolai attempted to valorize the indigenous medium of value for the Tolai and Duke of York Islanders, to valorize their shell money itself. By invoking contrasts between shell money and Western-derived currencies, he represented the Tolai and Duke of York Islanders as having maintained a distinctive cultural heritage and rootedness that was not anachronistic but enabled functioning in the contemporary world. He argued, in effect, that because shell money remained both economically viable and morally superior, it should represent the successful emergence of the nation as a whole from the inequities of a colonial history. That the effort of this Tolai was likely to be rejected by Papua New Guineans from other groups speaks to the difficulties of creating a national identity in a postcolonial Papua New Guinea. Many residents of Papua New Guinea, who have engaged in long-term struggles to maintain and establish their own worth and identity in significant reference to a colonial presence, would be extremely reluctant to give up their cultural distinctiveness. This would be especially the case if they became not only subsumed within a unified nation but subsumed under the cultural banner of another group.

The third chapter, "From Darkness to Light in the George Brown Jubilee: The Invention of Nontradition and the Inscription of a National History in East New Britain," follows from the second in that it also provides historical grounding for a contemporary argument about the basis of national unity. This argument was made to Duke of York Islanders in 1991 by the then–prime minister of Papua New Guinea at an annual jubilee, a local commemoration of the Reverend George Brown's 1875 arrival. The prime minister argued that what united Papua New Guineans was having ancestors who had once all been equally savage until brought from "darkness" to "light" by the early missionaries. In other words, he suggested that what Papua New Guineans had in common was a savage past that, through acceptance of Christianity, they had all left behind.

This message was reiterated in a skit central to the commemoration in which the ancestors of Duke of York Islanders were portrayed as bumbling savages who were then "civilized" by Brown and his entourage of Fijian missionaries. In particular, we investigate why Duke of York Islanders found this skit hilarious inasmuch as it incorporated remarkably racist imagery about their ancestors. By contrasting the jubilee performance we witnessed in 1991 to those described in the late 1920s we demonstrate that what was funny in 1991 was not funny before. This change signals an important shift both in power relations and in the way local identity was affirmed from the period of colonial domination to that of nation formation.

In the fourth chapter, "First Contact with God: Individualism, Agency, and Revivalism in the Duke of York Islands," we continue to explore the relationship between Christianity and nationalism in the Duke of York Islands. Although Methodism has been the predominant Christian religion practiced there since Brown's arrival, increasing numbers of young and better-educated islanders have recently been converting to evangelical forms of Christianity. Many claimed, in effect, a contemporary and personal "first contact" with God, a contact that empowered them to redeem corrupted understandings of Brown's initial "first contact" teachings. These converts, moreover, have begun to confront their fellow villagers and kin by challenging the prerogatives of an all-male ritual organization. This organization focused on the *dukduk* and *tubuan* sacred figures, which have become primary symbols of Duke of

York (and Tolai) identity. The evangelicals, however, regarded these figures as "satans."

Members of this ritual organization on Karavar, fearing that the evangelical men would reveal ritual secrets to local women in general, asserted their power by destroying property belonging to the evangelicals. In response, the evangelicals invoked the power of the state—the police—to protect their property and their right to worship as they chose. In analyzing the ensuing police hearing, we show that the evangelicals used the power of the state to define themselves as *individuals*, as autonomous relative to other Karavarans. In this regard, they were coming to view themselves more as citizens of a country than as members of a cultural group.

In the fifth chapter, "The Triumph of Capitalism in East New Britain? A Contemporary Papua New Guinea Rhetoric of Motives," we continue to explore Papua New Guinean considerations of what sorts of persons with what sorts of commitments should compose their nation and govern its people. We focus primarily on a speech given by the then–prime minister, who was campaigning among his Tolai and Duke of York Island constituency for re-election to his parliamentary seat. He had accepted a Karavaran invitation to speak at a "traditional" mortuary ceremony honoring a long-dead and somewhat mythical Karavaran ancestor, Tovetura—an ancestor to whom the prime minister claimed kin ties. In his speech, he recognized the importance of colonial history in providing the context for present struggles over identity and worth in contemporary Papua New Guinea and provided his own interpretation of these events. He suggested that Tovetura not only taught the Germans how to govern but, in so doing, had made it possible for him, the prime minister, to be a successful national leader. All power, he thereby implied, was locally derived, and moreover, Karavar was an especially powerful place. Indeed, it was his local connections (in several senses) that enabled him to exercise national power. Thus, Karavarans should be assured that a vote for him would not be a wasted vote, since he was mindful that he would remain a powerful national politician only as long as he acted as their kinsman—only as long as he provided strong support for their particularistic interests.

We argue, however, that it was very difficult for a politician to act as kin to more than a very few local groups, a very narrow constituency. Certainly, the electoral turnover among politicians was high. Perhaps, in consequence, many politicians tried to court local interests while at the same time grabbing as much as possible for themselves (and their "real" kin) in the limited time available. In the face of what was widely perceived as political pandering and corruption, some Papua New Guineans had begun to argue that politicians should adopt a vision of themselves as "statesmen," as representatives beholden only to the national good. We speculate, though, about the consequences of such an arrangement for local groups. We suggest that these "statesmen" might well define the national good in class terms, favoring, for instance, multinational interests (in the exploitation of timber and mineral resources) over local ones. Thus in our view, local people might simply become more peripheral to the centers of power, losing whatever limited influence and protection they currently could exercise through their elected politicians.

In the conclusion, we return to a consideration of the erroneous models of change that we have introduced here. Taking into account both Western and Karavaran perspectives, we seek to interpret what a European shipping magnate living in the New Britain port city of Rabaul called Karavaran "bloodymindedness"—their "irrational" opposition to a plan he said would help them. He had built a tourist facility on the island of Kambakon that would provide some of the nearby Karavarans with an income, but they sabotaged his efforts, in part by vandalizing his "state-of-the-art ablution block."

We treat this encounter as a parable, both instructively similar and dissimilar to the one just related about the Reverend Rickard and the Duke of York chief: By comparing the two, we can reflect upon important continuities as well as transformations occurring over the more than a century of often-troubled relations between locals and more powerful outsiders. Moreover, in exploring why Karavarans behaved as they did in destroying the ablution block, we are led to some final speculations about the future of Karavar in the contemporary nation of Papua New Guinea and about the future of the nation itself. What might the foreseeable prospects be for a nation composed of groups such as the Karavarans who have long insisted upon defending their identity and worth with contentious obstinacy?

NOTES

1. Anton Ploeg (1991) elaborated these issues specifically in relation to Papua New Guinea. For other recently published considerations of nationalism in the Pacific see Babadzan 1988; Mangi 1989; Feinberg 1990; Hirsch 1990; Linnekin 1990 ; LiPuma and Meltzoff 1990; and Thomas 1990. See, as well, Gewertz and Errington (1991: 169–195) for an analysis of how the Chambri of East Sepik Province negotiated with the state. Finally, Robert Foster (1991) has provided an excellent summary of the recent nationalist literature cross-culturally.

2. Among those who have most completely theorized these processes, see Bourdieu 1977; Bloch 1986; and Comaroff and Comaroff 1991, 1992.

3. In an earlier work (Gewertz and Errington 1991), we argued that in the face of the postmodern critique of ethnographic representation as hegemonic (see, especially, Clifford and Marcus 1986; Clifford 1988a), anthropologists must acknowledge political responsibility and not simply justify their research in terms of misguided scientism.

4. For a discussion of how this film affected the people in it, see Gordon 1992.

5. We use the term "European" to refer to those of European descent, even those currently American or Australian. Although the term does not refer to the substantial number of those of Chinese descent who had come to live in Papua New Guinea, the interests of these people became, by the late colonial period (and after considerable discrimination), substantially allied with those of the "Europeans."

6. William Roseberry (1992) made a fascinating case that this commitment to understanding political relationships in a historically contingent world differentiated many anthropologists from most multiculturalists.

7. In recent years, anthropologists have become increasingly concerned with the extent to which they, both in their field research and in their writings, may have reproduced colonial power differentials. See, among many others, Asad 1973; Clifford and Marcus 1986; and di Leonardo 1989. Our own perspective is that although representations are political, to remain mute does not counter the hegemony. See Gewertz and Errington (1991) for further discussion.

8. This term was widely used to describe Papua New Guinea. See, for instance, Gavin Souter's 1963 book entitled *New Guinea: The Last Unknown.*

9. We do not intend this book as a comprehensive anthropological monograph about Karavar. The ethnographic data provided are primarily those necessary to understand the circumstances under consideration and the arguments at hand. For readers interested in more ethnographic detail—for discussion, for example, of social organizational features such as the operation of the matrilineages and matrimoieties in ritual—see Errington 1974a.

10. Brown came to be regarded by Karavarans as having made "first contact" with them in 1875. However, in 1776, Philip Carteret, on the *Swallow,* had observed many "'coconut plantations,' houses, and inhabitants with handsome well made canoes" (Rubel and Rosman n.d.: 77) on the Duke of York Islands. In 1791, William Bradley, on the *Sirius,* had "exchanged some Cocoanuts and pieces of Iron hoop" (1969: 256) with locals there. In the several decades prior to Brown's arrival other Europeans "came in naval vessels on exploring expeditions and in trading or whaling ships. In addition, Duke of York Islanders had been taken as crew members 'for a whaling cruize or pearl shell expedition,' and observers in the 1870's noted their ability to communicate in English" (Neumann 1992: 50).

11. Technically, no part of what became Papua New Guinea was a colony of Australia. However, practically speaking, Australia administered it as a colony.

1

Resistance Through Emulation

On Patrols, Reports, and "Cults"
in Colonial New Britain

W E BEGIN our discussion of the social and cultural changes that have occurred among Karavarans following European arrival with an inquiry into the nature of the Australian colonial regime in the Territory of Papua New Guinea. To this end, we examine and contextualize an incident of late colonial history in which the administration disciplined two anthropologists for unintentionally engaging in the production of a disquieting article that differed significantly from officially sanctioned texts. Fred had spoken to a European reporter on a colonial newspaper who then published an article conveying that the Karavarans were greatly—perhaps violently—discontented with the regime. This incident proved to be a historically complex colonial conjuncture, both in its antecedents and in its consequences. The incident itself touched on a chronic colonial raw nerve, since it suggested that, contrary to the administrative reports, matters were not under proper control: The natives were restless and the anthropologists, inappropriate in their speech. The administrative response was to subject both natives and anthropologists to close surveillance—concerted patrolling and additional reporting. (Newspaper reporters were already suspect. However, the relationship—both of opposition and complicity—between what was defined as a free press and the administration is not the subject of this chapter.)

In an effort to provide a more thoroughly historicized analysis of this colonial encounter, one that does justice to the manifold changes wrought by colonial control, we explore an important aspect of colonial life: the ways in which documents—official as well as unofficial—about natives, Europeans, and their mutual interactions both contended with each other and were articulated with action. In other words, we explore the often-complicated and important intersections between particular colonial texts, characteristic colonial practices, and specific colonial events.[1] Thus, in our interpretation of the incident we pay special attention to different texts and to responses to and negotiations about these texts. We show that to interpret the significance of what was, for both the administration and the anthropologists, embarrassingly unregulated speech, we must understand the contrast of this speech to certain fully authorized and formalized discourse concerning the relationship between Europeans and natives (neither of which, of course, was an entirely homogeneous group). We must understand the incident of the irruption into a colonial newspaper of an anthropological account of native unrest against a background of discourse embodied and embedded in official patrol reports. As we shall see, not only were patrol reports and the patrols they represented and shaped central mechanisms of colonial control, they also contributed to the circumstances in which the control was challenged.

THE INCIDENT

In 1968, shortly after arriving to do field research on Karavar, Frederick Errington, along with Shelly Errington attracted the unfavorable attention of the Australian colonial regime. While purchasing supplies in Rabaul, the commercial and administrative center of what was then the New Britain District,[2] Fred was asked for an interview by a reporter on a European newspaper, the *South Pacific Post*. He declined the request, explaining (naively) to the reporter that because there was considerable anti-Australian feeling on Karavar, his work might be compromised if he became too closely identified with European interests. The reporter, disregarding Fred's concerns, forthwith published the following article.

Villagers are Hostile Say 2 Americans
RABAUL: *Suspicion and hostility towards the Australian Administration have been expressed on the Duke of York Islands by some of the local villagers.*
   Two American anthropologists at present on a study trip of the islands said they had been surprised at the attitude of the villagers.
   The villagers concerned could be Johnson Cultists. ...
   The Johnson Cultists until now mainly found on New Hanover, have in the past refused to pay council taxes but have subscribed to an unofficial "American tax" to buy President Johnson from the US. ...
   Recently the Johnson Cult has appeared to be dying out as more and more villagers have shown an increasing co-operation with the administration.

However, after a preliminary tour of only a few days on the Duke of Yorks, in which the Erringtons looked for a base camp, they became aware of what they called the hostility of the local people.

"NOTHING"

Mr. Errington said he heard such remarks as "Thank God the Americans are here, now we will get some help—the Australians are doing nothing for us."

He said he did not know if the attitude of these villagers might develop into civil disobedience or not. (*South Pacific Post* 1968: 4)

This newspaper article, thus, reported both the situation in the Duke of York Islands and the presence and activities of the American anthropologists. In response, the district commissioner went on the radio to deny that inhabitants of the Duke of York Islands were cargo cultists on the brink of civil disobedience. ("Cargo cults," minimally defined, are Melanesian efforts by ritual means to acquire "cargo," a Pidgin-English term referring to European manufactured goods.) Everything was under control, he assured his largely European audience.[3] At the same time, he sent a letter to the errant anthropologists, summoning them to see him immediately. The anthropologists did indeed seek him out immediately. After they had abjectly apologized and claimed they had been misquoted, they were provisionally forgiven and allowed to resume their work. However, it was clearly understood on both sides that if they were again to challenge the rules of public discourse concerning native peoples, as that discourse was defined by the administration, they would probably be evicted from the territory. The administration also indicated that it did not want the anthropologists to be used by Duke of York Islanders for antiadministrative purposes. In fact, the administration later required that the anthropologists give a radio broadcast in the Duke of York language explaining that their interests lay not in the promotion of cargoistic politics but in the study of traditional customs.[4] Both anthropologists and "cargo cultists"—to say nothing of the conjunction between them—obviously merited considerable administrative concern and attention.

SOME INTERPRETIVE PRELIMINARIES

The late colonial context in which this incident took place was, importantly, unlike those in which the class relations of hierarchy had become thoroughly entrenched (see, for example, Mitchell 1990; Scott 1985). Certainly in the Karavaran case, the imposition of hegemony—a way of life that in this circumstance would accord with the hierarchical interests of the European colonists (Gramsci 1977)—had become neither so complete as to appear fully convincing nor so evidently irrevocable as to appear immutable. Indeed, as we shall see, the weapons of resistance employed by these Papua New Guineans were *not* predicated upon their acceptance of either the fundamental assumptions or the inescapable fact of colonial hierarchical difference. They were not predicated on their acceptance of either the intrinsic or the permanent superiority of Europeans (cf. Genovese 1975; Sider 1986; Beckett 1987; Cowlishaw 1988; Trigger 1992).

On the contrary, the Papua New Guineans whose discontent the newspaper reported had obdurately resisted the imposition of a system of hierarchy in which distinctions would become ontological, that is, incommensurate. This was the case because Karavaran social life (as well as social life more generally throughout much of Melanesia) had, since European contact, remained the product of innumerable, often material transactions between individuals who regarded each other as essentially equal (see, for example, the story in our introduction of the chief who offered the Reverend Rickard betel nut; and cf. Strathern 1988). In addition, throughout Melanesia, local groups such as the Karavarans had long pursued their strategic interests through regional trade that included the acquisition of the novel and powerful by importing (and exporting) exogenous cultural traits and complexes. (A number of features of Karavaran ritual—songs, dances, and figures—were obtained from groups in New Britain and in New Ireland.) Hence, many aspects of European life— both practices and possessions—were of intense interest to Melanesians. Yet although Karavarans came quite willingly to emulate many European practices as superior to—perhaps more powerful than—their own, they refused to capitulate to European judgments of them as inherently and categorically inferior.

Although not denying that a "colonization of consciousness" (Comaroff and Comaroff 1991: 26) had to some extent taken place, we argue that this "colonization" was for a considerable time limited in important aspects, since Karavaran emulation of Europeans was in steadfast pursuit of indigenous objectives. Emulation, we must stress, did not mean capitulation (cf. Ohnuki-Tierney 1990). Indeed, on the whole, emulation became what might be seen as a particularly Melanesian form of resistance, one by which local groups attempted to maintain or enhance their own worth. Significantly shaping the historical processes of colonialism in Papua New Guinea was, then, the presence of local groups committed to egalitarianism (albeit competitive egalitarianism); differences must remain commensurate—matters of degree rather than kind (Gewertz and Errington 1991). As we shall see, what made this particular colonial context—and the incident we are especially concerned with—

refractory for Europeans and gave a special cast to the ongoing negotiations that constituted colonialism was that locals were willing to grant colonists great power but not inherent superiority.

PATROLS AND PATROL REPORTS IN
COLONIAL PRACTICE AND DISCOURSE

As we have already said, Fred's injudicious remarks to the reporter—his unregulated speech—must be understood in contrast with another type of then contemporary discourse concerning the relationship between Europeans and natives. The patrol report was a rhetorical form that had been well established during the Australian colonial regime in Papua New Guinea. It was, at least in colonial New Britain, an influential *model of* "correct" speech and thought concerning Europeans and their relationship to natives. The patrol report was also an important *model for* structuring the terms of engagement between Europeans and natives (Geertz 1973), since the expectations concerning the way the report should be constituted served in significant ways to delineate the activities that constituted the patrol. Patrol reports operated, then, as both record of and pattern for administratively correct thought, speech, and action. Moreover, simply expressed (but complexly enacted), these discursive practices helped create the threatening natives, the vulnerable colonists, and thus the situation in which the words of the American anthropologists that appeared in the newspaper might be *heard* as alarming and discordant (cf. Lindstrom 1990).

Patrols and their reports were, in other words, a significant part of the ongoing colonial encounter. There were, of course, other kinds of engagements mutually (and in many cases, unequally) affecting both locals and colonists. For groups such as the Duke of York Islanders, contact with Europeans had, by 1968, also included a long period of missionization, years of employment on plantations and in other enterprises, the devastation of war, and, more recently, Western forms of education. Yet without claiming special privilege for our focus here on patrol and report in this encounter, we do think they were significant in the process by which colonial differences as well as similarities were constructed and negotiated—imposed and eroded, affirmed and (as in the case of the incident with which we are concerned) challenged. At least in the Duke of York Islands, the patrol deeply penetrated and affected the local community, and the report substantially informed the administration's understanding of and response to that local community as it was so penetrated and affected. Patrols and reports were thus central to a process of imposed surveillance and ordering (Foucault 1979). They played a considerable role in the "colonial encounter [that] entailed struggles over differing forms of knowledge, over group boundaries, over moralities, over the intimate details of work and life" (Cooper and Stoler 1989: 620).

As part of this struggle, local people to some extent came to turn this scrutiny—this colonial eye—in on themselves, initially to their own discomfit. However, administration "strategies of containment" (Jameson 1981) at least partly defeated themselves. Importantly, perhaps ironically, by accepting many of the administration's strictures about the significance of control, Duke of York Islanders undermined the administration's capacity to exercise control over them and so became a manifestation of European fears. In this context, Fred's anthropological authority (his eye/I, after all, was "there" [Clifford 1988a])—that which made him credible to both colonists and the locals—was a resource that each sought to employ in the ongoing contestation.

Although much of our knowledge about patrols comes from patrol reports (and we have argued that each was mutually constructed such that patrols and reports constituted a critical aspect of the ongoing encounter), we initially, albeit provisionally, separate the two in our presentation. One reason for this is that each had a different primary audience: The local people were the immediate audience for the patrol, whereas the European administration was the immediate audience for the report.

The Patrol

At least after World War II (the only period for which we have reliable evidence), the Duke of York Islands were patrolled only once or twice a year, and most villages were visited for no more than a few days each time. But the disturbing consequences of a patrol officer's visit long outlasted the frequency and duration of his patrol. This was not because the officers were arbitrarily coercive. Patrol officers were expected to be resourceful in the field (see Schieffelin and Crittenden 1991) but were by no means free agents. After all, many of them were young, often only in their twenties. They were expected to carry out prescribed duties in prescribed fashion and to report the execution of these duties in a relatively standardized way. And so far as we can tell, most—in the Duke of York Islands anyway—obeyed their directives and fulfilled their duties.

Central to these duties was inspection. The patrol officer was accompanied to a village by several native constables and sometimes by a cadet patrol officer or a medical officer. Their arrival was frequently known in advance so that the village could prepare itself. The patrols on Karavar, as locals described them to

Fred and as he witnessed in one case, seem typical. After summoning, or at least being joined by, the village *luluai* and *tultul* (the administration-appointed headman and his assistant), the patrol officer, together with his party, would walk through the village judging the quality and condition of housing and sanitation and the degree of general tidiness. Deficiencies were commented upon and directives given for their prompt remedy. (Pidgin English was the language used. Developed on plantations, it often lacked subtlety of expression. Nonetheless, it was more than sufficient to convey commands and reprimands. It was, in fact, the only practical means of communication insofar as few patrol officers [and other European] understood any of the local languages, and at least in the Duke of York Islands prior to independence, few locals knew English very well.) There might also be a tour of the village cemetery and gardens with instructions requiring, for instance, more thorough clearing of brush from grave sites or improvement of fences around gardens to keep pigs out of crops.

Moreover, the villagers themselves were often assembled by the patrol officer and attendant native constables for inspection. Patrol routine frequently included "lining the village." Karavarans and other villagers were told to arrange themselves in orderly lines so that they—their bodies—could receive a medical inspection. (This inspection could be performed by a patrol officer and did not require the presence of a medical officer.) If yaws, filariasis, or other maladies were found, either immediate treatment (perhaps injection) would be given or recommendations for treatment would be made. Villagers might also be comparably assembled so that a census could be taken or taxes collected.

Two sorts of written records were kept of these visits of inspection: the patrol report, which will be discussed shortly in detail, and the village book. The village book was left in each village with the local *luluai* and was consulted and augmented by visiting patrol officers. A village book contained various preprinted headings, the most inclusive of which was "General Information (notes on village officials, roads, gardens, water supplies, walking times, etc.)." In the Karavaran village book, for instance, the following comments appeared under this general heading:[5]

30.4.56–6.5.56
   Arrived here ex KUMAINA [another Duke of York Island village] late afternoon 30th. Census Revision made 2.5.56. Village Inspection 30th.
   Concur with latter remarks of J. Martyn [entered in village book about a year earlier]. TONGA, luluai, is a surly lad—never saw him smile once. P'raps the responsibility of Trade Store weights heavily on his narrow shoulders.

The village book contained the names of individuals cited for delinquencies in housing or sanitation. These citations were followed by statements made on subsequent patrols indicating whether the deficiencies had been rectified.

Rest house [where the patrol officer stayed] and kitchen very recent. No latrine or Police Barracks on arrival but matter rectified the next day!

Other entries in the village book under such fixed headings as "General Instructions" and "Results of Instruction" contained the names of individuals cited for delinquencies in housing or sanitation. These were followed by statements made on subsequent patrols indicating whether the deficiencies had been rectified. The village book, hence, enabled patrol officers to maintain an ongoing process of surveillance and discipline even if particular personnel had been transferred. Indeed, one wonders whether, as an ongoing manifestation of colonial scrutiny, the village book functioned in much the manner of a panoptic eye (Foucault 1979).

The village book constituted a dialogue between patrol officers in which they asserted not only continuity of colonial control but the continuity of difference between the colonizer and the colonized. Because at the time of Fred's fieldwork, few if any Karavarans would have been able to read the village book left among them, patrol officers probably regarded their comments in the book as facilitating confidential and administratively important communication among officers. Yet these village books likely conveyed other kinds of communication as well and to a broader audience. For instance, the Karavaran village book during the mid-1950s was left in the care of one of the very persons it denigrated. It would be the *luluai* Tonga—the "surly lad" of "narrow shoulders"—who would be required to produce the book for the (perhaps amused) perusal of the next patrol officer; it would be Tonga who would accompany the officer on his rounds of inspection and who would perhaps watch while the officer wrote a note corroborating his predecessor's observation concerning the inadequacies of the current *luluai*.

Left in the village itself because it was written in a language it was assumed local people were virtually incapable of learning, the village book thus embodied and at least indirectly conveyed not only a continuity of colonial surveillance and discipline but also a continuity of colonial frustration, if not outright disdain and contempt. Whether centered on the village book itself or implicit in the context in which the book operated—that of the patrol (and by extension, that of the administration and colonial life more generally)—these mechanisms and attitudes whereby differences were created and maintained certainly affected local people.

Although local people such as Karavarans soon learned what to expect from a patrol, they continued to find much of the regimentation and scrutiny onerous, demeaning, puzzling, and unsettling. For them, the key experience was that of being "ordered" (in both senses) by those more powerful than they. At the same time, the basis and rationale for this ordering and for the maintenance of colonial difference remained at least somewhat mysterious.

Patrol Reports

The reports we consider cover patrols in the Duke of York Islands after World War II, these being the only reports surviving for this area. As they appeared on file—as they came to constitute the official record—these reports were embedded in a hierarchy of evaluation and appraisal covering several levels of administration. The individual report identified the members of the patrol and usually assessed the performance of those subordinate to the patrol officer himself. These included the native constables and, on some occasions, cadet patrol officers. K. J. Lang characterized one of the native constables who accompanied him on his patrol of the Duke of York Islands in 1950 as follows: "Const. PARANA-6022 P.A. A hard working constable, not overbright, but reliable" (Rabaul Patrol Report [RPR] 1950–1951, Appendix A). Moreover, the immediate superior of the patrol officer would pass the report on to his own supervisor with a cover letter that evaluated the patrol officer in terms of his report (and the patrol it described) and summarized, often in some detail, the significance of the report. His superior did much the same, and in some cases the chain extended to the most senior official in the territory.

Patrol officers were obviously following a standard form in writing their reports. Although this form shifted some over time, the reports covered essentially the same topics for the period on which we have information. The reports did, as well, key into previous reports for the same area, indicating continuity or discontinuity with the circumstances covered in them.

They began with a brief outline of the personnel conducting the patrol, the location, objectives, and duration of the patrol, sometimes even a specification of the map used. Following this, a detailed patrol diary indicated the time, place, and activity of the patrol for each day. For instance, on August 28, 1950, Patrol Officer Lang also recorded the following: "0715 Departed PALPAL [another Duke of York Island village] per native cutter for KERAWARA [Karavar]. 0815 Arrived KERAWARA. 0815-1600 Amended census, issued new village book, inspected village, completed war damage payments. Discussed housing, gardens and advisability of restocking village [with livestock replacing those killed in war]. Returned PALPAL" (RPR 1950–1951: 2).

After the diary came the body of the report, which often began with a description of the geographic area in terms of location, rainfall, and soil types. Then came a section entitled "Native Affairs." Here the focus was on the general state of the local population, particularly with regard to its development and what might be termed its "administratability," the extent to which local people were responsive to the wishes of the administration. A specific measure of this was the degree to which locals complied with the instructions of the immediate patrol officer or his predecessor.

For example, in 1957, Patrol Officer A. D. Steven began a one-page section on native affairs with the following sentence: "The foremost general impression gained of the native situation in the group is the lack of material progress made by these people despite their long contact with the Government and Christian Missions" (Kokopo Patrol Report [KPR] 1956–1957: 2). He ended the section in this way: "Recent patrols, particularly the last patrol of three months, have had a beneficial effect. Villages were cleaner, and with one or two exceptions every co-operation was given to the patrol" (p. 3).

Subsequent categories in the report often included "Agriculture and Livestock"; "Medical and Health"; "Education and Missions"; "Law and Justice"; "Housing and Hygiene"; "Roads and Bridges"; "Census"; "Villages and Village Officials"; "Anthropology"; "Non-Indigenes"; "Standard of Living". The discussions under such headings were both descriptive and evaluative. Importantly, the patrol officers were particularly careful to record the degree of order (cf. Packard 1989): Were the pigs properly penned? Were the roads and paths cleared? Were houses sturdy and symmetrically arranged? Were latrines adequate in number and sufficient in depth? Were locals processing copra properly and efficiently? Were they utilizing available medical services? Were there nonlocal Papua New Guineans living among them? Was everyone on the census register accounted for? Was clothing clean? Were village officials cooperative?

In 1957, Patrol Officer Steven, under the heading "Law and Justice," noted:

> The previous patrol prosecuted several natives in various villages for minor breaches of the N.A.R.s [Native Affairs Regulations]—principally in respect of latrines. There is now a marked improvement in village hygiene and cleanliness.
>
> Two glaring exceptions to this improved state were INLIMUT and KABIBIAI, the only two inland villages on the [Duke of York] island. Both villages had been warned by previous patrols to improve the state of sanitation and housing. Although they had ample warning of the patrol's arrival the main tracks leading to the villages were overgrown and the villages dirty and housing inadequate. Thirty two male natives were convicted under Regulation 119(a) of the N.A.R.s and sentenced to one month's gaol at KOKOPO. (KPR 1956–1957: 5)

In contrast, in 1950, Patrol Officer Lang, under the heading "Roads and Bridges," recorded that he found native tracks sighted by the [previous] patrol all cleared and in good condition" (RPR 1950–1951: 8). Lang, under "Villages and Village Officials," also described Karavar itself as follows: "The village is comprised of three hamlets which are scattered over a fair area of the island. Houses range from fair to good although one family was found living in an old Army tent. It was pointed out to them the non-suitability of a tent as permanent living quarters and the male was advised to build a house in the interests of his family's health" (p. 10). And in language echoing that of the Karavaran village book, Lang represented the Karavaran officials in this way:

> *LULUAI*—TOKOIKOI—an official big in stature, but small in intellect.
> *TULTUL*—OUKA—solid official, appears to carry out his few duties allocated by Luluai in an efficient manner. (p. 10)

Frequently in their reports, the patrol officers ignored, denigrated, or challenged local systems of order that were different from their own (cf. Lawrence 1964).[6] In 1971, for example, Patrol Officer G. R. Medaris made a number of pronouncements about the ways indigenous forms of sociality were impeding economic development:

I would like to see the people move away from the villages and settle on whatever ground they may own. This could help to increase their sense of responsibility towards providing the needs of a family, to bring about a sense of pride
and achievement in ones work—and to lessen the influence of any undesirable
element in the village. ...

   The number of individually owned copra dryers is ever-increasing and many
licenses are held to buy copra. The current dominant attitude is to only harvest
sufficient produce to meet a certain need. Belief in the Duk-Duk [a ritual figure
and complex, it will be recalled] also imposes a two-three month ban an work.
Thankfully, there are a number of men in almost every village that strive to
make as much as possible. These men are the ones that disassociate themselves
from village affairs and concentrate on earning a decent income. (Molot Patrol
Report 1971–1972: 3)

                         *   *   *

Patrol officers concerned themselves on their patrols and in their reports with
all aspects of life: Backward locals had to be taught the fundamentals of
proper living and were judged and represented according to their willingness
and capacity to conform to European standards. Much of the significance of
the patrol and the patrol report, it seems to us, was that they served importantly in colonial strategies of containment. Together they effected and mani-
fested the capacity of the regime for surveillance. In this system of surveillance few details of native activity were exempt from administrative scrutiny
and representation. In short, patrol and report together composed part of a
highly ordered—and ordering—process of intrusion, differentiation, and
control.

Local Responses

We do know that Karavarans often resisted as demeaning, misinformed, or
foolish some of the enjoinders of the patrol officers who visited and inscribed
them in their reports. For instance, by the time of Fred's 1968 research,
Karavarans were reacting to the administration's preoccupation with latrine
construction with wry amusement, deciding simply that being required to
build them did not mean they were required to use them. After all, as they
commented to Fred, it would be truly embarrassing to them to have their affines see them entering or leaving the outhouses; also no one would want to
use the outhouses because the tide would not be able to wash away the excre-
ment and they would stink. Moreover, they told Fred that any *luluai* who
cooperated extensively with the patrol officer would simply have additional

(often irrational) demands made of him and he would not have time for his own important activities.

Certainly, Karavarans were not likely to agree with the patrol officer's demeaning appraisal of their *luluai* Tokoikoi. They regarded him (as well as his comparably maligned successor, Tonga) as among the most powerful and wealthy men anyone could remember. And far from regarding the *dukduk* ceremonies as interruption of meaningful work, locals regarded them as among the most significant aspects of their lives. In fact the eminence of big men such as Tokoikoi (or Tonga) came from their sponsorship and supervision of the intricately structured sequence of exchanges and feasts that were part of the *dukduk* and *tubuan* ceremonies. These ceremonies mobilized and coordinated the activities of hundreds of Duke of York Islanders, often from different villages, for weeks if not months.

Nonetheless, Karavarans (and other Duke of York Islanders) clearly recognized the administration and its emissaries as very powerful. And at least by 1968, few of them objected to the presence of the administration and to the fact per se that they were subject to its control.[7] In this regard, long-term exposure to European power seemed to have affected the evaluation locals made of aspects of their lives. European power lay not only in its capacity to jail those whose latrines were not up to standard but also in its capacity to impose a regime based on surveillance (Foucault 1979). This surveillance, which almost always found—and represented—local people as wanting in fundamental respects, had its consequences. For Karavarans, its effect seems to have been that they frequently regarded themselves as deficient. Specifically, Karavarans often (though by no means always) regarded themselves as *inadequate orderers* who needed to revise their conduct.[8]

We do not mean to argue that Karavarans and their Duke of York neighbors were content with their position in colonial society. Indeed, as we have indicated, throughout their colonial history they continued to react with anger at the condescension—paternalistic or otherwise—if not outright disdain they encountered from Europeans (or Asians). (See Chapter 3 for examples.) Although Karavarans might, for instance, cheerfully call the colonial government their "father," regarding it as a source of wisdom and assistance, they deeply resented being treated as children. Nor are we contending that Karavarans and their neighbors necessarily were greatly impressed by the particular patrol officers and other emissaries of the administration they encountered. Some Karavarans, as we have seen, told Fred with glee how they managed to trick and otherwise aggravate inexperienced patrol officers. However, we *are* suggesting that many Karavarans and Duke of York Islanders were painfully and recurrently convinced that they were vulnerable to a colonial evaluation of them as less than equal. Correspondingly, they had developed an abiding desire to rectify this source of ongoing inequality.

Cargoism in the Duke of York Islands. At least one of the important Karavaran responses to inequality seems to bear the imprint of the message redundantly expressed through patrol and report (as well as, of course, in other of their encounters with Europeans): From at least the 1930s, Karavarans and many of their neighbors embarked on a sequence of "cargoistic" movements in which they sought, through internal surveillance and regulation, to replicate European levels of *order* and so represent themselves as fully self-supervising.[9] Moreover, they believed that if they ordered themselves properly, the prosperity would soon follow that would provide the material basis of the transactions that could effect equality with Europeans.

Whereas we are not presenting a general discussion of cargo cults or cargoism in this chapter, some comparisons between the cargo activity of Karavarans and that of others might be suggested. There are, indeed, similarities between Karavarans and the Kaliai cargo cultists that Andrew Lattas (inspired by Fanon's [1968a] psychiatric perspective) described elsewhere in New Britain. About these Kaliai, striving through ritual means to acquire Western goods, Lattas wrote:

> Colonial and neo-colonial inequalities come to be personalized, in that they become expressions of moral identities and moral differences. ... Here social inequalities become part of a moral economy where the whiteman's power and wealth are seen as extensions of his moral laws and moral personhood. ... Such moral beliefs are part of the process of internalizing the conditions of colonial domination; that is, they are part of the process of making one's race morally responsible for the conditions of its own subjugation. (1992: 32)

Inasmuch as such colonial definitions of unequal worth were propagated and in some cases accepted as true, they were strategies through which the differences on which colonial society rested were maintained. Yet in our view, although Karavarans did blame themselves as inadequate orderers, *they did not internalize as fundamental to themselves that which marked them as different from Europeans.* Though Karavarans clearly regarded themselves as in some ways deficient, *they never regarded their deficiency as the product of inherent nature; rather, they saw it as the result of immediate and rectifiable circumstances.* They did not see the differences between themselves and Europeans as incommensurate, as precluding the transactions through which equality could be established (cf. Strathern 1992). Indeed, Karavarans understood their cargoism as a set of activities critically important in effecting these transactions.

In this regard, Karavaran cargoism was a program of "self-containment" designed to efface colonial differences through emulation. If one were to follow Lattas's interpretation of the Kaliai circumstance, this emulation would be regarded as a "doubling process" whereby locals reflected themselves "into the image of the whiteman" (Lattas 1992: 36). Moreover, this doubling process would be seen as "in part instituted by the colonial authorities themselves," who "along the way ... lost control of this mimetic function and doubling process" (p. 36). However, it is our view that among the Karavarans it was not so much that colonists lost control of mimesis as that Karavaran mimesis had always been intended to negate colonial control by abolishing colonial boundaries: Karavaran emulation was an instrument of fundamental noncapitulation.

*   *   *

Karavarans, through their cargo activities, did eventually gain a welcome measure of colonial respect, although not for the reasons they anticipated. Their emulation—their self-imposed regulation based (in part) on the injunctions of patrol and report—came to prove disconcerting to the administration and others in the colonial audience when it raised the specter of "cult" behavior, behavior out of control (cf. Kaplan 1990).

Moreover, in replicating aspects of European life—those focusing on the great importance of acquiring manufactured goods—Karavaran (and many other) "cargo cultists" struck Europeans as familiar but *perversely* so and thus as both reassuring and threatening. From the European perspective, their movement reassured, since the message of colonial superiority based in part on European lifestyles and on control of material goods seemed to have been absorbed; but it also threatened, since the emulation, especially as it appeared in "cult" form, served local and often seditious purposes. To some extent, European standards, preachings, and teachings were turned against their sources in such oblique ways as to render difficult any head-on refutation of, and confrontation with, what was identified as a potentially out-of-control circumstance.[10]

The Kaun and Its Predecessors. By the time of Fred's 1968 fieldwork, many Karavarans and their Duke of York neighbors had come to believe that for them to generate and maintain European levels of order and prosperity, they must fully master European knowledge. To achieve rightful equality with Europeans, they must learn to live in the well-regulated harmony thought typical of European existence. As steps toward achieving this equality, they must increase everyday discipline and, correspondingly, move ever further from the state of chronic conflict they had come to see as characteristic of their precontact past—their existence prior to European intervention.[11]

From the Karavaran perspective, the key manifestation and source of European power, especially the capacity for order, was the European knowledge of how to conduct the disciplined activity of "business." (In regard to the importance of disciplined activity, Karavaran cargo movements were not significantly different from many others reported in Papua New Guinea. See, for classic analyses, Schwartz 1962; Lawrence 1964; and Worsley 1968.) Business, clearly a major European preoccupation, was seen by locals in this area as the source, not only of superior European levels of control over material resources but of superior European levels of control over people—of social regulation and order (cf. Gregory 1982). To the end of understanding and conducting "business," the Karavarans created an organization they called the Kaun (a transformation of "account," as in "savings account"), which was designed to replicate European business practices.

The Kaun was, at the time of the 1968 fieldwork, only the most recent of a series of Karavaran efforts to reconfigure their relations with Europeans. The antecedents of the Kaun went back to at least the 1930s. At that time, a series of meetings were held on Karavar, attended by big men from the various communities in the Duke of York Islands. The question addressed with perplexity and anger at these meetings was why the Europeans persisted in treating them like dogs rather than like human beings (Worsley 1968). Indeed, during Fred's 1968 and 1972 fieldwork, the Karavarans continued to feel that the Europeans treated them like dogs. He was told again and again that Europeans—in particular, patrol officers—refused to eat their food, to sit and talk with them, to give them significant assistance. Instead, they said "raus" (Pidgin English for "get out") as though they were dogs. This treatment was a clear indication to the Karavarans that the Europeans still regarded them as savages. It was a denial that the Karavarans had been able to achieve an acceptable level of order in their lives.

The Karavarans referred to these meetings in the 1930s as the "dog affair" and said that at that time no conclusions were reached and no action was taken. They came to realize later, after World War II, that the solution to their problems might be to make a business. By the early 1950s (partly in response to international pressures promoting decolonization), the administration, through its patrols and other modes of engaging locals, was actively promoting native development in the form of cooperative societies (cf. Pomponio 1992). Thus, by the mid-1950s, the Kaun was formed by Karavarans as a business activity.

By the late 1950s, the influence of the Kaun had spread to the extent that its members dominated in the majority of Duke of York communities and its business enterprises had expanded and diversified. Controlled by big men, these largely unsuccessful enterprises were focused on constructing and stocking trade stores throughout the Duke of York Islands, purchasing and operating two boats for copra transport, and placing large orders for goods—cargo—to arrive from abroad. In addition, regular contributions of money and copra were collected as a tax from the membership. Significantly, although the Karavarans and other Duke of York members spoke of the potential profits of the Kaun, they had very little interest in and no concrete plans about what should be purchased with this money. Instead, their emphasis was on the *activity* of business itself.

In talking to Fred in 1968 about the nature of business, Karavarans emphasized the hard work and discipline of Europeans. Kaun leaders stressed the importance of self-surveillance as they exhorted their followers to work hard in the activities of the Kaun. Europeans, they said, did not spend the day fishing or loafing on the beach at the men's ground. They spent their time working, all day, every day, and the members of the Kaun must do the same. The leaders argued that the Europeans would be impressed with the amount of money raised by the Kaun, with the copra coming in every month as it did on plantations,[12] and with the regular collection of taxes. This would be proof that the Karavarans were capable of the same kind of disciplined, ordered control that was implicit in European business and life. (The importance of this discipline was also suggested by a patrol officer who described an early meeting of the Kaun at which members were dressed in uniforms and engaged in marching [Wals 1961].)[13]

Not surprisingly, the local anthropologists, as resident Europeans, were enlisted in the business activities of the Kaun. For instance, when taxes in money or copra were collected, they were asked to be present to record amounts contributed, to attest that an orderly procedure had been followed, and to advise more generally about how to make a business. Karavarans hoped that if they could impress Europeans—including the local anthropologists—with (what might be termed) their "business potential," the Europeans might fully share their still superior knowledge of business. Also, they hoped that through mastery of the knowledge inherent in such business procedures, their society could be transformed into one comparable to European society and they could, thus, become the equals of Europeans.[14]

Locals reorganized themselves—in part through the self-imposition of the system of surveillance the patrol officer implemented and the patrol report instantiated—so that colonists would accede that Europeans and natives had a common humanity. This suggests that Europeans had, in important measure, triumphed in the colonial encounter. They had, after all, set the standards for emulation. However, the emulation by Karavarans and other members of the Kaun of at least aspects of European life continued to vex the colonial government. Although conceding aspects of the struggles "over differing forms of knowledge, over group boundaries, over moralities, over intimate details of work and life" (Cooper and Stoler 1989), Karavarans were still intent on achieving equality with their colonial masters.[15]

COLONIAL AMBIVALENCE AND THE
APPROACH OF SELF-GOVERNMENT

Even after the errant anthropologists had made their radio broadcast in the Duke of York language, stating that they were living on Karavar to study traditional customs, not to help the Karavarans make a business, the administration was not finished with them. Some four months later, Patrol Officer M. J. Brereton came to Karavar and, according to the official patrol diary, "talk[ed] with Anthropologists" (KPR 1968–1969: 30) between 8:00 and 9:30 AM on August 27, 1968. Also, according to the patrol report, Brereton had been directed to establish a new base camp in the Duke of York Islands so that an officer could be permanently stationed there to collect census data. And in an inclusive instruction, he had been told to "complete any outstanding general Administration matters which will probably have built up" (p. 32).

The patrol was deemed successful. Brereton submitted his report to his immediate supervisor, the acting assistant district commissioner. He in turn submitted it to his superior, the district commissioner, along with a letter congratulating Brereton for the work he had done and for writing an exemplary report: "Mr. Brereton has submitted a long and informative report, which covers nearly all aspects, this would be a good documentary report of the island for future officers" (KPR 1968–1969: 35). The district commissioner forwarded the report to his supervisor on the national level, the director of the Department of District Administration, assuring him that the "report and covering memorandum by ... [the] Acting Assistant District Commissioner indicate a sound appreciation of the problems they are dealing with in the rather difficult situation of the Duke of Yorks" (p. 41).

What had been admitted as a "difficult situation," one attracting the attention of the full administrative hierarchy, was the subject of Brereton's conversation when he met with the anthropologists on Karavar. Of primary concern to him and of continuing interest to the administration was the fact that many locals were adamantly opposing the administration's concerted efforts to introduce local government councils. (By way of background and elaboration, under pressures both from the Australian government, which found Papua New Guinea expensive to administer, and from the international community, which regarded Papua New Guinea's colonial dependence to be a postwar anachronism, the administration had begun preparing the ground for eventual independence. An initial and crucial step was an effort, beginning in the 1950s, to introduce councils so that Papua New Guineans could acquire the skills and responsibilities necessary for citizens in a modern democracy.) The councils, composed of elected members, were to raise taxes and allocate the revenues in support of schools, roads, and other aspects of life necessary for Papua New Guinea to function as a self-governing society. Significantly, the council system, premised as it was on the forthcoming political independence of Papua New Guinea, was opposed by many, both Europeans and local people. Although by 1968 no definite date had been set for independence (after more than a decade of promoting the council system), fears abounded on both sides that independence would come before the territory was "ready."

On the European side, the move toward self-governance and eventual independence aroused deep-seated colonial fears that the white few would fall prey to an out-of-control—perhaps vindictive—black many. (See Chapter 3 for elaboration.) There were, for instance, immediate anxieties that the propagation of local government councils would signal that colonial rule was on the wane and, thereby, might encourage insurrection. And even if the transition to independence occurred smoothly, there were whites who feared that their persons and property might not be adequately protected in a prematurely self-governing Papua New Guinea.[16] At the very least, there were concerns that colonial privileges would be curtailed as Papua New Guineans replaced expatriates in business and government. In this latter regard, to the extent that members of the administration were successful in fulfilling their task of preparing Papua New Guineans for independence, they were doing themselves and a number of their friends and associates out of jobs. Independence was thus regarded by many of the colonial community with, at best, considerable ambivalence.

On the local side, and here we again speak primarily of the Karavarans and other Duke of York Islanders, opposition to the council was widespread, though by no means universal, and came to crystallize around the Kaun. As we have shown, Karavarans and many of their neighbors, having partially accepted the criteria on which colonial distinctions were based, thought that they would not be ready for independence until they had become more nearly equivalent to Europeans in their skills and powers. Indeed, the Kaun came explicitly to define itself through opposition to the council.

Anticouncil sentiment had been one of the major subjects of patrol reports in the Duke of York Islands for the decade prior to 1968. (A 1957 patrol report, for example, described "500 villagers truculently demonstrating against the establishment of councils" [KPR 1956–1957: 8].) By the time of Brereton's 1968 patrol, the Duke of York Islands (and adjacent parts of New Ireland and New Britain) had become polarized as villages defined themselves (to some extent on the basis of traditional patterns of alliance or rivalry) as supporters of either Kaun or council.

Also, the Kaun was of concern to the administration because it was "cargoistic." Whether the Kaun was a cargo cult had been preoccupying the administration for some time. Thus, when Brereton visited with the anthropologists on Karavar, he wished to discuss a variety of intersecting topics with them concerning the Kaun. Especially, he wanted to know whether the Kaun's objectives suggested cargoism and whether the anthropologists had become caught up in its activities. Indeed, if the Kaun was a "cargoistic" activity, much less a "cargo cult," any anthropological compliance with or support of its activities would be particularly prejudicial toward administration interests.

During his conversation with the anthropologists, it was agreed that it was hard to tell how cargoistic the Kaun was. Brereton said that although the Kaun focused on what appeared conventional business activities such as operating trade stores and marketing copra, the high expectations for these enterprises did not seem at all "realistic," since few of them made any profit. That the hopes for success of Kaun members were greatly inflated suggested either the strength and volatility of conviction underlying a "cult-like" quest or the passionate commitment to the pursuit of "development." Brereton admitted that he was frustrated and perplexed. He found the Kaun a formidable force he did not know how to respond to or appraise. He did not know whether it was a cult led by naive local leaders or, perhaps, charlatans. He did not know whether it was only what it appeared to be, a nascent business led by fledgling and fumbling entrepreneurs. And given this uncertainty about what the Kaun was, Brereton seemed at a loss to know what arguments to make to Kaun members concerning why they should give up the Kaun and cease their opposition to the administration-sponsored council. Correspondingly, it was not clear to him how he, and by extension the administration, could remain in control of what (as mentioned) had become defined as the "rather difficult situation of the Duke of Yorks." (It was largely to contain this situation that Brereton was charged in his patrol with constructing a base camp in the Duke of York Islands so that an officer could be resident full time.)

Hence it seems that as Karavarans and other members of the Kaun began to control themselves in what they thought was a European manner—as they began to emulate and, in so doing, reconfigure European directives and forms—Europeans began to fear that they would lose control over them. The self-imposed regulation by those in the Kaun, based in part on the injunctions of patrol and report, proved disconcerting to the administration and others in the colonial audience. In this context, the principal European concern became less that locals would continue to lead slovenly, backward, or otherwise "untidy" lives. That was more or less expected of them. Rather, there was the exacerbation of a primary colonial fear: that the "natives" would get seriously out of control. To return to the incident with which this chapter began, there was a specific fear that local discontent might intensify and flare up into "cult" activity, especially if stimulated by the presence of anthropologists, whose commitment to colonial strategies of containment was uncertain.

REESTABLISHING CONTROL

Significantly, Brereton, in what was regarded as an exemplary patrol report, did not mention the particulars of his conversation with the anthropologists. And rather than admitting the extent of his perplexity about how to think and act concerning the Kaun, he stated that its members needed more supervision because they were still backward.

"In short," Brereton wrote, "although independence is a good thing and it is necessary to stimulate the use of initiative, guidance is even more important to these people" (KPR 1968–1969: 24). As explicit evidence of their economic and political backwardness, Brereton reported the following:

> The anti-council faction object to councils on the grounds that once all the Territory comes under council influence, self-government is imminent. This is virtually true, but the point is that these people in their present lethargic state

would be lost in the rush. Their alternative to the council, the "Account" is, as predicted, not turning out to be a great success. Business wise they have not the education, as yet, to run such an enterprise properly. ... At the stage when the proposed Duke of York Council was discussed, the "Account" purchased another boat of workboat size. The reason being that council villages in the islands considered that a new council should buy a workboat as one of its first projects, and the "Account" not to be beaten, decided to buy one immediately as a token of their strength. Needless to say, buying in haste they made a bad decision and the particular boat has been in dry-dock most of the time since then, and is in danger of being repossessed as it has not been paid for. The people, however, follow in blind faith and do not query their leaders' actions. (p. 25)

Brereton's official report (which was, to reiterate once more, examined, commended, and then, passed on to the highest administrator in the territory) represented the Karavarans and other members of the Kaun as obviously unready for self-government. He thereby denied them the agency of their protest against the council, the body leading to self-government. Their protest against the council and by extension, the administration—was hence discounted as no more than a reflection of their backwardness. In effect, Brereton sought to render nugatory their emulation (and reconfiguration) of European practices by describing Kaun members as lethargic and lacking economic and political sophistication. Thus, in what was appraised by his superiors as exemplary colonial discursive form, Brereton expressed the dominant truth claim of the regime: "They" are backward and "we" are advanced and everything is, and should be, under our control.[17]

Brereton's visit to Karavar was not only to check up on the Karavarans and by extension, the Kaun, but also, as we have said, to look in on the resident anthropologists. The claims attributed to these anthropologists in the *South Pacific Post* were in many ways the opposite of those he was to make in his report. The publication of these remarks embarrassed the administration, which in turn found itself compelled both to refute them in a radio report to the colonial public and to discipline the anthropologists who had conveyed them.

The *South Pacific Post* had been accurate in publishing that "suspicion and hostility towards the Australian Administration have been expressed on the Duke of York Islands by some local villagers." And it was true that "Mr. Errington said he heard such remarks as 'Thank God the Americans are here, now we will get some help—the Australians are doing nothing for us.'" The purported interview with the anthropologists may have been welcomed by some portions of the colonial public inasmuch as it confirmed and publicized their suspicions that locals were far from ready for self-government. However, it probably also exacerbated their fears. Not only were there "restless natives," but so too were there irresponsible—out-of-control—Europeans who might undermine European interests. The newspaper article, thus, was doing more than reporting a disquieting situation in the Duke of York Islands as described by anthropologists. It was also reporting the anthropologists to the adminis- tration and the larger European community.

In so speaking about native people from their firsthand knowledge, these anthropologists were assuming for themselves the administration's role as a mediator between local people and the European population. They were, thereby, challenging an administration strategy of containment that was, at least in part, based on the control of knowledge generated through the patrol and its reports. They were suspect as points of "leakage" in this system of con- trol. Their anthropological authority was subject to subversive uses. As an- thropologists who actually lived with the people rather than as patrol officers who administered them, their loyalties were unclear. And, one might add, they were Americans rather than Australians at a time when Australia was un- der increasing international pressure to relinquish control over Papua New Guinea. Simply put, they might side with locals rather than with other Euro- peans, use their European prestige to undermine European interests, and gen- erally exacerbate colonial tensions.[18] Thus, for many of those invested in the colonial truth regime, these anthropologists might, in what appeared short- sighted and otherwise misguided ways, take seriously the Karavarans claim that the Australians were "doing nothing"; these American anthropologists might be induced to try to provide the "help" that locals sought. At the very least, they might become caught up—either wittingly or not—in local efforts to reconfigure the colonial system of differences.

STRATEGIC EMULATION

We have argued that through such means of surveillance and control as the patrols and patrol reports, Karavarans and other Duke of York Islanders came to see themselves as deficient orderers relative to Europeans. In consequence, they sought the procedural knowledge necessary to engage in such orderly ac- tivities as European business. In the course of their attempts to efface these differences between themselves and Europeans through emulation, they be- came more and more difficult for the administration to control and appeared increasingly threatening, additionally formidable. As their insistence on emulating European forms became publicized, the colonial strategies of containment appeared less effectual and the colonists, increasingly vulnerable.

The district commissioner appears to have been aware of this vulnerability. He was certainly concerned that the purported interview published in the *South Pacific Post* might have unpleasant consequences for the administration. It revealed that European control had made natives intractable rather than docile, resentful rather than compliant. Karavarans, it was reported, were angrily maintaining that if they were deficient, it was because the administration had done nothing to help them; that if they lacked European power, it was because the administration had denied them European knowledge. Moreover, the article implied that with their own resident European (anthropological) advisers—advisers who might (if their unregulated speech was any indication) try to help them fulfill their objectives to be the equals of Europeans—Karavarans would come to regard the administration as dispensable and perhaps to act upon this view.

The district commissioner's concerns, as we have shown, were not without cause. Karavarans were obdurately egalitarian and would not capitulate to the incommensurate differences of colonial evaluation; they would not accept, as they put it, being treated like dogs. Though the district commissioner had become aware of the "rather difficult situation of the Duke of Yorks" (KPR 1968–1969: 41), the newspaper article suggested a far higher degree of discontent than did the reports. Moreover, the process by which the reports were gathered—the process of colonial surveillance and control—was likely to engender further discontent (which might, in turn, be underestimated in the reports, giving rise to further unpleasant and public disclosures, etc.). In other words, the texts and the processes by which they were constructed contributed to specific events that mattered, such as the business activities of the Kaun; these in turn gave rise to other, different texts such as the newspaper account reporting the presence of cargoism and anthropologists, which in turn generated other reports and events, and so on.

In this chapter we have described what might be considered a "dialectics of culture and power, ideology and consciousness" (Comaroff and Comaroff 1991: 6) that shaped complex articulations between texts and events, articulations that constituted a portion of the late colonial history of the Duke of York Islands. Unfortunately, this dialectic did not result in equality with Europeans for the Karavarans and other members of the Kaun who sought to emulate the practices of European business. The Kaun did not succeed as a "business"—the world proved refractory—and only disappointingly meager quantities of cargo were obtained. Neither did equality follow for those members of the council in the Duke of York Islands who sought to emulate the practices of European local government. If Duke of York consciousness had been colonized, it was to the extent that locals attempted to understand their position in the colonial hierarchy by asking the wrong questions about themselves—by asking what *they* were doing wrong. As many have observed (see, for example, Memmi 1965; Fanon 1968a, 1968b), even the most assiduous and precise emulation of the colonizers by the colonized usually failed to transform significantly those the colonizers regarded as the demeaned other: The colonial strategies of containment were likely to be sufficiently resilient to guarantee that emulation could never be structure-breaking. To the extent that emulation was an effort to *meet* standards rather than *set* standards, the locals' truth claims remained vulnerable to the arbiters of the dominant discourse.

Yet in the case of the Kaun, although members did not win the equality they sought, they did take a measure of satisfaction from the grudging respect their intransigence eventually received from the administration. However, when Papua New Guinea gained independence in 1975, the dialectic shifted. Colonial dependence gave way to postcolonial economic influence and the Kaun lost much of this respect. It survived as a moribund enterprise only until about 1980, when its most eminent leader died. By that time, many Karavarans had come to be disillusioned, believing that its leaders had long been little more than outright thieves. Nonetheless, Karavarans continued to refuse to pay taxes to the council (and to its successor, the community government) until 1990. As a result, the East New Britain provincial government eventually withheld from them most services, including schooling. Consequently, during the 1980s, most Karavarans received little education; by the time of our 1991 research, they had come to realize with distress that fewer from their community were educated than in any other community in the Duke of York Islands.

During the late 1960s and early 1970s, the Karavarans had confronted the evident inequalities—the racial distinctions and social barriers—of the colonial regime with a mixture of anger and excitement. They regarded themselves as real contenders, as on the brink of achieving recognition from Europeans as equals. By the early 1990s, many Karavarans were not sanguine about their prospects for future importance.[19] This seems to have followed from the growing class differentiation that characterized the "development" in recent decades of a free-market economy in Papua New Guinea. With class differentiation, many of those who had remained villagers in the Duke of York Islands (and elsewhere) increasingly found themselves disadvantaged and peripheral.[20] We argue that Karavarans were not especially optimistic about their prospects not only because equality remained elusive despite decades of struggle but also because the nature of the struggle itself had changed.

As a colonial system of caste difference based on racial differentiation gave way to a postcolonial system of class difference reproduced (significantly in Papua New Guinea) through educational achievement and kinship networks, the oppositions became less obvious, the dialectic less dialogic. Inequality in the postcolonial context could not be as readily understood and confronted as a clear "us-them" dichotomy.[21] Simply put, class in Papua New Guinea proved more subtle (though perhaps no less durable) in its operation than caste.

Thus despite the end of colonialism, Karavarans were still troubled about their identity and worth. Indeed, during 1991, they still asked their visiting anthropologists why things had not worked out for them and for so many Papua New Guineans. It seems that in this perpetuation of inequality, the hierarchical system of incommensurate differences importantly propagated by the patrols and their reports, although not fully colonizing the egalitarian consciousness of all, proved far more tenacious than did the particular colonial administration that first implemented it.

*   *   *

In looking at the basic practices of colonial interaction as they affected Karavarans' lives, we have seen that the Karavarans have long been caught up in processes of cultural construction, historical contingency, and mutual determination. Though strongly affected by the European presence, Karavarans were neither crushed nor completely transformed by the colonial regime. Instead, they continued with (dogged) resilience to negotiate their worth and identity with each other, their Duke of York neighbors, and colonial powers of various sorts. In the next chapter, we show how contentions over media of crucial importance in determining such worth and identity—shell money versus European money—got played out against the background of the procedures of colonial administration and discipline. We continue to explore the nature of colonial interactions, including their effect on the politics of postindependence Papua New Guinea, wherein some were trying to control—to represent and subsume—others much as the colonists had attempted.

NOTES

1. This inquiry, in other words, takes seriously Nicholas Dirks's warning that analyses of colonial situations all too often obscured the historical experience of colonialism in "the elegant new textualism of colonial discourse studies" (1992: 175).

2. Subsequent to Papua New Guinea's independence in 1975, Karavar came to be located in the province of East New Britain.

3. The district commissioner's speech was in English, a language few Karavarans and other Duke of York Islanders understood. Moreover, although there were some radios on the Duke of York Islands, there were none on Karavar at that time.

4. Fred felt thoroughly shaken by this incident that threatened to cut short the research on which his dissertation was to be based; he also felt uncomfortably delinquent. Told in graduate school that a cardinal rule of fieldwork was to avoid embarrassing the local administration, he blamed himself for what appeared a thoroughgoing breach of discipline, both of the administration and his chosen profession. Not only silenced but also wishing for silence, he vowed to watch himself in the future. He was determined, at least for the time, to be prudently self-surveillant.

5. In citing these records of inspection, we present them as written without the use of "sic" or other such devices.

6. Some of the reports contained startling errors indicating no knowledge of basic social practices. A few, in contrast, contained quite accurate accounts concerning, for instance, kinship, inheritance, and land tenure.

7. If we follow Lila Abu-Lughod's (1990) elaboration on Foucault (1982), Karavaran resistance can be seen as an index of European power. Still, there was much about the colonial administration they had come to accept and, at least by 1968, welcome.

8. In certain limited ways Karavarans were likely to regard themselves as better than Europeans. For instance, on particular occasions focusing on the male *dukduk* and *tubuan* ritual, Karavarans (and their Duke of York Island neighbors) thought they were able to establish a level of order exceeding that of Europeans. However, such moments were seen as transitory. (See Errington 1974a and 1974b for further discussion.) As we show in Chapter 2, Karavarans, at least on occasion, also considered their indigenous shell money superior to European money in that the former entailed, and thus built social relations, in a way that the latter generally did not.

9. In contrast to Errington's (1974b) discussion of Karavaran cargoism, in which the Karavaran preoccupation with order was seen as indigenous, the position advanced here is that this concern was, in at least significant respects, a product of interaction with Europeans.

10. The replication in cargoism of aspects of colonial life did seem to disquiet colonists. Perhaps for some this was because in seeing themselves refracted in the dominated other who in some regards emulated them, they disliked themselves both for what they had done to natives and for what they were.

11. By this point in their colonial history, Karavarans and many of their Duke of York neighbors had come to view their precontact past as the *momboto,* a time of darkness when people could not see the path of proper conduct, a time when incest, cannibalism, and other "savage" behaviors were rife (cf. Young 1977; Shore 1982; White 1991). As we show in Chapter 3, this view of their own precontact state had been strongly influenced by mission teachings that stressed the dramatic enlighten-

ment effected by those intrepid Europeans who had brought the gospel. But as we have also been arguing with respect to patrol and report, many of their encounters with members of the colonial administration (as well as with other sorts of colonists) had conveyed to locals that, relative to Europeans, they were deficient in their present material and social lives. In this regard, it might be noted that many of these colonial pronouncements conform strikingly to Fanon's general description of colonial policy: "When we consider the efforts made to carry out the cultural estrangement so characteristic of the colonial epoch, we realize that nothing has been left to chance and that the total result looked for by colonial domination was indeed to convince the natives that colonialism had come to lighten their darkness. The effect consciously sought by colonialism was to drive into the natives' heads the idea that if the settlers were to leave, they would at once fall back into barbarism, degradation, and bestiality" (Fanon 1968b: 210–211). However, it must be noted that, although Karavarans did accept as accurate the portrayal of their past as characterized by the *momboto* and the portrayal of their present as characterized by the deficiency of order, they did not regard these circumstances as in any way justifying Europeans treating them as less than potential equals.

12. We have, of course, avoided the claim that patrols were the only mechanism by which colonial order was imposed on local people. As the reference to plantations suggests, Karavarans—especially Karavaran men who had engaged in contract labor (in most cases prior to World War II)—had encountered other forms of discipline that had impressed (and oppressed) them.

13. Although we do not intend to provide a general discussion of cargo cults or cargoism in this chapter, we might mention that cargo activities elsewhere in Melanesia often displayed apparently similar concerns with order. Thus, for example, Peter Lawrence in his classic *Road Belong Cargo* (1964) reported the construction of special villages carefully laid out with an emphasis on neatness and sanitation. In some cases, there was the inauguration of paramilitary order. Lawrence described an instance in which the cargo cult replicated important hierarchical aspects of the European administration, such as going on patrol.

14. In their effort to become like Europeans, the Karavarans and other members of the Kaun sought to initiate a process of virtually instantaneous transformation instead of gradual transition. This corresponded to a view that time was episodic rather than evolutionary. See Errington (1974b) for further discussion of Karavaran ideas of process and time as they became significant in the activities of the Kaun.

15. In addition to their activities within the Kaun, Karavarans and some of their Duke of York neighbors were pursuing other means of redressing colonial inequalities. For instance, they were actively—in fact, sometimes militantly—seeking the return of European-held plantations in the area, claiming that they had never received proper compensation for the land. (Some of these land claims proved successful subsequent to Papua New Guinea's independence.) They also sought help from such in-

stitutions as the United Nations and the queen of England in fostering their economic development.

16. During the late 1960s and early 1970s, many of the conversations Fred had with nonofficial European colonists living in the Rabaul area revealed fears concerning independence. These conversations focused largely on speculations about what would happen to white-owned property once the black majority came to control the government. Also, colonists felt their own safety was at stake, in particular the safety of women and children, when the as-yet-uncivilized natives were no longer regulated by white officials.

17. Although we do not think that Karavarans and other members of the Kaun were threatening serious civil disobedience, they were posing a serious problem. Yet Brereton chose not to so report because his competence and his patrol report would be judged by whether things were under control.

18. In regard to colonists' fears that visiting Europeans might undermine white interests—might let their side down—consider the following passage from a 1935 edition of the *Rabaul Times* to welcome the second tourist ship to Rabaul. (It was published when the "dog affair" was active on Karavar.) "There is another point that should be stressed for the benefit of our visitors and ourselves: It is the matter of deportment before the natives. One of our most important assets in this country is the prestige of the White Race; this must be maintained by all classes of Whites in order to obtain the respect of a subject race for those in authority" (n.p.).

19. As we show in Chapter 4, however, there were Karavarans (some 20%) who had left the United Church to become members of the evangelical New Church and were decidedly upbeat about the future and their role in it.

20. For an analysis of class formation throughout the Pacific, see Hooper et al. 1987.

21. Of course, class was important in colonial Papua New Guinea. However, as Albert Memmi (1965) suggested, class differences among colonists were frequently collapsed into categorical racial oppositions. See, in this regard, note 18 concerning the importance of maintaining a "united front" in support of white prestige.

2

Dueling Currencies in East New Britain

The Construction of Shell Money as National Cultural Property

WE PURSUE OUR general interest in exploring the changes that have led Karavarans and their neighbors to become preoccupied about their own identity and worth in the nation of Papua New Guinea by examining in this chapter one instance of a political process increasingly engaged in by indigenous and minority groups throughout the world. These groups have begun to promote and defend their own representations of identity by invoking images and other embodiments of tradition, history, and ethnicity.[1] Here we describe such a politicization of culture in East New Britain, one that centered on a recent phase in a history of contrast between native and introduced currencies. As part of an ongoing struggle to determine the representation of self and other, *both* certain East New Britains and their colonizers had long invoked contrasting sets of essentialisms—powerfully and dramatically simplified contrasts—about the nature of shell money and (for want of a better term) money.[2] In the case we consider, locally generated essentialisms had also become part of the efforts by these East New Britains to define and validate themselves in the contemporary world of Papua New Guinea: They sought to portray a set of their activities centering on shell money as national cultural property and, moreover, as a matter of special national concern—as constitutive of national identity. In our discussion, we explore a range of different his-

---

An earlier version of this chapter will appear in James Carrier, ed., *Occidentalism* (Oxford: Oxford University Press, forthcoming).

torical factors at work in the emergence of these politically significant essentialisms, in this case those focusing on currency. In so doing, we stress the importance of these essentialisms as they contributed to the self-representations that were asserted as constituting national identity.

The effort to establish national identity through the creation of national cultural property has, of course, been reported elsewhere (see Morphy 1983; McBryde 1985; Dominguez 1986; Handler 1985, 1988). Here we seek to elucidate the process by which certain activities, objects, and events became eligible for promotion to national cultural property and hence definitive of national identity. We do so by examining an instance in which the central and contrasting essentialisms on which national identity so often rested were generated and invoked. Exploring this process is especially important to an understanding of postcolonial politics in such places as Papua New Guinea. Nationalism, necessitating both the creation of unity and the maintenance of a relatively coherent cultural distinctiveness within the world at large, was likely to be especially difficult to achieve in a context like Papua New Guinea where there was enormous cultural pluralism and little collective history.

In short, we examine one strategy for establishing national identity, specifically, an attempt by members of a particular group, one that had become relatively powerful during the colonial and postcolonial periods, to promote, through invoking historically salient essentialisms concerning currency, certain of their cultural practices as representative of the nation as a whole. These cultural practices, as we shall see, had much to recommend them in providing one possible basis of a Papua New Guinea nation, a polity both unified and distinctive. However, that they were needed at all to consolidate Papua New Guinea's diversity virtually ensured that they would be strongly contested.

SETTING THE SCENE

Near the end of our 1991 fieldwork in Karavar, a collection of postcolonial characters converged to engage in a drama which struck us at the time as typical of this general process by which essentialisms were employed to construct identity. The drama featured what has become a relatively standardized cast and plot as well as events that were indeed of enhanced—dramatic—significance. Yet, particularly on reflection, this drama seems to have been more than merely typical. It was especially instructive both in its form and its content (cf. Silverman 1977). As a confrontation between locals and those foreigners wishing to exploit them, it was an assertion of the political autonomy prototypic of a postcolonial, nationalist will (cf. Kapferer 1988, 1989). It also starred, in this assertion, a set of local cultural practices remarkably well suited for promotion to national cultural property. Clearly, not any set of cultural practices would do; not any set could convince a critical audience to suspend its disbelief (and distrust) and entertain the idea that the portrayal represented more than matters of local concern.

The case we observed focused on the media of value and transaction themselves. It focused on what became presented, by means of essentializing contrasts, as the relationship between indigenous and western currencies—between shell money and money. In thinking about the drama, we came to realize the extent to which these currencies were (to paraphrase both Malinowski [1954: 44–47] and Lévi-Strauss [1963: 89]) good to use as well as good to think. Shell money and money were thoroughly embedded in the daily lives of most we knew of these East New Britains. Moreover, for them, the relationship between shell money and money encapsulated and embodied the colonial and postcolonial encounter in a remarkably salient way. In addition, the two currencies conveyed that encounter in a way that could be readily recognized by Papua New Guineans generally. As we shall see in the drama and our discussion of it, the representational value in East New Britain of shell money—in its contrast to money—might (to paraphrase Bourdieu 1977: 167) have come without saying, but it had long ceased to go without saying.[3]

THE DRAMA

The Characters (all names except ours have been changed and identities, as far as feasible, obscured):

> *The Foreign Missionary* (Father Joseph Crane, an American priest stationed in the Duke of York Islands, interested in increasing church revenues through the sale of native artifacts)
>
> *The Artifact Dealer* (Herr Franz Müller, owner of an artifact gallery in Munich, Germany, specializing in Papua New Guinea *Kunst*)
>
> *A Member of the Indigenous Elite* (Dr. Isaac Tolanger, director of a Papua New Guinea research organization empowered to grant or deny export permits)
>
> *The Expatriate Adviser* (Dr. Martin Brown, an American anthropologist and expert on indigenous arts and crafts)
>
> *The Tolai Elder* (Mr. Paulis Toling, businessman and politician of a Tolai village)

The Community Government Officer (Mr. Patrick Sulia of the Sepik region, who was stationed in the Duke of York Islands)

The Field-Workers (Drs. Frederick Errington and Deborah Gewertz, periodically resident on Karavar Island in the Duke of York group)

The Tolai Youths (a sardonic assortment)

The Plot: Before the curtain goes up, community government officer Sulia informs the audience that there has recently been trouble concerning the export of a *tubuan* figure—a mask, as mentioned, that was used in the male ritual of the neighboring and closely related Tolai and Duke of York peoples; Father Crane had tried to send one to Müller in Germany but was stopped when Sulia discovered that the elders giving Crane local permission to export were none other than his catechists.

Scene 1: The Berlin Museum. Franz Müller researches traditional arts and crafts of New Britain, part of the German colony of New Guinea prior to World War I. He collects photographs and descriptions of "traditional" masks and ritual figures—many, such as those once made for the cannibalistic *iniet* organization, no longer in use—and of coils of shell money decorated with archaic designs. He sends these to Father Crane, who contracts with New Britain villagers to reproduce them. The villagers are happy to earn money and are also moderately interested to learn about their forgotten heritage.

Scene 2: Port Moresby, Papua New Guinea. Müler has sent Brown photographs allegedly covering the entire contents of the two large shipping containers of artifacts and shell money he and Crane wish to export. Suspicious of both Müler and Crane and unfamiliar with the cultural area from which the artifacts come, Brown is reluctant to approve their export until he consults with Tolanger, a Tolai. Tolanger is particularly alarmed at the proposed export of the shell money, which is of central importance in the *tubuan* organization and in many other social interactions. He flies to Rabaul, the capital of East New Britain and the center of the Tolai homeland, to intercept and examine the shipment.

Scene 3: Rabaul. Tolanger, in the company of Paulis Toling and Tolai youth, meet Crane by his two containers at the Rabaul international wharf. (Müller by this time is no longer in Papua New Guinea.) Crane removes some innocuous artifacts from the front of the first container and evasively claims that all the rest are just like these. Tolanger, smelling a rat (if not a *tubuan* mask), insists that all the contents be revealed. He, Toling, and the Tolai youth watch with angry amusement—chewing betel nut and smoking in the shade of a nearby tree—while Crane, perspiring freely, begins to unpack the containers in the noonday tropical sun. Soon a *tubuan* mask not included in the list of contents submitted for export is revealed, as well as a number of coils of shell money. Tolanger blocks export permission for the entire shipment.

Scene 4: Port Moresby. Tolanger describes his encounter with Crane to the field-workers, who are paying him a courtesy call. He explains the need for a policy on national cultural property that would protect Papua New Guinea as a whole against cultural loss. In addition, the policy would protect objects associated with secret organizations, even those objects explicitly made for sale and export, from being displayed to the public—any public. He would have this policy cover objects of significance to contemporary secret organizations, such as the *tubuan,* as well as objects of significance to those organizations that have not existed for decades. Rather than viewing Müller and Crane as perhaps stimulating crafts production and reviving culture, he sees them as encouraging natives to debase their tradition and as stealing their heritage. Of most concern to Tolanger, importantly, is their attempt to export shell money. Under no circumstances, he explains, should this be permitted, since shell money is "vital to the culture and to the country." Perplexed by the intricacies of the cultural politics of representation—the dispute about preservation and self-determination—the field-workers leave to begin thinking about this conflict.

INITIAL THOUGHTS

As we have already suggested, whenever we thought of these East New Britain events they took the form of a drama because the characters—their conversations and concerns—had become relatively standardized not only throughout Papua New Guinea but elsewhere in the "third" and "fourth" worlds. Moreover, the events were presented with respect to the actors and audience alike as having enhanced significance, as being particularly compelling. Indeed, variations of this drama, generated by histories of comparable disparities in power, have also been enacted in recent years among, for example, the Maori, Australian Aborigines, and Native Americans. In these cases, as in the East New Britain drama, an overriding concern has been the ownership and display of objects—generally sacred objects—expressing (and inventing) particular cultural traditions.[4]

What struck us as remarkable, though, about the East New Britain drama was that it focused not primarily on sacred objects but on shell money. Certainly contentions over Hopi kachina dolls and Aboriginal sacred sites had prepared us to understand why Tolanger and other Tolai might object to the export and profane viewing of sacred objects such as the *tubuan.* (Presumably,

Tolanger placed the newly made *iniet* objects in the same category of the sacred as the *tubuan*. We might mention that the justification for restricting access to ritual objects regarded as secret by long-dead ancestors can be complex. And the complexity was augmented in this case because the *iniet* objects, for instance, were used for cannibalistic sorcery, an activity generally disapproved of by most, if not all, of the practitioners' long-Christianized descendants.) The controversy over shell money, however, concerned an object that by its very nature was thoroughly, quintessentially, public.

Shell money, called *tabu* (or *tambu*) by the Tolai and *divara* (or *diwara*) by the Duke of York Islanders, consisted of small cowrie shells (*Nassa camelus*) strung onto strips of rattan and counted either individually or measured on the body in standard lengths. The most important length has been described by European commentators as the "fathom." Continuously spliced, these strips could be arranged in large wrapped and sometimes decorated coils containing hundreds of fathoms. (In regard to their shell money, the neighboring Tolai and Duke of York Islanders were identical.[5])

Although there was some (mostly early) debate challenging the status of shell money as money (Malinowski 1921; Roheim 1923; Einzig 1949; Douglas 1967), most of those who have worked among these East New Britains have agreed that it did have the status of money. T. S. Epstein, for instance, described it as "true money. It acted as a generally accepted medium of exchange: food was bought and sold for money; it provided a measure of value; forces of supply and demand determined the tambu price for most articles sold. Moreover, it was a liquid asset as well as a store of value: large coils represented the accumulated wealth of the Tolai [and Duke of York Islanders] (1968: 26). We must also add that shell money was the single standard by which not only everything but everyone was distinguished. The differences in the amount of shell money that an individual owned and used in public ceremonies distinguished a person of importance from one of mere respectability and the latter from one of no consequence. Shell money was fundamental to the prestige system and to the ordering of social life. (See, among others, Errington 1974b; Bradley 1982; Neumann 1992: 183–190.)

Finally, it should be noted that in the modern era shells were purchased with money (now the Papua New Guinea kina), often from trade-store owners who acquired them from as far afield as Malaita in the Solomon Islands. So the shell money that Crane and Müller wished to export in the form of coils, although entirely acceptable for exchange, might never have been in circulation. It might, for instance, have been purchased by Crane from outside

Shell money was fundamental to the prestige system and to the ordering of social life.

Papua New Guinea and strung by his parishioners. In our discussion with Tolanger concerning the source of Crane's shell money, neither its actual provenance nor economic history seemed especially relevant to him. He was far more concerned with its cultural than with its fiscal significance. (We subsequently discovered that the shells had been used by local people to purchase trade goods at the Catholic mission store Crane ran. We also think that if we had suggested to Tolanger that he charge Müller and Crane enough money so that he could import shells from the Solomon Islands sufficient to replace (or exceed) the shell money they wished to export, he would probably not have been satisfied.) Consistent with what we interpreted as his concerns, the nationally circulated daily newspaper ran a picture of Tolanger, Toling, and two unidentified Tolai standing beside some fifteen coils of shell money. The caption read: "Cultural shipment confiscated" (*Post Courier* 1991: 3).

Given that shell money in various forms from unstrung shells to long lengths could be bought and sold for money and was itself a public medium of exchange, our initial response was, Why all the fuss? As we shall see, although the effort to export shell money as artifact was new, the antecedents of the fuss were of long standing. Because shell money had been both means and marker of intercultural negotiation, it had acquired a particularly salient representational value. Shell money embodied the condensed essentialisms that constituted for local people a particular version of colonial history; its continued use in everyday life imbued common and pervasive transactions with emblematic significance. Tolanger's indignation, in other words, was well justified.

In our initial speculations on this drama, we began to see that by virtue of their political potentialities, the events precipitated by Crane and Müller were remarkably serendipitous. The Tolai were well educated and prosperous relative to other Papua New Guineans. Because of their early European contact and, with the move of the German administrative center to New Britain, their close and long-term proximity to the center of government, Tolai were—even in comparison to Duke of York Islanders—"given a headstart in educational and economic development" (Bray 1985b: 191). Therefore, these events were an opportunity to promote local self-identity and so to augment national influence and prominence.[6]

ESSENTIALISMS IN THE GENERATION OF
SHELL MONEY AS CULTURAL PROPERTY

Unlike a great many indigenous currencies employed elsewhere in Papua New Guinea, the shell money used by the Tolai and Duke of York Islanders retained the full range of uses that it had at the time of contact. It remained of great significance as a means of paying for goods and services and as a means of establishing and maintaining social relationships. All modern field-workers among the Tolai and the Duke of York Islanders have recognized the continuing centrality of shell money in social life, its status as a "social fact" (Durkheim 1964). T. S. Epstein (1968), A. L. Epstein (1963, 1969), and Richard Salisbury (1966, 1970) were primarily interested in the uses of shell money in Tolai socioeconomic organization and change; Frederick Errington (1974a) focused on the importance of shell money in ritual processes of social reproduction in the Duke of York Islands; A. L. Epstein (1979) extended his economic analysis to account for the persistence of shell money in psychoanalytic terms; Christine Bradley (1982) examined the effects of shell money on Tolai relations of power, particularly as they pertained to gender; Klaus Neumann (1992) studied the shifting patterns of shell-money use among the Tolai in colonial and postcolonial contexts; and most recently, Jacob Simet (1992) documented the complex and pervasive articulations of shell money with other aspects of Tolai social life.

All of these approaches have illuminated the meanings, functions, and uses of shell money in social life itself, whether for the Tolai or Duke of York Islander, even while that social life was changing. However, we suggest that what has been written so far as to the centrality of shell money does not fully account for the alarm that the prospect of its export as artifact created. To explain this alarm, we need to understand not only its centrality but also its status as cultural property. (After all, the U.S. dollar has been central to American life, yet Americans have generally been pleased when foreign investors sought to acquire dollars. To be sure, there have been restrictions on the export of large quantities of dollars, but dollars have not usually been regarded as cultural property.) Thus, we need to understand not only how shell money operated for Tolai and Duke of York Islanders but what it signified vis-à-vis its proposed export to Germany.

To elucidate the alarm, and the drama, we must recognize that it was around the essentialized similarities and differences, some clearly recognized from the first and some emerging only gradually, between shell money and money that much of the history (histories) of interaction between colonized and colonizer coalesced. Such perceived similarities and differences, not only between currencies but between those who used them, had long been part of the politics of representation that both reflected and shaped Tolai and Duke of York Islander histories. Although much, including much about the relationship among currencies, will probably never be known (it would now be difficult, for example, to determine in detail how European currency was indigenously evaluated when introduced in the late nineteenth century), there are some provocative data in the colonial record that may serve to illustrate the general process.

Consider, for example, the following early account: In 1888, the Reverend Benjamin Danks, one of the first Methodist missionaries to work in the region, represented his (potential) flock, which then consisted primarily of Duke of York Islanders and Tolai, as largely the product of their shell money and their use of it. He believed that because they valued shell money, they were "frugal and industrious" and that "their commercial transactions extend to places they have never visited" (1888: 316). He also believed, however, that shell money fostered undesirable traits: "A people whose greatest love is reserved for money, and whose highest aim is to get money, is an exceedingly hard-hearted and an intensely selfish people" (1888: 316). Interestingly, and a point we shall return to, Danks's perception of these local people as both industrious and avaricious reflected the contradictory perceptions, the ambiguous moral value, of money that has existed in *Western* ideology. Evidently, in his view (but, as we will show, not in theirs), their actions were both social and antisocial because their money was like our money: both "devilish acid or ... instrument and guarantor of liberty" (Bloch and Parry 1989: 30).

The colonial record also suggests that, at least initially for the indigenous peoples of the region, shell money prevailed over money as the more desirable currency.[7] This preference was noted in the German administration's annual report for 1900–1901: "It was often very difficult for the European firms to obtain the shell required to purchase copra etc. In this respect they were completely dependent on the natives, and at times the exchange rate for shell money was forced up absurdly high. ... In view of these facts, the Government, by an Ordinance of 18 October, 1900, prohibited trading in *diwara*. ... From the same date the use of any kind of shell money in commercial transactions was forbidden" (translated by Sack and Clark 1979: 220).

Apparently, then, from early in their (and Papua New Guinea's) post-contact history, Tolai and Duke of York Islanders were perceived as adept in controlling Europeans so as to drive hard bargains that yielded them good returns in shell money. In this encounter, shell money remained so strongly the currency of preference for indigenes that its use had to be limited by colonial law.

Indeed, it would appear that during much, if not the entire course, of colonial history shell money had an oppositional role to money, perhaps serving to sustain local identity through resistance to what were perceived as extraneous forces.[8] Certainly, as mentioned, during the periods of Fred's 1968 and 1972 research and our 1991 joint research, shell money was frequently described by Duke of York Islanders in terms of an essentialized contrast to money: Shell money was extolled as "heavy" (*mawat*)—as substantial and significant—as capable of generating the activities on which both male and female reputations were built and social order rested; money was denigrated as "light" (*biaku*)—as flimsy and inconsequential—as incapable of creating or sustaining personal worth or enduring social relationships. (See Errington 1974a.) Additionally, we were frequently told by our Duke of York assistants that they would have preferred for us to pay them in shell money, if only we had enough shell money to give them. Their stated reason was that shell money stayed on the island or region to generate further exchanges; money merely flitted away in the purchase of easily broken, imported goods. Locals actively sought opportunities to convert money into shell money; men often wished us to photograph them next to their rolls of shell money.[9]

This relatively contemporary evidence suggests that the preference for shell money expressed early in colonial history, much less so more recently, was not a preference for one morally ambiguous medium over another, as Danks might have thought. Rather, it was a preference for a medium that through its

Men often wished us to photograph them next to their rolls of shell money.

acquisition, accumulation, and distribution established personal reputation, social good, and cultural identity and worth.

Yet the ongoing negotiations concerning cultural identity and worth also transformed the system in which Duke of York Islanders and Tolai were negotiating. Subsequent to the enactment in 1900 of the ordinance prohibiting transactions between Europeans and indigenes in shell money, local peoples in such contexts as labor and land values, world copra prices, taxes, and the cost of trade goods have been strongly affected by international capital and its fluctuations.[10] Although, as indicated, most Duke of York Islanders and Tolai continued to value shell money highly, they certainly became interested in acquiring money. Without doubt, they became fascinated with it: As shell money was the basis of an indigenous leader's power, money appeared the basis of colonial power.

Hence their fascination with money went well beyond a need to pay taxes or to purchase trade goods. (In fact, in parts of East New Britain, it has recently become possible to pay taxes not with money but with shell money.)[11] As we have already seen, from the 1930s until the mid-1980s, many Duke of York Islanders and some Tolai organized themselves under traditional leadership into cargo movements. They wished not simply to acquire money for European goods but also to engage Europeans as comparable in power, as social equals.

*In parts of East New Britain, it has recently become possible to pay
taxes with shell money.*

Certainly, as we have suggested, Karavaran cargo activities had this latter objective. Their "dog" movement, to reiterate a point we made in Chapter 1, was
designed to determine why Europeans repudiated them as if they were dogs.
Locals eventually decided that they were treated with such little respect, as so
powerless and insignificant, because they did not know how to participate in
European business practices: They did not know, for instance, how to build a
factory, to order goods, to acquire money. Their postwar Kaun movement, as
we have shown, was a collective effort to raise large sums of money in order to

duplicate such European business practices as ordering from overseas.[12] It was an effort designed to duplicate these practices so as to affirm local identity, to represent themselves as equivalent in worth to Europeans. Indeed, some, such as the Tolai who joined the Mataungan Association—a micronationalist movement that emerged in 1969 and was dedicated to immediate self-government—believed themselves already equivalent in worth to Europeans.[13] To be a Mataungan, one analyst of the movement said, was "to stand on one's own two legs in front of Europeans and to decide for oneself whether to say 'Yes' and then, whether to add 'Sir'" (Grosart 1982: 142).

We can piece together a number of such instances of local resistance, differentiation, qualified emulation, and self-confident assertion. These did not, of course, make the Tolai and Duke of York Islanders unusual in Papua New Guinea. However, it is our speculation that the colonial experiences of these shell-money users were importantly distinctive. In this part of East New Britain, some of the risks of historical action (Sahlins 1985: 143–156)—the likelihood that events would disprove cultural assumptions—were reduced in that both shell-money users and Europeans shared, and perceived with *relative* accuracy that they shared, *somewhat* comparable organizing principles: Both relied upon a universal currency. This, we suspect, contributed to a contact situation in which crucial aspects of colonial hegemony could be countered rather effectively and over a long period. Simply put, much of the discourse between colonizers and colonized was conducted in terms that, for shell-money users, both validated their concepts and enabled them to negotiate their autonomy with considerable skill.

From the very first, each found the other able and willing to transact, to do "business." Furthermore, the initial sense of mutual similarity did not dissolve into one of *great* difference, as was so often the case in contact situations.[14] And as far as we currently know, the Duke of York Islanders and Tolai did not come to regard themselves as diminished by virtue of the differences they did recognize between themselves and the Europeans.[15] Unlike many Papua New Guinea groups, these shell-money users did not apparently come to experience their ritual complexes and attendant valuables as "rubbish" in contrast to those of Europeans. For instance, the leaders of their cargo movements were "big men" whose power continued to be based—as it had been before the Europeans arrived—on the use of shell money in ritual and marriage transactions. Shell money and money, in other words, remained sufficiently similar so that the latter did not invalidate the former.

Although shell money and money were in many important ways comparable, there were also areas of subtle but significant differences. These differences, as we shall see, eventually became for locals the basis of an essentializing critique of money that would provide cultural animation for Tolanger's alarm. This critique stemmed from their perception, shared with Europeans, that money itself had an ambiguous moral value. In this respect, locals regarded shell money as superior to money.

From the Western perspective, the ambiguous moral value of money may well have been rooted, as Bloch and Parry suggested, in the disjunction in capitalist societies between short-term and long-term interests and between matters of everyday strategizing (often in pursuit of individualistic, self-indulgent pleasures) and matters of social reproduction (1989: 23–30). In Western capitalist societies, therefore, it was likely to be a matter of concern and contention whether those activities focusing on the accumulation of money subtracted from or augmented the social whole (thus the ambivalence in the fascination with which Americans watch Donald Trump). Yet such a distinction between short-term personal and long-term public interests did not arise within this East New Britain context concerning the accumulation and use of shell money. Duke of York Islanders and Tolai viewed sociality as generated by the use of shell money, especially, at least until recently, through the shell-money exchanges and other transactions of big men. The shell-money expenditures of big men were the politics of both self-aggrandizement and social reproduction. (This is not to say that big men could not act asocially as, for example, with the practice of sorcery. However, the possession of shell money seemed to be regarded as inherently socializing, as we shall see in Chapter 5.) As Richard Salisbury said for the Tolai, a big man "creates a name, not for himself alone, but in terms of which other people can organize themselves" (n.d.: 30). (See also Bradley 1982; Neumann 1992: 183–203.)

The fact that these East New Britains and Europeans might readily have agreed that "money maketh the man" but far less readily have agreed that "the [monied] man maketh society" generated, as one might expect, misunderstanding and conflict. To judge from their cargo activities, including the "dog" movement, Duke of York Islanders and Tolai (like many other Papua New Guineans) were troubled that their transactions in money had not established enduring relations with Europeans. (Recall, once again in this regard, the chief who attempted to exchange betel nut with the Reverend Rickard.) Unlike their transactions in shell money, which generated local sociality, transactions with Europeans frequently led nowhere. (See Parry 1989 for a comparable point.) The difference in the capacities of shell money and money to establish relationships that not only were enduring but effected social reproduction was, we think, interpreted by many Duke of York Islanders and Tolai as indicating the superiority of shell money: Shell money was "heavy" because it entailed transactors in pervasive and ramifying ways, as money apparently did not. (See Counts and Counts 1970 for supporting, comparative evidence.) In this regard the cargo activities we have discussed among the Duke of York Islanders and the Tolai can be seen as efforts to bring money up to the standards of shell money to effect social reproduction. (We stress again that we are concerned here with the relationship between essentializing—and hence partial—*perceptions* of these currencies. It must be noted, therefore, that not all transactions in shell money actually established or were meant to establish ongoing social relations. Such relations, after all, could be burdensome. Nor, of course, was it impossible for monetary transactions to establish enduring relations.)[16]

Thus shell money not only had retained its value as a medium of exchange in Duke of York and Tolai social life but had remained the exemplar of what a medium of exchange should be. (Perhaps the capacities of the Duke of York and Tolai universal currencies to resist displacement might provide oblique confirmation of Kopytoff's appraisal of money as "fundamentally seductive," as inexorably conquering the internal economies of all societies into which it is introduced [1986: 72].)

Although most Europeans were no doubt unaware of the criteria against which their currency was being judged, they certainly understood that local people wished to alter their social arrangements with Europeans. Cargo movements in this East New Britain area and elsewhere in Papua New Guinea were chronic sources of European concern. At best, they were seen as distracting local people from (what Europeans regarded as) productive labor and at worst, as politically subversive. Indeed, many Europeans feared industrial action, if not insurrection. For instance, in January 1929 during what has become known as the Rabaul police strike, native police and contract workers left their jobs to protest low wages and practices of corporal punishment. Although their demonstrations near the Methodist and Catholic mission stations were entirely orderly and their walkout suppressed in a few hours, the European community was thrown into a panic and rage at what many feared was an effort by the black majority to seize power through a general strike. A citizens' committee was formed to ensure that the strike leaders were imprisoned and that efforts to improve native education were curtailed.

To be sure, some Europeans admitted that local people were justified in viewing economic and social differentials as unfair. But even the more sensitive of these Europeans were likely to regard these differentials as unavoidable, at least for the time being. In this regard, a 1941 edition of the *Rabaul Times* explained the robbery of a Chinese carpenter, relatively well paid by non-European standards, by three of his Papua New Guinean plantation coworkers in the following manner: "The three felt considerably annoyed [by the disparity in pay] … for was one not a senior lorry driver, another a 'boss' boy, while another was an old hand copra cutter? To them it was a very unjust world, even as millions of low paid workers have felt in every country before them. They adopted the primitive method of remedying this injustice—of effecting an equal distribution of wealth" (1941a: n.p.).

Eventually, in a gradual move from their own "primitive method" of control through outright oppression, Europeans pursued more sophisticated ways to remedy their anxieties about the possible consequences of colonial injustices. Consider, for example, a set of European-published pamphlets about money and its uses. In these pamphlets money, and by direct extension European life and the colonial presence, were represented as proper and inevitable. These pamphlets are especially interesting, for they illustrate a process by which increasingly explicit meanings—in this case those embodied in money and in shell money—came to have additionally enhanced representational value. These pamphlets, which contributed to the ongoing transformation of what came without saying into what could no longer go without saying, proceeded through a set of European-generated essentialisms distinguishing between "us" and "them."

These European essentialisms, in turn, we believe, laid some of the ideological groundwork for the creation by local people of cultural property. Shell money was to become more than a medium of exchange that contrasted with money; it became cultural property and the subject of the alarm that was central to our drama.

THE PAMPHLETS

During the late 1960s, the Reserve Bank of Australia, in association with banks operating in Papua New Guinea, issued a series of clearly written, though disingenuous, pamphlets entitled *Your Money, Prices, Banks and Banking, Keeping a Checque Account,* and *What Is Wealth?* These pamphlets were designed "for use by secondary school children and others who want to learn something about money and saving" (*Your Money* n.d.: i). They were widely available throughout the country at banks, libraries, and schools. Not surprisingly, these pamphlets failed to deal directly with colonialism and its effects. Presenting the desire for wealth as "natural because we all like to make progress and have a better standard of living" (*What Is Wealth?* n.d.: 8), they answered the question of why some people fulfill this natural desire more completely than others by referring to hard and efficient work:

> Some people do not understand how richer persons get good homes, motor cars, refrigerators, radios and furniture while other people who also work hard, still have to live in small huts.
>
> The people who own these things have got them ... by saving, by working and earning money, by growing crops for sale, by raising livestock, by trading or by obtaining them from relatives. Most of them have worked hard but also efficiently. People train as Teachers and Government officials. Others train as Doctors, Lawyers or Engineers, and so on. They earn more money in this way because of their training. Other people train as organisers of businesses and factories so that they can also earn more money.
>
> In every country of the world, there have always been some people who are more wealthy than other people. (*What Is Wealth?* n.d.: 9–10)

Nowhere in these pamphlets was there any mention of race, class, or relative position in colonial society—all those factors that determined access to training. For instance, those with sufficient training to read the pamphlets must have been aware that even they had to transact their banking at a desk apart from those used by Europeans.[17]

Local readers of the pamphlets, moreover, were told nothing about the importance of ownership in the productive process and about the potential profits ownership conferred. Instead, one pamphlet answered the question "Why cannot we be given Motor Cars, etc.?" by portraying high prices as reasonable, indeed, as fair (*What Is Wealth?* n.d.: 10). Factory owners, it seemed, had to charge high prices because "it costs a lot of money to make a motor car and the people who buy cars must pay a big enough price for each one so that the people who own factories can get back all the money they have spent" (*What Is Wealth?* n.d.: 11).

In both implicit and explicit opposition to the European self-representations of their money-based economic system as rational, reasonable, fair, natural, and leading to progress was the native system. Those who did not recognize the inherent superiority of Western socioeconomic relations were backward, misguided, and patronized as foolish. The many thousands of Papua New Guineans who noticed that Europeans rather than they owned most of the motor cars were pleasantly told, in effect, that their questions concerning colonial patterns of distribution were based on ignorance of how an economic system must operate.

Throughout the pamphlets, moreover, indigenous systems were portrayed as curtailing progress, as fundamentally unproductive in a narrow materialist sense, because they channeled wealth into the ownership of pigs and the staging of feasts (*What Is Wealth?* n.d.: 10); conversely, the indigenous systems did not encourage appropriately focused savings or investment. Thus, of the nine "main ways of increasing wealth in the Territory" with which *What Is Wealth?* concluded, the first was "saving by people so that savings can be put to some purpose which is productive" (*What Is Wealth?* n.d.: 20).

Native economic systems were, as well, presented as cumbersome and inefficient in the modern world: "Can you imagine the difficulty in exchanging, at a shop or a store, a pig for a radio set or a guitar? Even if you could bring the pig to the shop or store which had the radio set or guitar for sale, the shopkeeper might not want the pig. However, he would always accept money. Besides, the pig might not be worth the same as the radio set or guitar, so how would you settle the difference in value?" (*Your Money* n.d.: 2).

We do not know to what extent these pamphlets were actually read; in addition, they composed only a small portion of a late colonial discourse. Yet they illustrated and contributed to a process of increasing self-consciousness about critical differences between "us" and "them" and about the power of representations. The pamphlets and the kind of discourse they embodied were likely, in our view, to fail to convince a Tolai and Duke of York Island audience for two reasons: on the one hand, as already implied in our discussion of the increasingly recognized incomparabilities between shell money and money, many locals would have found the pamphlets' premises both implausible and amoral. On the other hand, the very training advocated in the pamphlets so that native people would be able to progress was to have the unexpected consequence of producing an indigenous elite highly suspicious of the particular essentializing contrasts meant to inspire them. (Such an elite would become relatively strong in East New Britain, where there was a higher proportion of students, mostly Tolai, in secondary schools between 1972 and 1982 than in any other province in the country [Bray 1985a: 17].)

Most Tolai and Duke of York Islanders would have rejected the European self-representations presented in the pamphlets as implausible largely because they did not believe that colonial patterns of distribution were just.[18] Local people had long understood that factory ownership was important and that owning a factory (or its fruits) was not simply a product of efficient work.[19] Furthermore, they did not think that prices—certainly high with respect to their limited earning capacities—were reasonable and fair.[20]

Concerning the European representation of natives, we surmise that many of these villagers would have objected to the European evaluation of their investments in social relations as nonproductive. Although accepting that "we all want money ... for the things that money can buy" (*Your Money* n.d.: 5), villagers would have depicted themselves as valuing the social uses to which money could be put lest they seem selfish, socially naive, and irresponsible. To illustrate this latter point, during our visit to the Duke of York Islands in 1991, people were pleased when we noticed that our gifts—whether watch, pocketknife, flashlight, or shorts—changed hands multiple times, often before our eyes, and that even soft drinks, purchased by us or by others, were passed on several times before finished.

Conversely, we were asked by villagers on numerous occasions to tell stories that essentialized the contrast between "them" and "us": tales of the homeless (about whom they had heard on radio and in newspapers) and about impoverished isolation and social dislocation.[21] These stories, indigenous parables really, all conveyed the ambiguous moral value of money—its aspect as "devilish acid." These tales confirmed for these villagers the asocial individuality and social inequality of European society; they confirmed the truth of one of their own essentialisms about the West, which can be formulated as "no money— no food—you die!"[22] Simply put, our village informants would not have accepted as likely or desirable the European essentialisms in the pamphlets, in part because these representations contradicted their own essentialisms.

The indigenous elite would also have rejected the European representations of self and other. This elite had emerged in part because with independence in 1975, many positions formerly held by Europeans had been localized. Members of this elite, who had begun to "earn more money ... because of their training" (*What Is Wealth?* n.d.: 9), knew very well the practical and moral difficulties of efforts to sequester income from the social claims of kin and others.[23] Moreover, despite the implicit promise of the pamphlets (and of late colonialism) that training could lead to socioeconomic equality, that backward tribalists who brought pigs to exchange for radios could readily become respected bureaucrats and bankers in the eyes of Europeans, members of this elite knew the process was more complex. In particular, their training or work had often taken them abroad into the racially divided West, where the discrimination they encountered, their formal qualifications notwithstanding, made them very sensitive to demeaning characterizations.

THE DENOUEMENT

Tolanger, as not only a member of the national elite but as a shell-money-using Tolai, was unusually well suited to reject the kind of essentialized representations the pamphlets portrayed. He was also able, we suggest, to reformulate them. His people would have readily recognized the dissonance of bringing a pig to exchange for a radio. Their own currency could be accurately represented as having retained its full range of uses and as having long been the standard against which European currency was evaluated. Shell money, in this depiction, although a "true money," was not a "devilish acid," the root of all evil. Both economically viable and morally superior, it could be convincingly regarded as encapsulating the virtues of a particular local tradition. Moreover, we surmise, if properly promoted as representation, shell money could denote the postcolonial nation as a whole. It could be elevated to the more powerful status of national cultural property because it could represent a successful emergence from the inequities of a colonial history.

We can now speculate more fully concerning the bases of Tolanger's alarm. If shell money was to retain its special salience among these East New Britains—much less be feasible as national cultural property, as a matter of national interest—it had to be *defined* as inalienable. It had to be defined as, perhaps paradoxically, beyond price. It certainly could not be allowed to appear as *subject* to European currency, as might any ordinary commodity. To have permitted Crane and Müller to transform shell money from currency into artifact would, we suggest, have negated shell money's status as money, its capacity to act as a medium of value. It would have been intolerable for Crane and Müller to be allowed to submit shell money to their measure. Moreover, to let them define shell money as an exportable tourist object would be to relinquish its special power to represent, to embody, cultural heritage.

Thus, we think it likely that from Tolanger's perspective the purchase of shell money was not simply a matter of its convertibility—the value of one currency relative to another—but a matter of its appropriation. Crane and Müller were perhaps adding insult to injury because they were buying large amounts of shell money in order *not* to use it. They were, in effect, reengaging Tolanger and others in East New Britain in the colonial battle that the Tolai and Duke of York Islanders thought they had already won. Once again, the basis and matrix of indigenous social entailments were threatened with dissolution by an alien "devilish acid." (It is interesting in this regard to speculate about the possible cachet on the German market of the artifacts Crane and Müller wished to obtain. There was little doubt that their experience with artifacts had been sufficient to teach them about the international value of the locally authentic and significant. In fact, the less willing local people were to part with objects, the more valuable they were likely to be in Germany. That an alarm was raised at the proposed export of these "artifacts" must have confirmed to Crane and Müller that they had chosen potentially profitable items.)

Appropriately, given the threat to social entailment the proposed export of shell money created, Tolanger, by raising the alarm, asserted a unity among what had in actuality become a fairly diverse group. He not only was invoking indigenous essentialisms to counter and supplant those of Europeans but was, we suggest, also using them to obscure what had become substantial differences among shell-money users.[24] Although, as we have seen, dense networks of social relations constituted sociality among both Tolai and Duke of York Islanders, Tolanger was surely quite aware that some among them had become considerably wealthier than others both in shell money and in money and, more consequentially, that their interests and possibilities had begun to diverge.[25]

The reasons it was important for members of the elite to maintain links within their own cultural groups were various and included the importance of maintaining a local power base in electoral politics (as we shall see in some detail in Chapter 5), retaining a place of refuge if life away became too precarious, and ensuring personal identity in a multicultural nation. From the point of view of villagers (and there were, as well, increasingly important economic and educational differences among villagers), connections with the elite were also important. They provided sources of donated income, access to jobs, points at which power and influence could be exercised, and ties to the broader world known increasingly through the media.

By raising his alarm, it seems to us, Tolanger was not only keeping his home fences in good order; he was also validating a vision of local life as focused on shell-money use. At a time when class distinctions were becoming increasingly evident in Papua New Guinea (as the "devilish acid" did its work), Tolanger was providing substantiation to the idea that a moral community of concerned shell-money users still existed, that he, Toling (the Tolai elder), and the Tolai youth were united in a way that denied, or at least played down, the extent to which their interests and possibilities had become disparate. (One Tolai member of the East New Britain provincial government had a rather cynical vision of how shell money helped maintain this moral community. He said that shell money was "the opiate of the people—it keeps villagers thinking that they are equal to those with more money.")

THE SOCIAL LIFE OF METATHINGS

We have documented one attempt by a local culture to promote and defend its own representations of identity. For Tolai and Duke of York Islanders this process focused in significant measure during the colonial period on the relationship between what we have termed "dueling currencies." Unlike most indigenous currencies in Papua New Guinea, shell money proved both durable and of important representational value: Each characteristic contributed to the other. Indeed, European currency appeared to have been given a run for its money and to have met its match. Furthermore, in the most recent and postcolonial period, shell money had gained additional value: As a still vital indigenous currency—again, one of the few monetary survivors of the colonial wars—it could, we suggest, in the context of Papua New Guinea as a whole, come to represent the successful survival and continued vigor of a local tradition.

Thus, the drama Tolanger helped stage was directed at least as much to a contemporary Papua New Guinea audience as to the likes of Crane and Müller. It was a drama for several reasons: It focused on a political circumstance commonly encountered with emergent nationalisms; it employed a somewhat standardized cast and utilized a familiar "rhetoric of motives" (Burke 1969); it had an audience or, more accurately, audiences; and it sought to present events as portentous. The themes of Tolanger's drama, focusing on freedom from foreign influence and determination, were, of course, of wide pertinence to those in many former colonies. However, because his audience was largely composed of Papua New Guineans, these themes were meant to have, we speculate, more local referents, ones articulating the country's particular nationalist concerns.

As mentioned, Papua New Guinea as a state was characterized by extensive cultural pluralism, and national culture was still largely composed of the heritage of particular groups. (National Day celebrations at the national high schools, for example, involved performances by students of the "signature events" of their particular cultural groups.) National politics involved contestation about which cultural groups would become most representative of the state. Or at the very least, these politics involved argument about which cultural groups were sufficiently strong and cohesive to become and remain major national players. Political survival often depended on the successful manipulation of contrasting representations. Politicians might have to justify, for example, their promoting an islander rather than a Highlander or a Sepik for the next prime minister, or they might have to convince an international investor to locate a timber project or resort or processing plant among the Tolai rather than among the Chimbu or the Chambri. (The National Parliament building is one example of the results of regional leaders' influence. It was constructed during the tenure of Prime Minister Michael Somare, a man from the Sepik region, and had the overall design of a somewhat generalized Sepik men's house [see Rosi 1991]. When we were in East New Britain in

1991 there was considerable national concern that there were too many Tolai in government, particularly because the prime minister then was a Tolai.)

Tolanger's drama, focused as it was on shell money, was likely to engage both local and national audiences. For the shell-money users, it encapsulated a long colonial history of successful resistance and defined the Tolai (and, by extension, Duke of York Islanders) as part of the current community of shell-money users. As well, the drama through its evocation of contrasting essentialisms—the essentialisms of locals were presented as successfully displacing those of Europeans—powerfully validated local life more generally to the extent that this life continued to focus on shell money as a medium of exchange and value.

For the national audience, the drama, though well attended, undoubtedly merited decidedly mixed reviews. Given the nature of national politics, no claims for the priority of any cultural group would go uncontested.[26] (Some on the local level might also pan the drama. For instance, one of the minority representatives to the East New Britain Parliament [whose constituency did not use shell money] complained to us about the shield, the symbol of provincial authority. It pictured items important only to the Tolai and Duke of York Islanders: the *tubuan* figure, a large roll of *tambu,* and the two birds representing the matrimoieties common to both groups.)

Yet at the very least, Tolanger asserted—through his alarm and the national publicity it received—that the Tolai and Duke of York Islanders, unlike most other Papua New Guinea groups, had an indigenous universal currency that was still powerful.[27] They were shown, in this respect, to be strong and cohesive as well as preadapted to modernity.[28] In other words, more than any other group in Papua New Guinea, they were presented as both traditional and modern.

In this regard, the drama was addressing a more general nationalist dilemma: how to maintain both a distinctive cultural heritage and a rootedness that were not anachronistic but enabled functioning in the contemporary world. The proposed solution to this dilemma was inspired. Shell money, as it emerged from the contrasting sets of essentialisms—both local and European—had come to represent, to embody, and to enable both traditional and modern values. As we have outlined here, Tolanger's alarm at Crane and Müller's proposed appropriation of shell money concerned not only the valorization of the medium of value itself but its valorization as a matter of national significance.[29]

*   *   *

We have sought here to explicate a set of events—Tolanger's "drama"—in terms of both historical antecedents and contemporary political context. Our objective was not only to render change complex and yet comprehensible but also to make recent negotiations concerning identity and worth in Papua New Guinea, as they played out both locally and nationally, more intelligible. Through clarification of these changes and negotiations, we hoped to reduce the differences and the distances between Duke of York Islanders and ourselves such that we might understand their aspirations and those of, for example, Father Crane and Herr Müller.

Tolanger's drama was the focus, the embodiment, of many of these changes and negotiations. He provided a contemporary argument over the basis of national unity that was convincing to some and problematic to others. In the next chapter, we again provide a historically grounded analysis of another strategy for achieving national unity. Interestingly, this strategy was also presented in the form of a drama, but a comic drama about the arrival of the Reverend George Brown in the Duke of York Islands and his pacification of the "savage cannibals" he met there. In this drama, unlike the one we have just considered, cultural roots were presented as truncated and the significance of deep cultural distinctiveness was thereby denied. In other words, because some of the grounds of difference and competition were diminished, various groups were portrayed as relatively comparable.

NOTES

1. The literature concerning attempts on the part of minority groups to promote and defend their own representations of identity has proliferated in recent years. For provocative presentations, see Gwaltney 1981; Whisnant 1983; Clifford 1988a: 277–346; Handler 1988; Nadel-Klein 1991b; and many of the essays in Hobsbawm and Ranger 1983. For recent analyses focusing on the Pacific in particular, see Babadzan 1988; Keesing 1989; Linnekin and Poyer 1990; LiPuma and Meltzoff 1990; and White 1991.

2. These particular paired essentialisms might be called "orientalisms" and "occidentalisms" (see Said 1978; and Carrier 1992). Through such paired essentialisms, both "they" and "we" are dialectically constituted in a process of both mutual opposition and construction.

3. We recognize that the value of money is always significantly a matter of representation—one of perception. See, in this regard, Virginia Dominguez's (1990) interesting study of how dollars came to be regarded in Israel as more "real" than shekels.

4. On the Maori, see, among others, Hanson 1989; and Wilford 1990. On Australian Aboriginals, see Morphy 1983; Myers 1988, 1991; and Nadel-Klein 1991a. On

Native Americans see Clifford 1988a: 215–251; and Raymond 1989, 1990. For works of more general interest see Fischer 1989; Karp and Levine 1991; and Terrell 1991. See also, Hillerman's (1989) fictional account of the controversy surrounding the Smithsonian's claims to Native American bones in the name of "science."

5. As we have already said, the Tolai and Duke of York islanders were not the same people; their languages, as well as other aspects of their culture, were distinct though closely related. In our effort to understand the drama with its focus on shell money, however, we concentrate on certain important similarities between them, including a largely common colonial history.

6. Indeed, in 1982 East New Britain had a higher percentage (31%) of students enrolled in grades 7 through 10 than any other province in the country (Bray 1985a: 17). But Tolai fared even better educationally than others within East New Britain. For example, in 1983, 81 percent of elementary-age children among the Tolai were enrolled in community school; 63 percent among the Duke of York Islanders; 59 percent among those in the two Baining census divisions; and 36 percent among those in the three Pomio census divisions (data extrapolated from Bray 1985b: 189).

7. Writing at the turn of the century and basing his analysis on German colonial sources, Oskar Schneider confirmed this point. It was because shell money was more valuable than European currency to local people that the German administration both remunerated and fined them in shell money. Schneider wrote: "All work is compensated with diwarra; the administration, thus, pays those who have been sent away to work one strand monthly, along with food once a day. It is not only due to the buying power of the diwarra, but also its value [literally, belovedness], that it is taken as atonement for everything, even the worst crimes. ... The administration also makes use of the value of diwarra. In 1896–97 the government pulled in 923 strands in fines from the natives, and, in addition, on various punitive expeditions, the islanders would only be granted pardon for their misdeeds after a payment of strands of diwarra" (1905: 31–32, translated by Margaret Gates).

See, as well, the history of New Britain–European contact in Salisbury (1970) and the history of New Ireland–European contact by Rubel and Rosman (n.d.) for additional confirmation of the preference for shell money.

8. See Thomas (1992b) for discussion of the development of the Fijian concept of *kerekere* in opposition to the ideology of European business. See also Keesing and Tonkinson (1982) for an overview of the development of the concept of "kastam" and Foster (1992) for a discussion of the importance of "kastam" as opposed to "bisnis" among the Tangans of New Ireland.

9. Strings of shell money were rarely purchased directly with money; unstrung shells sometimes were, at rates that varied considerably over time for the volume acquired. The most usual way to acquire shell money was through selling locally grown foodstuffs or consumable trade goods (such as biscuits and tobacco). See, for confirmation, Neumann 1992: 183–190.

10. For an informative discussion of the sequential responses by the nearby Tangans to capital penetration, see Foster 1988: 22–70.

11. Some Duke of York Islanders had begun to pay community government taxes with strings of shell money: two and one-half fathoms per nuclear family was considered an amount equivalent to the annual tax of K5.00 (approximately US$5.50). These fathoms of strung shells were later converted into money when individuals purchased them for use, primarily in mortuary and marriage ceremonies. As we watched the Duke of York Islands community government president collect the taxes on Karavar Island, we saw several individuals buy the strings of shells their covillagers had contributed. The president said that Tolai, as well, often bought Duke of York shell money in this manner, but he was adamant that "none would leave the Province."

12. As Counts (1971), McDowell (1988), and Kaplan (1989) have made clear, to use the more familiar term of "cargo cult" would be inappropriately ethnocentric. "Cults" existed only from the outside looking in.

13. Although the Kaun and the Mataungan Association were contemporaneous and were both committed to achieving social equality with Europeans, members of each had very different views concerning the desirability and feasibility of self-government. See Errington (1974b) for a more complete comparison.

14. In this regard, the early encounter between Europeans and Karavarans was, for instance, significantly unlike that described by Sahlins (1981, 1985) in which the Hawaiians regarded Captain Cook as the God Lono. (For a critique of Sahlins's account of Cook as Lono see Obeyesekere 1992.)

15. For a contrasting case, see Burridge 1969. See also MacFarlane 1985.

16. James Carrier (1992) made the important point that it was an essentialistic error to define premodern economies as exclusively the realm of entailed gift-giving and to define capitalistic economies as exclusively the realm of individualistic commodity exchanges.

17. A 1957 edition of the *Rabaul Times* reported, in this regard, that "the Commonwealth Bank will invite native village councilors and native clients to attend the opening of the new 'Native Accounts' premises at the Rabaul branch. ... The bank has had native accounts for many years but has only recently opened extensions to the buildings specially designed for native clients" (n.p.). The number of active native clients in the Rabaul area had grown considerably during the late 1950s; by 1957, they numbered nearly 20,000. Presumably, white depositors had begun to find banking side by side with so many native investors discomfiting.

18. We recognize, of course, that Europeans were also exposed to, and in some cases also rejected, comparable, essentialistic messages intended to convince them that their own system of economic differentiation was equitable. Thus, in a series of moralistic advertisements for the Commonwealth Bank of Australia that appeared over a twenty-year period in the *Rabaul Times,* Europeans in Papua New Guinea— also subject to the vicissitudes of a coconut economy—were enjoined to be thrifty

and save regularly in order to achieve economic autonomy and self-sufficiency. They were told, for instance, that "the petty borrower loses prestige and friends. He is trading on the thrift of others whilst practicing none himself. He is selling his pride on the installment plan—a pound at a time. The man of self-respect, the man who values the good will of others, takes care that he is never in the position of being 'short of a pound'" (1941b: n.p.).

19. Indeed, as we mentioned in Chapter 1, Fred's arrival on Karavar in 1968 was welcomed largely because it was hoped he (as a generous American) could help build a factory or, barring that, provide access to the fruits of factories by teaching them the secret numbers necessary to receive large amounts of goods with little or no payment.

20. As Hank Nelson pointed out, "For much of the time labour was so cheap and so ineffective at pushing for higher pay that there was little incentive to reduce the size of the labour force (1982: 80).

21. One Papua New Guinea journalist recently reported her shock at discovering homelessness in her own country. She wrote: "There is no reason why Papua New Guineans should live in poverty. We have an abundance of agricultural land available where people can grow their own food and hunt or fish from their own traditional hunting and fishing grounds. ... [As she and a colleague drove into the Baruni rubbish dump outside of Port Moresby, all they] could see near the huge mound of rubbish that was just thrown out by a garbage truck were women and children all bending down and retrieving whatever was edible from the refuse. I could not believe my eyes that this was happening in our own country" (Seneka 1991: 12). Her response, however, can be regarded as perhaps somewhat stereotypic, as this condition had existed in Port Moresby for at least a decade.

22. This apt phrase was coined by Thomas (1992b: 76) to capture Pacific-Island perceptions of Western societies.

23. For discussion of the degree to which members of the Papua New Guinea elite remained socially entailed, see Gewertz and Errington 1991: 101–125.

24. Again, for data about class formation in the Pacific, see Hooper et al. 1987.

25. Interestingly, we often heard wealthy Tolai described by marginal peoples in East New Britain as like Europeans. Thus, the wealthy might provide food but would not eat with someone they regarded as of low station. In fact, one man told us that "the Tolai think of themselves as a master race." Similar perceptions of Tolai condescension have been reported by Andrew Lattas among the Kaliai of West New Britain and by Jane Fajans among the Baining of East New Britain (personal communications). Tolai were, certainly, aware of possible ethnic discontent among these marginal peoples. Tolai provincial government officials had, for example, employed two Western anthropologists to study their ethnic minorities.

26. J. Mangi (1989) made a similar point and suggested that it might be necessary to refer to prehistory in order to establish a unitary identity for Papua New Guineans.

27. After the essential completion of this chapter, we read of a similar East New Britain attempt to valorize shell money as of national importance: to make it, in fact,

a national currency. The *Times of Papua New Guinea* reported that "about 20 prominent East New Britain leaders have petitioned the [national] government to recognize the role of traditional shell money, *tabu,* and establish ... the financial institution based on the value of it. The leaders, including the provincial Speaker James Agi and deputy premier Henry Saminga, want parliament, the Department of Finance and Planning and the Bank of PNG to consider their petition" (1993: 9).

28. This formulation, in its celebration of the distinctive and superior qualities of shell money with respect to money, would be importantly different from T. S. Epstein's (1968) account of Tolai as primitive capitalists.

29. We have heard much of late about British objections to the substitution of a currency common to the European community for the pound; we have heard, as well, worries about the intentions of the various republics formed from the former Soviet Union to use different currencies. Much commentary concerning these objections and worries involved, it seems to us, a rather limited definition of value: It focused on fiscal encumbrances—on the difficulty, for instance, of measuring one currency against another—rather than on representational importance. Commentators should be reminded that it was no accident that the coins and bills issued by most nation-states generally depicted either historically significant figures or contemporary occupants of historically significant positions, for example, Abraham Lincoln or the queen of England. Tolanger's drama about the valorization of the medium of value (albeit without his concern with the alienation of cultural property) had, in this respect, a worldwide cast.

3

From Darkness to Light in the George Brown Jubilee

The Invention of Nontradition and the Inscription of a National History in East New Britain

I N THIS CHAPTER, the complexities concerning the ways Karavarans and their neighbors got to be as they were, including the aspirations they had come to hold for the future, are further explored in a description of another strategy for achieving local worth and national unity. Unlike Tolanger's strategy celebrating indigenous accomplishments, this strategy, also taking the form of a drama, surprised and perplexed us because it enacted many of the racist stereotypes characteristic of the colonial era.

We were to discover that we were not the only anthropologists surprised and perplexed by such a drama. Indeed, this chapter began in response to a challenge from Don Kulick and Margaret Willson, anthropologists who witnessed a comparable event while in the field among the Gapun villagers of the East Sepik Province of Papua New Guinea. A visiting friend of Kulick's wished to videotape a traditional ritual to show his friends at home in Sweden. The villagers obliged him by dressing up as savages and cavorting about. They engaged in what had become for them a rather common type of performance, referred to locally in Pidgin English as a "konset" or "drama." In these performances, they portrayed their ancestors as "bus kanakas," or country

An earlier version of this chapter appeared in *American Ethnologist* 21, 1 (February 1994). Reprinted by permission of the American Anthropological Association.

bumpkins. According to Kulick and Willson, the actors "generally appear shirtless, dressed in ragged sago-frond skirts with flowers drooping from their hair. Their speech is loud and boorish, often it is gibberish, conveying an image of senseless babble. The actions of the actors tend to be exaggerated and over-large: gestures are sweeping, arms are thrown about, walking becomes stomping" (1992: 147). In other words, according to Kulick and Willson, Gapun villagers displayed racist assumptions about themselves within their dramas. These assumptions appeared not only in their gestures but also in their narratives: Many of the skits concerned natives who were incapable of following the appropriate advice of colonial officials or western missionaries.

Kulick and Willson were troubled by these performances because they saw Gapun villagers as incorporating in them "a Western stereotype of the savage" (1992: 149)—what might be called an auto-orientalized view of native life (cf. Said 1978). Some anthropologists have analyzed comparable self-representations as modes of resistance, or at least as creative appropriations of Western imagery for indigenous purposes (see, among others, Comaroff 1985; Lattas 1992; Taussig 1987). Kulick and Willson rejected this view for the Gapun context. After they had questioned Gapun villagers about what the participants believed themselves to be doing, Kulick and Willson argued that it was "more reasonable to see the villagers' actions as reinforcing, entrenching and embodying the colonist discourses which permitted the development of the image of 'the savage' in the first place" (1992: 149). They challenged ethnographers to explore comparable "echoing images" (1992: 150) for what they could teach us about the complexity of colonial power relations.

In accepting the importance of this challenge, we turned our attentions to a "drama" we observed in August 1991 while living on Karavar. (The Karavarans also used the term "drama" in this context.) It was a reenactment of the past performed regularly by Duke of York Islanders, as well as by the Tolai (peoples very different from the Gapun). In this East New Britain drama and in the other festivities of an annual event locally termed the Jubilee, villagers celebrated the August 15, 1875, arrival of the Reverend George Brown and his Fijian assistants. To the great hilarity of a large local audience, villagers recreated the transformation of their "ancestors" from wild, indeed precultural, savages into staid and civilized Christians. They recreated the transition from the *momboto,* a time of darkness in which people could not see the path of proper conduct, into the enlightened present.[1] Some villagers, clad immaculately in white and singing hymns, portrayed Brown and his entourage. Others, covered in mud, vastly unkempt, and trembling with cannibalistic frenzy, portrayed the ancestors. In the course of the drama, the ancestors were pacified—literally cooled—by the seductive harmonies of the Methodist hymns and enculturated by the display of such Western items as money, steel tools, and salt.

Perhaps most striking about these annual dramas, filled as they were with negative stereotypes of savage and stupid ancestors, was that the local audience so thoroughly enjoyed them and viewed them as so remarkably funny. No one to whom we have spoken came away from these dramas feeling in the least demeaned, although many had frequently expressed anger when they remembered past interactions with racist Europeans and Asians (particularly in the context of plantation work and forced labor during World War II).

One possible explanation for the villagers' great amusement at the depiction of their ancestors as cannibalistic incompetents can be found in Bruce Kapferer's argument that the comic aspect of a performance "tells participants to question the truth of all statements appearing within it, that what appears within it has no strict necessity" (1983: 209). As "conscious reflexive mimesis" (Calkowski 1991: 644), moreover, comedy provides the possibility of "rerealization," whereby objects, actors, and events may be transformed. But what statements were opened to question during the Jubilee? Whose verisimilitude was challenged? And what was being reconfigured?

The scholars whom Kulick and Willson questioned for viewing comparably racist self-depictions as creative appropriations of Western stereotypes might answer that the Jubilee performances projected the metamessage "This is how some might view our ancestors, but you and I know that it is a hegemonic view that can be contested and transformed." They might compare the Jubilee to the cargo-cult narratives Lattas described as "allegories for present relations of inequality" (1992: 28) and suggest that as a performance—as an alternative social structure on the margins of society (see Bauman 1975)—the Jubilee was additionally efficacious. As a means of rerealizing these relations of inequality, it created "an objectified medium outside the self" (Lattas 92: 27) through which racially subordinated Papua New Guineans could reconfigure existing lines of fragmentation and distinction—could, in other words, remake themselves as the equals of Europeans in the "resistance spaces" (Seremetakis 1991: 5) of the performance.

And so, we believe, some early Jubilee dramas did indeed operate, when those enacting them were aware of themselves as subordinated in what was, in effect, an Australian colony. But since independence, when these long-contacted East New Britains emerged as among the most enterprising and best educated in Papua New Guinea, the "strict necessity" of the statement within the drama—that "civilizing" changes had been effected by the European missionaries and colonists—had long been granted in this context and had also been encoded in many other historical memories (see Errington 1974a).

Those who staged, performed, and witnessed the contemporary Jubilee drama may have wondered about their identity and worth. But they also viewed themselves as among the most sophisticated of Papua New Guineans. (Recall, in this regard, that the Tolai-dominated East New Britain provincial government had recently hired two Western anthropologists to study its ethnic minorities.) Among those who attended, for example, were several who had observed to us that, unlike Highlanders, who still sometimes wore leafy coverings over their genitals, the Duke of York Islanders wore a "native dress" consisting of *laplap* and *meri blaus* (wraparound skirts and blouses) introduced by the missionaries in the mid-1870s. (In fact, at a beauty contest we attended in 1991, several East New Britain contestants objected that a defining characteristic of the "native dress" event was the wearing of "primitive" clothing and the baring of breasts.) For them, the coming of George Brown had become a historical *event,* much as the coming of the Pilgrims or the signing of the Declaration of Independence was for others. (On events of this type see Biersack 1991; Sahlins 1991.)

In most cases, our East New Britain informants accepted *as fact* that their ancestors had once been savages (cf. Young 1977). And as fact, ancestral savagery was definitely not within the 1991 Jubilee "play frame," to use the term adopted by Kapferer (1983) and others. It was not, thus, to be evaluated as an arbitrary depiction, one possibly to be rejected and reconfigured. Rather, what made this contemporary Jubilee performance funny—its challenge to strict necessity—was the assumption that depictions of ancestors *were* depictions of self. The metamessage of the contemporary performance, we suggest, was that there existed *no* implicating connection between those portrayed as savages and the audience viewing their shenanigans.

Indeed, the 1991 Jubilee drama presented the total eclipse of ancestral savagery by Brown's arrival as what might be called an "anchor event," one that convincingly defined the appropriate basis and nature of national life in contemporary Papua New Guinea. It was one strategy for addressing the question of how a nation could incorporate tribal multiplicities and include both those who still wore leafy genital coverings and those who had not done so for over a century. (As we shall see, the transformative significance of this event was made explicit by the then–prime minister of the country, who was himself a Tolai, when he attended the 1991 performance.) The 1991 Jubilee performance, in other words, did not challenge the depiction of a savage past. Instead, it rerealized Papua New Guineans as citizens of their own country by separating them from their common precultural pasts—by separating them from what was, in effect, an invented and ubiquitous nontradition. Moreover, as an anchor event in the contemporary nation of Papua New Guinea, the Jubilee performance effected different ideological work than it had once done: No longer providing a resistance space for East New Britains, it had become for them a dominant discourse that substantially precluded resistance.

From the first stagings of the Jubilee to those in 1991, the participants had altered both the nature of the performance and the play frame, repositioning the present relative to the precontact past. There had been a change from improvised to standardized performances, which marked the emergence and development of official history corresponding to the development of a nation-state. (For a description of the standardization of history in a similar performance event, see Neumann 1992: 81–90.) There had been, too, a corresponding and significant change in what was considered funny. What was thrown into question and at whose expense and with what kind of laughter had all changed. Moreover, we suggest (and adduce additional evidence from similar performances in the Solomon Islands [White 1991: 133–156]) that these changes could be regarded as the fulfillment of what seemed only a distant possibility during the early Jubilees: that the resistance to European domination might prove ultimately successful, that (to return to Lattas's discussion of cargo narratives) black skins might assume the roles of white ones.

In sum, by taking a historical view of this performance—by attempting to draft a social history of a particular enacted auto-orientalism—we demonstrate that what cannibal ancestors might signify was not fixed. The point is straightforward: The uses and meanings of laughter at what might be considered racist self-representations were complexly negotiated in a context of shifting power relations. In other words, we demonstrate that to understand the "echoing images" we were enjoined to explore, we must investigate the changing harmonies of their echoes.

THE EARLY JUBILEE

The minutes of the New Britain District Synod of October 18, 1923, described the decision to provide a "Jubilee of Methodism in the District" (p. 61). It was to be celebrated on August 15, 1925, not only in the Duke of York Islands, where Brown had first arrived in the area, but throughout the district. Indeed, as we have said, by this time much mission activity was centered in New Britain among the numerically dominant but culturally similar Tolai.

The Jubilee was at least partially designed to raise funds from both Papua New Guinean and overseas sources. Special souvenir issues of the *Missionary Review* and the Tolai *Nilai i ra Dowot* were to be issued to mark the occasion. (*Nilai i ra Dowot* means "voice of the truth"; Tolai had become the language of Methodist education throughout the district.) The synod hoped to raise a Jubilee fund of not less than £1,500, which would be "devoted to the erection of a new and up-to-date building to be known as the George Brown College, with provision for a theological institution" (Minutes of the New Britain District Synod: 62).

The special souvenir editions were, in fact, published. Both proclaimed the extraordinary success of the mission in the years after Brown's arrival. The Reverend John W. Ackroyd wrote in 1925:

> This year is the jubilee year, celebrating the beginning of missions in New Britain, and as the interest of missionary enthusiasts in all Methodist circles in Australia will be more or less directed to this field of labour, it is appropriate that our friends be given an insight into the work of the church in this little-known country. ... Fifty years ago the first missionary came to this land, and if it were possible for him to pay it a visit to-day, he would have every reason to thank God for the planting of Methodism in this corner of the world. Fifty years of future work in New Britain will tell of a wonderful increase of Christianity and uplifting of these people. (1925: 5, 7)

We know something of the celebration itself from church sources. The general secretary of the mission, J. W. Burton, traveled from Australia to New Britain in order to see the Jubilee and kept a journal of his trip. Unfortunately, he was delayed by bad weather and missed the Jubilee by a few days. He did, however, visit several of the Jubilee sites in the Duke of York Islands and New Britain and described several church services he attended. On August 23 he witnessed a "thrilling sort of service" at Molot, in the Duke of York Islands, the site of Brown's first arrival. At this service,

> the old men told how they remembered Dr. Brown landing at that very spot fifty years ago. How they made up their minds to frighten him away. They kept their war dances going all night long close to the hut where the Fijians slept, and brandished their spears as they yelled their war cry; but he could not be terrified. They described with a vividness and a detail that could not be translated the old bad days and there was unmistakable gratitude in their eyes as they spoke of the present time and of all the joy and happiness the Lotu [church] had brought them. (Burton 1925: 14)

These old men had themselves experienced Brown's arrival. They were among those who were to become the "ancestors" in later Jubilee performances. However, as Burton presented their accounts, they had not been bumbling savages at the moment of missionization but rather ferocious, if benighted, warriors. Perhaps they did credit the *lotu* with bringing joy and happiness—certainly many of our friends and informants were grateful to the church for helping to end indigenous warfare—but they did not at this time think the church had transformed them from clowns into Christians. They remained formidable rather than foolish.

None of our sources reveals with certainty whether these vivid recollections of Brown's arrival were presented in the form of a drama or whether this drama was humorous. The idea that a commemoration should take place was clearly at the church's initiative, but we think it likely that the comic elements were an indigenous contribution. After all, there was a long tradition of the comedic, as William Mitchell has demonstrated in a masterful survey of Pacific performance humor. He concluded that "the ritual and theatrical comedic forms of Oceania, although roughly analogous to those in the West, are indigenous inventions long antedating contact with Western colonialism" (1992: 33). Moreover, for both Duke of York Islanders and Tolai, clowning was an expected component of many rituals. For example, when the powerful *tubuan* figures were about to "die," they moved throughout the villages with exaggerated and hilarious decrepitude, limping and brushing flies from their sore-ridden bodies. As commonly, at least in the Duke of York Islands, individuals might voluntarily burlesque ritual proceedings by, for instance, dancing with exaggerated lewdness while others remained serious and controlled. (See Shore [1982: 259–260] for discussion of a circumstance in which this opposition was an expected part of ritual structure.)

Our first clear indication of the performance of a humorous Jubilee skit—in this case, obviously an indigenous improvisation—comes from Burton's journal covering a later visit to New Britain. In 1929 he and several Methodist dignitaries traveled to Matupit, a coastal Tolai village immediately adjacent to the Duke of York Islands, on the occasion of its Jubilee. Although the improvisation in 1929 was performatively distinct from the established Jubilee drama of 1991, a point we will return to, the contrast between the humor displayed in each, both in kind and in focus, is most suggestive. (The contrast can be no more than suggestive, however, because any comparison between Tolai and Duke of York Island Jubilees must be somewhat imprecise. Nevertheless, as we have already stated, Tolai and Duke of York Islanders were culturally and linguistically very similar and had a largely common colonial history.) Burton wrote:

> As we neared Matupit there was not a soul to be seen and we thought this very strange. As we got nearer we saw a high placard about 12 feet long I should think and perhaps 7 feet deep. On it was printed:
>
> WELCOME
>
> | REV. FRANK LADE, M.A. | J. W. BURTON, M.A. |
> |---|---|
> | PRESIDENT-GENERAL | GENERAL SECRETARY |
>
> We dropped anchor, but still there was no sign of human life and Margetts [a missionary working in the district who was a member of the visiting party] guessed that they were up to some of their dramatic tricks again. At length, Lade, Margetts and I got into the dinghy to go ashore and even when we were close in to the beach there was no sign of anyone though we heard a little sound from behind the placard that made us suspect that the people were in hiding thereof. As the dinghy grated on the beach, however, four nearly naked and highly painted savages rushed out with up-raised clubs and poised spears. They rushed at us dancing around the boat and splashing in the water making the most hideous yells. Afterwards Margetts translated to us what they were saying. It was roughly this—"Who are these white men. They are bad white men. They have come to disturb our peace, let's kill them. They are worthy of death." Then after a while they said—"Perhaps they are not bad white men for they have no weapons." And eventually after a lot of dancing and shrieking and palaver they said "Perhaps these are missionaries coming to bring us the Lotu, let us not prevent their landing."
>
> It appears that they were re-acting what had taken place when Dr. Brown landed fifty odd years before. We then walked up toward the placard and when we got close to it suddenly it was drawn up and some three or four hundred natives, who were hidden beneath it, burst out into a song of welcome. Afterwards the mass opened and formed two long lines down which the President-General and myself walked to see the Native Minister's house. ...
>
> We then went on to the big Missionary Meeting in the Church. There was a fearful lot of singing and then by and by a collection bowl was passed round but it came back with only a few shillings and some odd coppers in it. I thought that this was a rather poor collection from a crowd of people such as this, but after they had another hymn the old Chief came forward carrying a bag and he went up to the bowl, and poured from the bag a vast quantity of florins and shillings whereat the people clapped. They had another hymn and then another Chief from another part of the building came with a similar bag. The result was that they had a collection of £137. They do this dramatic thing rather well. Margetts was telling us of a case where he went to a Missionary Meeting and they said how sorry they were that they were poor and could only give these few odd shil-

lings, and by and by a man came up and said he was too poor to give anything and all he could offer was a coconut, but when Mr. Margetts received the coconut it was fearfully heavy and lifting off the top he found it was packed with notes and silver. On another occasion they gave a poor collection but presented an excellent model of the "Montoro" and in the hold of this model [mission] boat was about £400. Still on another occasion the people had given a very meager offering and one of the Missionaries noted that there was a wire stretching from the ceiling of the Church down to the pulpit and he could not understand what it was for, but after they made a great exhibition of their poverty there came sliding down the wire the model of an aeroplane and in the aeroplane was two or three hundred pounds. These are all their own ideas without any suggestions from Europeans so that they have not only generous hearts but a very keen sense of humour. (1929: 35–38)

This "keen sense of humour," displayed in both the skit of welcome and the ruse of offering, was at the expense of the European visitors. A placard welcomed specific visitors to an apparently uninhabited village where they were tricked into participating in a skit about George Brown's arrival but then were treated with deference as honored guests. Later, offerings were collected, but at first little money was given. There was, thus, the momentary assertion that the natives did not have to celebrate Brown's arrival, did not have to greet the missionaries, and did not have to contribute money to the church. Though they did celebrate, greet, and contribute, it was in such a way that their compliance became a critique of the circumstances enforcing that compliance (cf. Scott 1985).

The fact that "Margetts guessed that they were up to some of their dramatic tricks again," taken in conjunction with the likely existence of an indigenous satiric tradition, suggests that practices of resistance through symbolic appropriation were well established. Moreover, these "tricks" should be understood with respect to widely held (and often reported) Melanesian views concerning the importance of reciprocal transactions—presentations and exchanges—in defining personhood, establishing sociality, and asserting power. Not surprisingly, local resentment was rife in this East New Britain context, where expatriate Europeans sought fortunes through an export-oriented plantation economy based on nonreciprocal and extractive relationships with natives. (Thus, as we mentioned in Chapters 1 and 2, there developed in the Duke of York Islands during the 1930s the "dog" movement, reflecting the natives' perception of how they were treated by whites.)

Indeed, it would be hard to think of more refined and distilled commentaries on the history and nature of colonial relationships in East New Britain than the cash-bearing coconut and the wealth-laden ship and airplane (cf.

Counts and Counts 1992). The locals overwhelmed the missionaries with gifts concealed and conveyed in appropriate, and appropriated, vehicles marking European domination. These gifts indicated, we suggest, both capitulation and resistance.

The compliance at the Jubilee and at the other missionary meetings acknowledged who really controlled the coconut plantations and the ships and planes serving as the economic basis of that colonial society. Power relations being what they were, capitulation was inevitable and resistance had to be indirect. Let us briefly augment our earlier exposition of colonial history with two texts illustrating what the natives were up against in the area of Papua New Guinea described by Hank Nelson as maintaining the most staunch racial separation (1982: 171). These texts, both written in 1925, were taken from the *Rabaul Times,* the newspaper of New Britain's administrative and economic center. One, a letter to the editor, appeared just eight days before the initial Jubilee. Written by a plantation manager, it was entitled "Corporal Punishment."

> To the Editor
>
> Allow me through the columns of your paper to express my views regarding the present system, which precludes any plantation man, or any other man who has the handling of natives, from administering, or at least in having the power to administer corporal punishment to delinquent natives. …
>
> I have invariably found that the average native labourer in these islands has the mentality and general characteristics of a child and should therefore be treated as one. … What child respects a weak parent, even in these days of infant emancipation?…
>
> I maintain that if the Administration should allow responsible plantation men to hold licenses for inflicting corporal punishment … there would be far less trouble arising between master and servant. Not for the reason that the master would be forced to exercise this privilege, but the mere fact of the master holding that power being known to the native would be conducive to better discipline and there lies the secret. (*Rabaul Times* 1925a: n.p.)

Although the paternalism, patriarchy, and prejudice expressed in this letter need no explication, the same sentiments in the following poem might need to be understood in context. Entitled "The Educated Native," the poem alluded to a debate then raging in the pages of the newspaper and elsewhere about what many planters regarded as the ill-considered missionary policy of educating the natives.

> For 50 years the native of this country has been taught
> To set aside his evil ways—and do the things he ought—

By faithful men and women (some departed and at rest)
Who gladly left their native land, their kindred and their best.
Their motive was a high one, they never thought of pay.
Their one desire—to lead the "coons" from "darkness" into "day."
So day by day and year by year, the bush kanaka grew.
In contact with his teachers, his ways and habits knew;
In course of time (we may presume) he passed his final test,
And, consequently, he went home to help "instruct the rest."
And so today we meet him—though at first it is hard to say
Which coon belongs to "darkness," or which coon belongs to "day."
So, if at any time perchance, you ever are in doubt,
I strongly recommend to you, don't leave your cash about;
If, on the other hand you do, as sure as you are born
You'll only have yourself to blame to find the lot is gone. (*Rabaul Times* 1925b:
    n.p.)

Perhaps the "very keen sense of humour" that Burton noted in Matupit was related to the jocular tone with which our European poet described the transition from savagery effected during the course of colonial contact. Although the poet indirectly blamed the missionaries for the misguided assumption that natives could be educated out of their darkness—"darkness"—was a word frequently used by Methodist missionaries to describe the precontact condition of villagers—missionaries themselves often had similar doubts, or at least had to fight against them.[2] Consider the following excerpt from a confidential report submitted to the Methodist Board of Governors in Australia by the official delegation to the first (1925) Jubilee.

> Our first impressions were surprisingly unfavorable. Usually the romance of a new people intrigues the observer and creates an atmosphere of charm. But such was not the case here. The filthiness of the women in and about Rabaul, and in the villages, was a smarting disappointment; while the dull apathetic expressions of so many of the men haunted us. We could not fail to reflect upon the impression that must be made upon the mind of the casual tourist and unfriendly critic as this picture meets his eye. Even in our Christian villages, except during Church hours on Sunday, we found people clad in dirty garments and showing very little outward sign of missionary influence. ...
>
> We were disappointed further in the low average intellectual level of the people and their lack of mental attainment. There are, of course, some outstanding exceptions to the above general statement, for we met some of our Native brethren who, when all circumstances are considered, are men of whom we as a Mission are justly proud; but we found [it] very hard to counter the criticism that the people of these islands are "low-grade humans." The explanation is probably

that of arrested development. For centuries they have been isolated in a way that is difficult for us to imagine, and their mental life in consequence has been stunted. We must remember this fact in all our judgments, and regard their state as a still more urgent call to us for help. We believe that, in spite of all outward seeming, they have dormant possibilities, and it is our God-given task to evoke these. (Jenkin and Burton 1925: 2)

Under these oppressive colonial circumstances—when many Europeans did not feel the least compelled to disguise their racist sentiments—it was little wonder that most expressions of autonomy and independence had to be placed in a play frame. The Jubilee skit of 1929, the subsequent offering, and the offerings at other missionary meetings incorporated props that were gems of oblique appropriation at a time when natives knew full well that most whites regarded them as thoroughly inferior.[3] Significantly, natives knew that they could not fully dissociate themselves from the roles colonists insisted that they play: They were not laughing at themselves as "savages," past or present. What could be rejected within this play frame—what could be rerealized in this allegory of inequality—was not the fact of colonial oppression but its legitimacy. Though grateful that the missionary presence had resulted in the cessation of warfare, the natives deeply resented the inequality that had also ensued. At least some of the statements locals presented as open to question were these: We are poor, benighted bush natives living in darkness; we are dull, apathetic, "low-grade humans." On the contrary, they asserted: We are clever enough to fool you, to frighten you, and to impress you—to establish ourselves collectively as persons of worth—with our presentations of that which you most value, money.

THE 1991 MIOKO JUBILEE: THE DRAMATIC
INVENTION OF A NONTRADITION

By 1991, with the entrenchment of an increasingly powerful indigenous elite responsible for economic policy and political governance in an independent Papua New Guinea, the play frame had changed. The Jubilee drama had become an official history and its humor, the dominant discourse. All could now laugh at their ancestors without, as far as we could determine, feeling compromised. Indeed, we argue that such a shift in the comic was virtually necessary given that no Europeans (apart from visiting anthropologists) were present and the honored guests included the prime minister and a United Church bishop[4] as well as local and regional clergy.[5]

In 1991, the Duke of York Jubilee was held not at Molot, George Brown's initial landing place, as was usual, but in the community of Mioko. Mioko was able to claim this honor because its parishioners had erected a cement marker, an *aim,* commemorating George Brown's arrival.[6] Prime Minister Rabbie Namaliu, whose constituency included the Duke of York Islands, was invited to unveil and place a wreath on the marker. Namaliu accepted the invitation, probably in part because national elections were impending.

We arrived at Mioko on the Jubilee day at about 8:00 AM to find that extensive preparations had been made. The main path was ornamented with palm-frond arches, flowers had been specially planted, and decorative sprigs fluttered everywhere. A mimeographed program, handed to us by the community government president, listed the events of the day as the Jubilee drama, a church service, speeches, lunch, and then a competition between village choirs.

We learned over a public address system that the prime minister would be arriving shortly by helicopter. As it turned out, he joined the program a few minutes after it had begun. A crowd of perhaps 400 had assembled on the lawn outside the church, near the newly erected *aim.* At one corner of the lawn, next to the *aim,* was a temporary shelter to protect the visiting dignitaries from the sun during the speeches. At another corner was a shelter (with coconut-frond walls but a sheet-metal roof) to house the savage ancestors during the drama. The latter shelter was referred to as a *marawat,* a word that had designated a ritual site of precontact cannibalism and sorcery. It housed some ten young men from Molot who, we were told, had participated in the drama before. They carried axes and spears, sported unkempt coconut-fiber wigs, wore leafy genital coverings (over underpants), and were covered in mud. A master of ceremonies (a former community government president), who provided a running commentary in Pidgin English over a bullhorn, described these savages as "having a strong tradition and preoccupation with fighting, killing and eating people."

Meanwhile, a motorboat filled with pastors from various Duke of York villages slowly approached. Dressed immaculately in white and playing the roles of George Brown and his entourage of Fijian missionaries, they stood singing hymns as the boat—named the *John Wesley* after Brown's vessel—stopped just offshore in front of the crowd. At their appearance, the savages began to tremble in what seemed a mixture of fright and cannibalistic agitation. Described by the master of ceremonies as "hunters of people, like hunting dogs," they urged each other on in the Duke of York language with shouts such as "What are you waiting for? Your ax is here; let us kill them." At this point "George

Dressed immaculately in white and playing the roles of George Brown and his entourage of Fijian missionaries, pastors from various Duke of York villages stood singing hymns as the John Wesley *stopped offshore. At their appearance, the "savages" began to tremble in what seemed a mixture of fright and cannibalistic agitation.*

Brown" tested the water, placing his hand in the sea. He found it hot, corresponding to the passions of those on shore.

But then the hymns began to work, and the savages made tentative overtures to the missionaries. Several attempted to paddle to the *John Wesley* but, to the vast amusement of the crowd, were conspicuously unfamiliar with the operation of a canoe, facing the wrong way as they paddled, nearly tipping over, and sprawling over the sides in their clumsiness. In this slapstick manner they eventually made it to the "ship" and offered a papaya for barter. But it was Sunday, and George Brown refused to transact. The master of ceremonies explained that the missionaries "wouldn't buy anything on this first day, but would only sing hymns, talk of the church and call the name of God." (Indeed, the real Brown stated in a letter that he had arrived at Molot on a Sunday and forthwith held a church service on board the *John Wesley.* He mentioned that villagers paddled out, "eager to trade," which he refused to do—thereby indicating, we imagine, his superiority as arbiter of exchange. Later that day, during the church service he held, they came on board and watched the "proceedings with quiet, respectful interest" [Brown 1875b: 594].)

The hymns began to work, and the "savages" made tentative overtures to the missionaries.

At this point occurred what the crowd found perhaps the funniest moment of all in the drama. On what was described as the second day of contact, the savages again paddled to the ship with a papaya for exchange. As they approached the ship, they exhibited what seemed the height of ancestral inappropriateness: They stood upright in their canoe and caricatured native dances to the music of the Methodist hymns.[7] The savages on shore were also dancing in this "traditional" manner to the hymns. Over the roars of amusement from the crowd, the master of ceremonies explained that the ancestors did not know about religious music but nonetheless "heard the hymns, which worked like the magic of attraction [*malira*]—the music pulled them." (*Malira*, frequently conveyed in song, was currently used to attract lovers and, in the distant past, to lure enemies to become cannibalistic fare. Those under the influence of *malira* were described as smitten, as without volition. However, we have never heard of hymns being used to attract lovers or enemies.)

Then, compelled by the hymns and their dancing finished, the savages could be instructed. As the master of ceremonies explained,

> You must understand, before [the missionaries' arrival] people didn't speak softly. They were angry and all they thought about was eating other people. When these ancestors wanted to sell food to the missionaries, they wanted the food to be purchased quickly. If the missionaries wouldn't buy the food, they

would be killed and eaten. But the missionaries kept saying *"kalou, kalou."* [This became the local word for God; missionaries introduced the term from Fijian when they could find no equivalent term in the Duke of York and Tolai languages.] At this time, no one understood well about God. No one understood about money either, and Dr. Brown taught them all how to exchange the papaya for money.

Indeed, those enacting the missionaries stopped repeating *"kalou, kalou"* and began uttering "money, money" while holding up coins.

The crucial transformation from savagery effected and essential lessons learned, George Brown once again tested the water and, finding it cool, knew that the savage passions had been quenched. The missionaries then came on shore, still singing hymns and uttering *"kalou, kalou"* for there was a bit of backsliding as the savages crowded around, smelling the well-fed bodies of the missionaries. But, in short order, the savages relinquished their weapons as commanded and were given a hymnbook in return. They were also given steel tools and salt.[8]

In the last set of events depicting the conversion of the savages, Brown purchased land for his mission station. The master of ceremonies then related that Brown was approached by big men from throughout the region, each of whom wished to buy the church for his locality. They were told, however, that the church was "a free gift from God."

$$*\qquad*\qquad*$$

The drama ended there. Thoroughly enjoyed by all, it had depicted events and employed rhetoric that were entirely familiar not only from enactments at other Jubilees but also from frequently recounted stories about the precontact epoch of the *momboto*. At least since Fred's 1968 field trip, the *momboto* had been defined as a time of darkness when, as mentioned earlier, people could not see the path of proper conduct (cf. Shore 1982: 158; White 1991: 138–139). The *momboto* was abruptly transformed into the enlightened present as the immediate result of Brown's arrival (cf. McDowell 1985). Significantly, those who lived during the *momboto* were depicted as not only savage but precultural. They were presented in the drama and in stories about the *momboto* as being unable, for instance, to paddle their canoes properly. Their one area of competence lay in killing and eating each other; in fact, stories about the *momboto* often depicted a Hobbesian war of all against all. Moreover, major cultural institutions such as moiety groupings and the use of shell money were often attributed to the arrival of Brown (or to his ostensible age-mate, the biblical figure Noah).

The missionaries came on shore, still singing hymns and uttering "kalou, kalou"—for there was a bit of backsliding as the "savages" crowded around, smelling the well-fed bodies of the missionaries.

In short order, the "savages" would relinquish their weapons as commanded.

Thus, the *cultural* past presented in the Jubilee drama and in accounts of the *momboto* was a shallow, sharply truncated one. The *momboto* exemplified what might be called *the invention of a nontradition.* (See Hobsbawm and Ranger [1983] for contrasting examples of the construction of a usable past.) The savages enacting the *momboto* in the drama would be as much at home in Gapun performing for Kulick's friend as they were in Mioko performing for the prime minister.

The widely held assumption that a momentous change of state had taken place with Brown's arrival provided the basis of the 1991 Jubilee play frame, namely, that these contemporary East New Britains were fundamentally disconnected from their precultural ancestors and thus were in no way compromised by a depiction of the latter as bumbling, bloodthirsty savages. Indeed, the laughter both marked and guaranteed that the change of state had been complete. Hence, a spectator could tell us not only that the drama was humorous but that its message was important: "It showed what life was like before the church came, and it was a message about the arrival of the good news. People should watch the drama, think about it and learn from it."

The significance of this Jubilee drama—what people should learn from it—concerned transformations not only from the past but from the present into the future. In the sermons and speeches that followed, its particular view of a past transformed, left entirely behind, and of cultural roots truncated became crucial to a nationalist vision of a future Papua New Guinea, a developed nation, united and prosperous.

The Sermons and Speeches: From Savagery to Citizenry in the Nation of Papua New Guinea

After the drama concluded, the master of ceremonies directed the by now almost 1,000 of us to the area next to the *aim* where the shelter had been constructed to shade the dignitaries. There a service took place, lasting over two hours. The service included prayers, sermons, and speeches by the bishop, several Duke of York clergy, and the prime minister. A central theme was change: change from savagery to civilization and from Australian domination to the political and economic autonomy of nationhood. And what was stressed as crucial to effecting such change was the unity that Christianity had brought to the country.

Thus, during the major sermon (in Pidgin English) we were told in images directly alluding to the change from the *momboto* to the present that

> no matter where you go in Papua New Guinea, there is only one Bible. All people of the country are Christian people; George Brown [and other early named missionaries] came to us to turn the world upside down. ... He came to change our lives, to bring us life. The missionaries eliminated our blindness; they gave us life. It is the life we will see when we go to Heaven. ... It is a new life. Our old lives are finished because the world has been changed; it has been turned upside down by these men who came here to live with us. ... Today we have good lives because of these men.

But it was the prime minister, Rabbie Namaliu, who most explicitly linked these themes of unity and Christianity with those of nationhood and socioeconomic development. Also speaking in Pidgin English, he said: "It's been 116 years since the Methodist Mission first came to our part of the country. ... I think we are happy that George Brown came to bring us light. During these 116 years, many changes have occurred. It is true that some changes have not been too good, but many have improved our lives. ... The government would not have been able to bring good changes into the country if these churches had not come first."

Namaliu elaborated on this theme in a subsequent speech, near the conclusion of the day's events:

> Today the Church is led by us; it is no longer led by Australians. In the same way, we are in control of the government. It was the church that handed over

power first, then the government. We are happy to celebrate today because it was the church that opened the way and showed us … how to run our own government in this country.

No matter where you go in this country today, the presence and influence of the church is strong; they are strong everywhere, particularly concerning spiritual development, community development and the development of education and health programs. … In many ways, the church can effect better changes than can the government. The government has the resources, but the church has the knowledge to put those resources to good use.

Moreover, the church strengthens the unity of the country: the church doesn't know any boundary marks. No matter what part of the country you come from, if you are a member of the United or Catholic Church and you go to the Central Province or to Bougainville, you will find members of your group there. … So the church is important in uniting the people, in uniting us here in Papua New Guinea and in uniting us with the people of other countries as well. …

But I think there is another important role for the church. … It won't be long before there's considerable development of our gold, oil and other resources. Soon the government will be receiving big revenues, and we will be seeking those who can help us spend them in order to improve the living conditions of all the people. There are not many groups that can help. Only the church has demonstrated that with just a little money it can bring development to improve the lives of the people in the villages. That is why this year and later, the church will be important in helping the government develop the country. The revenues from the big companies will open many things. I will be building many schools in villages where there are none now; I will be building many roads in areas which have none now. However, concerning all basic needs, such as education, welfare, and other needs, the missions will be able to help the government to strengthen development throughout our country. …

The influence of George Brown and the other missionaries will remain forever. That's why, 116 years after Dr. Brown first came, we spend a little time thinking about how it is we wish the church to continue to help us in the future. … And we think not only about the United Church, but also about the Catholic Church, the SDA [Seventh-Day Adventist] Church and the other churches of our country, because their teachings have been with us for a long time and will continue to be important because moral development and the development of ethics go along with education and health. We will not be able to improve our lives, to improve our customs, unless we strengthen our commitment to the churches in our various villages.

*   *   *

The themes of the past transformed—surpassed—were redundantly central to the Jubilee and to Namaliu's vision of Papua New Guinea as a united and prosperous nation. Namaliu was making an argument for unity in which church and state had to work hand in hand, and he did so not only because he was speaking at a church function. Papua New Guinea, in fact, defined itself in its constitution as a Christian country.

Namaliu appeared as an active participant in the enactment of what had become an official history. The imagery of the *momboto* transformed by the arrival of George Brown obviously reflected a view of history promulgated by the missionaries and framed in their language contrasting darkness with light. At some point between the 1929 Jubilee and the period of Fred's first research in 1968, these mission-motivated images of George Brown's arrival, that is, of the significance of the past and its relationship to the present, had become well established. No longer resisted by means of improvised appropriation, they had been performatively instantiated as truth. In 1929, the performers, deeply resenting the nonreciprocity inherent in European domination, had opened a resistance space by rerealizing their relationship to the vehicles of colonial domination—coconut, ship, plane, and money. But by 1991, neither resentment of nor resistance to the inequality of nonreciprocity was a salient theme in the Jubilee. The use of money, for instance, was noncontroversial and defined the transformation from savagery. Both performers and audience accepted without contention the definition and manifestations of commerce. (This is not to say, however, that money was regarded as appropriately displacing shell money.)

With the instantiation of these images there had been a transformation of the play frame in what was now an official drama—a shift in what was funny. White has described what might have been a transitional case—were it to have occurred in East New Britain—in his analysis of somewhat similar comic conversion dramas performed on Santa Isabel in the Solomon Islands. He argued that although these dramas enacted a disjunction between the present and the past, they also depicted what were interpreted as important continuities. In fact, the dramas were funny because they traded "upon emotionally and politically loaded topics" (White 1991: 143) concerning fundamental, ongoing ambiguities in people's identities as both Christian and customary, civilized and savage:

> By constructing images of violence and aggression in the exaggerated persona of the heathen warrior, the play makes the covert overt, taking real ambivalences and subjecting them to symbolic resolution through re-enactment of the conversion process and its hopeful transformation of "dark" passions.

> In like manner, the patent asymmetries between Western technological power and *kastom* [customary] ways continue to be sources of ambivalent reflection in Santa Isabel today. (p. 143)

Thus White's performers might be seen as attempting and reattempting a self-transformation, a reconversion, as they have accepted, at least in part, the self-blame that accompanied colonial power relations.[9] Theirs was not the resistance of the 1929 Jubilee improvisation; nor was theirs the dominant discourse of the official history performed before Prime Minister Namaliu and other members of the East New Britain elite. Theirs, instead, was an intermediary position ambivalently poised between anger at colonial inequalities and self-blame.[10]

By 1991, the Duke of York Islanders' anger and self-blame alike had largely abated, and the mission-motivated images of the *momboto* past could be accepted during the Jubilee as no longer denigrating and as the foundation of a modern Papua New Guinea nation. These images were not only thoroughly familiar to the audience but also the basis of Namaliu's construction of the future. This is not to say that Namaliu and the early missionaries had precisely the same agenda and historical position. However, both wanted to create structures and events that would incorporate disparate, contentious local groups into wider structures and events. In such an incorporation the work of church and state was akin; indeed, one was the basis of the other.

This work, we suggest, asserted or assumed a number of politically useful and somewhat overlapping propositions: All Papua New Guineans had culture; there were many different cultures in the country; yet all Papua New Guineans possessed comparable savage pasts and therefore an "ur-equality." In addition, differences among contemporary cultures were limited because they were to only a minimal extent primordial. Moreover, these (relatively) residual differences were ameliorated by the pervasive presence of Christianity introduced throughout Papua New Guinea by Brown and comparable missionaries.

Thus, Namaliu's speeches and the events of the entire Jubilee asserted what might be termed a *politics of nonculture*. They truncated particularist and primordial cultural roots by generalizing the savage past. As formulated in the 1991 Jubilee (and perhaps in the performance videotaped by Kulick's friend), cultural differences had become sufficiently "underdetermined"—compartmentalized rather than pervasive—and sufficiently alloyed by Christian commonality as to provide no inexorable barrier to unity. In other words, the argument of the Jubilee events and speeches was that for Papua New Guinea to be a nation-state, cultural traditions had to become equivalent through comparability. Because Gapun and Mioko, for instance, could be presented as having commensurate pasts, the differences between them could be presented as shallow. It might be said that for a Christian nation to be formed from a multiplicity of cultures (Papua New Guinea, as we have said, has over 700 linguistic groups), all God's children's ancestors had to have been bumbling savages. To resist this dominant discourse, this notion of an absolute disjunction between the present and the past, would be to run the risk of appearing anachronistic and peripheral, of appearing to be among the dwindling leafy-genital-covering crowd (perhaps one of East New Britain's ethnic minorities studied by the Western anthropologists).

This is not to say that the hegemony of this discourse was complete. As all the participants at the Jubilee undoubtedly recognized, very substantial cultural differences remained in Papua New Guinea and formed the basis of distinct cultural identities; [11] the project of the Jubilee was far from being realized, and national unity was frequently subverted by (among other things) competitive struggles between local groups. Perhaps for this reason, the final event of the Jubilee, the choir competition, provided a vision of intergroup "harmony" as one of well-regulated and restricted contestation.

The Choir Competition
as Constituted Equality

After the church service and a break for lunch, the president of the Duke of York community government announced that the choir competition was about to begin on the school playing field. Nearly 2,000 gathered to witness the male, female, and mixed-voice choirs from some twenty Duke of York villages compete in the precision of their marching and beauty of their four-part harmonies.

Each choir was decked in finery: The men of a particular contingent wore ties, white shirts, and *laplap* of the same color; women wore *laplap* and *meri blaus*. Some of the choirs were composed of ecumenical religious fellowships; moreover, no religion was excluded. One women's choir, for example, included members of both the United Church and the New Church (a recently established evangelical sect). Another was composed of those identified as the "Catholic mothers."

During the first part of the program, each choir marched around the playing field while singing two hymns, one prescribed for all and the other chosen by each group. During the second part, each choir appeared in turn to sing two additional hymns of its choice. The audience listened carefully to each of the performances. At least fifty people taped the singing, and several videotaped it. Our Karavaran friends were impressed. They thought that all the choirs were good—strong voiced, neatly attired, and well disciplined—and they could not decide which the judges should choose.

These Christian soldiers, as one of our companions explicitly characterized them, were very different from the motley savage warriors depicted in the drama with which the Jubilee had begun. Calmed by the hymn singing, the Duke of York Islanders had become the highly ordered hymn singers. The circumstances were no longer those of the Hobbesian war of all against all. The winners did not devour the losers. Nor was there either (substantial) gloating or grumbling over the judges' decisions. At least on this occasion, competition between groups was presented in highly structured and circumscribed terms as process involving ontological equals.

THE THEFT OF DEEP HISTORY IN THE
CONSTRUCTION OF NATIONALISM

Perhaps most generally, the Jubilee celebration, including the prime minister's speech and the choir competition, was addressing one of the central suppositions of contemporary nationalisms: that the nation must be composed of those sharing a particular cultural heritage. Handler (1988) has compellingly demonstrated, for example, that the demands of Quebecois separatists rested on the assertion that they had a distinctive cultural property, a heritage different from that of English-speaking Canadians. Such cultural property, often invented, was defined through reference to a primordial and inalienable past, a deep rootedness. Creation of the nation (as opposed to the state) in such terms would become highly problematic in contexts such as Papua New Guinea that were characterized by extreme cultural pluralism.[12]

We have suggested that one Papua New Guinea strategy for dealing with this problem involved articulating the objectives of nationalism with mission-induced, but pervasively accepted, views of the past. (See Kapferer [1988, 1989] for convincing demonstrations that nationalisms build on locally held conceptions of person and polity.) Those views of a sharply truncated past (crucial to the contemporary meaning of the *momboto*), which we have dubbed the invention of nontradition, had become the basis for claims of national unity.

During the period in which Jubilees have been celebrated, however, the meaning and political uses of the past seem to have changed. The available descriptions of the Jubilees in 1925 and 1929 suggest that the precontact past was remembered by a number of those still living. Despite the changes in life's circumstances after Brown's arrival, the present had real continuity with the precontact past. During this time of ardent colonialism, the most positive message of the European depictions of the precontact past was that natives should be grateful to their colonial masters for having changed their lives for the better. As we have seen in the 1929 Jubilee play frame (including the events at other missionary meetings that Margetts considered comparable), natives resisted this message by appropriating colonialist images—the coconut, ship, and airplane—in a limited but creative way. Indeed, in their comic improvisation they reconfigured social relations so as to emerge, however temporarily, the betters of their colonial masters.

By the time of Fred's first fieldwork and certainly by the 1991 Jubilee, the precontact past described as the *momboto* could no longer be contradicted by anyone's lived experience. The *momboto* had become a model of disconnection to be either established through effort or assumed as given. The Santa Isabel case, if it can be extrapolated to East New Britain, suggests a later period of colonial penetration (subsequent to that of 1929). Rather than a mode of confrontation and resistance, the comic had become a means of symbolically resolving ambivalences and ambiguities concerning identity and worth in a colonial context. As Karavarans came to blame themselves (to see themselves as inadequate orderers), the humor, it seems to us, became more painful than pointed. Eventually, by 1991, the humor had become easy and compelling. The drama celebrated a transcendent displacement of colonial conflicts; it had become the official and nonincriminating account of historical savagery, an anchor event.[13]

What this official history compelled—at least during the immediate time of its enactment—was the existence of a Papua New Guinea nation composed of equally cultured (or decultured) groups united through Christianity. The drama, of course, was a product of a specific (though not unique) ethnographic and historical context. Thus, the ideological constructions expressed in the contemporary formulation of the *momboto* would not "carry the force to become 'real,' to compel the imagination of community in a particular [nationalist] direction" (Foster 1991: 254)[14] among, for example, the Quebecois, whose task was to assert unbroken continuity with the distant past.[15] Furthermore, the ideological constructions had themselves changed so as to reposition the present with respect to the past. In 1929, they both served European interests and impelled local resistance to colonialism; in 1991, they served national interests and provided the basis for intergroup commensurability.

In trying to ascertain why contemporary Duke of York Islanders portrayed their ancestors as ludicrous, we have been drawn (perhaps by some *malira* of "echoing images") to illuminate and embody ethnographically not only the way in which a nationalist ideology disclosed its "ontological grounding" (Kapferer 1989: 180) but also the way in which that grounding had itself been constructed.[16] The harmonies of the echoes, although derived from Western tonalities in many regards, were no longer employed in a Western melody.

CODA

By the end of the afternoon, the community government president was rushing the program along. It was nearly 5:00 PM, the sun was beginning to set, and people had to start for home. The president suggested that we applaud God for having provided good weather. He then instructed us to bow our heads for a final prayer, in which God was thanked for having brought us from the darkness into the light so that now things were clear. As the audience dispersed—some on foot, some in motor boats, and some in canoes, paddling with considerable precision—Prime Minister Rabbie Namaliu rode off into the sunset in his helicopter, no longer only a model of a flying machine.

*   *   *

We have been trying in this book to do some justice to the complexity and significance of change in a colonial and postcolonial world—a world not only of the past and the present but also of the future. As seen by many Papua New Guineans, a satisfactory future had to involve shaping both local and national identity and worth. However, given cultural diversity and the widespread assumption that cultural groups were always in relations of potential competition, the feasible strategies for pursuing nationalism in Papua New Guinea were likely limited. The strategy we have outlined in the present chapter took the form of a comic drama in which cultural roots were presented as truncated and the significance of deep cultural distinctiveness thereby denied. In contrast, the strategy discussed in Chapter 2 consisted of efforts to promote the cultural characteristics of a particular local group as the national model. This strategy also took the form of a drama, but one perhaps potentially more tragic than comic. In it, deep cultural distinctiveness was asserted rather than denied and the field of competition was thereby enhanced rather than diminished. Thus, one strategy pursued unity through suppressing competition; the other (and probably ontologically more appealing to Papua New Guineans) pursued unity through suppressing the competitors, through achieving preeminence.

It seems to us that for both strategies, the play was the thing. The object of both performances was to catch actors and audience up in the action so that they could forget their habitual patterns of interaction. In other words, the object was to reconfigure existing lines of cleavage, fragmentation, and dis-tinction—whether cultural or class-based. Thus, actors and audience would be remade, however temporarily, as citizens. Oscillating as these dramas were, though, between the potential triviality of historical caricature and the poten-tial overreaching of cultural aggrandizement, it is not clear to us how effective they ultimately could be. We doubt that many of these prospective citizens would have suspended for long what were, after all, in this Papua New Guinea context, myriad and compelling disbeliefs.[17]

Certainly, as we shall see in the next chapter, many Karavarans became quickly aware of how much could be at stake in the making of citizens when some among them tried to assert and newly define themselves by standing apart from local social contexts. Interestingly, in so doing, these citizens adopted images of themselves comparable to those projected by colonial transformers of Papua New Guinea, explorers and missionaries.

NOTES

1. We do not know when the term *momboto* was first used in the Duke of York Is-lands. The word did not appear in George Brown's 1887 *Vocabulary of the Dialect Spoken in the Duke of York Islands*. Nor did it appear in the emendations to this word list made during the next few years by Benjamin Danks.

2. Our data confirm Thomas's (1992a) finding that in their writings, missionaries in the Pacific avoided essentialisms that defined the differences between natives and Europeans as absolute. After all, if differences were absolute, true conversion would be impossible. Not surprisingly, however, missionaries might on occasions of discour-agement slip into such essentialist comparisons, as in this confidential report.

3. White supremacists remained vigilant in defense of their interests. Consider, for example, an excerpt from a letter from J. Hoogerwerff, the manager of the *Rabaul Times,* to J. Mouton, its owner, who was living in Australia: "Our friend, Wallace [a rival printer], seems to be in hot water with the Government. As I hear the Govern-ment has found out that Wallace and his mother are having a bad influence on the native chiefs. I know from old Miss von Ziegler that the luluais [government-ap-pointed chiefs] visit the Wallaces, sit on chairs with them round the table and are given tea and cigarettes and good advice as regards their work for the Government which should be paid for. Well, the Government may get sufficient reasons to per-haps deport the Wallaces" (Mouton 1936: n.p.).

4. The Papua Ekalesia, Kwato Extension Association, United Church of Port Moresby, and Methodist Church of New Britain amalgamated to form the United

Church of Papua New Guinea and the Solomon Islands in 1968. For an excellent description of church history see Threlfall, 1975.

5. We should mention that skits and comedies have become widespread across the Pacific, occurring at events such as school graduations, agricultural shows, cultural fetes, and sporting competitions, as well as on religious occasions such as Christmas. Typically, the audience consisted not only of locals but of indigenous officials and, sometimes, tourists or even anthropologists. In the case of the modern George Brown Jubilee, it was unusual for the prime minister or Europeans to be present, but religious dignitaries and, perhaps, provincial leaders would attend.

6. Since the late 1960s, it had become increasingly common for the sponsors of mortuary ceremonies to erect a cement memorial—*aim*—sometimes to commemorate one particularly illustrious relative and sometimes to commemorate a matrilineal or cognatic line. The church had also encouraged erecting these to commemorate the early missionaries.

7. Don Handelman (1990: 236–265) offered an excellent discussion of clowns as providing both markers and mechanisms of transition in life-cycle ceremonies. Clowns, he wrote, embody processuality and oscillation; they are reified paradox. However, we contend that in the case of the 1991 Duke of York Jubilee, the ancestors became funny in their clowning once an absolute—unambiguous—distinction between the present and the past was established, one that did not admit a betwixt and between.

8. As mentioned, Duke of York Islanders traded with Europeans well before Brown's arrival. In fact, Brown's letter books indicated that they knew how to comport themselves in trade when he first made contact with them (Brown 1975a: 574). In the course of this trade, they had encountered metal substantially prior to Brown's arrival. More puzzling in the Jubilee drama, however, was the reference to salt as a trade item. Salt could hardly have been a scarce condiment for coastal Pacific islanders. However, one of our informants suggested a metaphorical interpretation: that just as salt made food savory, so too did the talk of the missionaries make the good news palatable.

9. Laughter in this context might be experienced as transformatory in itself. See Mosko (1992), who argued that ritually induced laughter served such a function among the Bush Mekeo.

10. The Santa Isabel Islanders resembled the Karavarans as Fred encountered them in 1968 and 1972. At that time, far more so than during 1991, Karavarans seemed preoccupied with keeping the *momboto* at bay. (See Errington 1974a, 1974b.) It was thought to be both a chaotic historical period that could abruptly return and an anarchical state of mind that could spill over into action. Unfortunately for purposes of comparison, neither the Karavarans nor Fred attended the Jubilee at Molot in 1968. (At that time, the Karavarans were claiming that in the late nineteenth century the church had unfairly appropriated their land on the neighboring island of Ulu in

order to make a plantation.) We would expect, however, that the dramatic ambience at that time would be more as White described than as we witnessed in 1991.

11. That cultural differences were, in fact, strong and important virtually goes without saying for anyone familiar with Papua New Guinea at this time. Among the Duke of York Islanders and the Tolai for instance, the importance of the *dukduk* and *tubuan* ritual complex and the use of shell money were significant markers of unique cultural identity. For discussion of this ritual complex in the Duke of York Islands, see Errington 1974b. For the most recent discussions of it among the Tolai, see Neumann 1992, and Simet 1992. It would seem that at this time, it was virtually impossible for anyone to have an identity simply as a Papua New Guinean without reference to a specific cultural group. Those using the nationalist strategy exhibited in the 1991 Jubilee were not trying to erase cultural differences; they were only trying to make them more commensurate and less exclusive.

12. The breakup of the former Soviet Union was only one contemporary example.

13. In this regard, Strathern's (1980) criticism of Errington's (1974a, 1974b) discussions of the *momboto* for employing Western concepts, such as the opposition between nature and culture, was misplaced. An account could be ethnographically accurate in describing certain ideas as locally salient, even though those ideas might prove to have been introduced. Neumann's (1992) criticism that Errington (1974a, 1974b) and Sack (1985) ignored the voices of many Tolai who might deny the significance of the *momboto* (the *bobotoi*, in Tolai) was similarly misplaced. Official histories, as dominant discourse, may be both compelling and contested. To judge by the Mioko Jubilee, as well as by conversations we had with villagers in other contexts during 1991, the rhetoric of the *momboto* was still the dominant discourse in the Duke of York Islands. Both Strathern and Neumann failed to consider the sociohistorical processes that would have persuaded native people to adopt, or to contest, the view of the *momboto*. It must also be recognized, however, that Errington's analyses of Karavar (1974a, 1974b) might have benefited from a fuller consideration of historical process. It was not, however, this deficiency that Strathern (1980) and Neumann (1992) criticized. If it had been, their criticisms might have been more telling.

14. Foster alluded here to Benedict Anderson's *Imagined Communities* (1983), a work important to all subsequent discussions of nation formation. In it, Anderson explored the manner in which citizens who will never actually know one another come to "image their communion" (p. 15).

15. Handler recounted many instances of what he called "cultural objectification" (1988: 14). In one, a performance at the Quebec City Coliseum about unique and indigenous ways of life, a "traditional if larger than life farmhouse interior [was constructed such that the] audience, willingly suspending disbelief, could imagine itself to be looking into an old-fashioned farmhouse parlor" (p. 12).

16. There may be further shifts in the meaning of the precontact past. For example, the notion of the *momboto* as precultural would be inherently implausible for those educated in a Western view of history and anthropology. As Tolai were probably

the best-educated group in Papua New Guinea, one might expect more Tolai than Duke of York Islanders to reject or challenge this positioning of the present with respect to the past. Neumann quoted a Tolai who said that such a view of the past was "bullshit" (1992: 204).

17. The achievement of nationalism in Papua New Guinea may, in actuality, lie ultimately with the predominance of consumer capitalism, however lamentable that may be for other reasons (see Foster n.d.). In other words, for nationalism to work, Papua New Guinea may need less of the dramatic and more of the everyday.

4

First Contact with God

Individualism, Agency, and Revivalism in the Duke of York Islands

W E HAVE BEEN writing about changes occurring among Karavarans and their neighbors since first contact with Europeans. One of the changes was the emergence of a postcolonial system of difference based on educational accomplishment, well-paying employment, and, as we will argue here, religious affiliation. In this chapter, we examine the manifestations among Karavarans of this increasing differentiation, focusing on the activities of a group of evangelical Christians to redefine the bases of identity and worth. Viewing themselves as modern in the face of anachronistic fellow villagers, these evangelicals saw themselves as "citizens" in a modern nation and sought to enlighten benighted others in their community. In so doing, they were, to some extent, replicating those "enterprising" Europeans who first brought the "wider world" to their ancestors.

Among the most famous and revealing of these Europeans was Michael Leahy, who documented his encounters and his sensibility in many vivid photographs. Leader of the first European expeditions into the hidden and densely populated valleys of the Papua New Guinea Highlands during the 1930s, Leahy, "captured brilliantly the drama, the fear, the elation of first contact, of the highland people responding to *him*" (Connolly and Anderson 1987: 99). Indeed, Highlanders could hardly have encountered a more concentrated embodiment of colonial individualism than Michael Leahy: Mauser slung over one shoulder and Leica over the other—his person in this

---

An earlier version of this chapter appeared in *Cultural Anthropology* 8, 3 (August 1993). Reprinted by permission of the American Anthropological Association.

way augmented by the most technologically advanced of Western mechanisms of domination and objectification—he felt fundamentally superior to, and detached from, the contexts through which he moved in his entrepreneurial pursuit of treasure and fame.

It is clear that Michael Leahy thought of himself as an intrepid agent of colonial transformation. That is apparent from the unusual care he took in recording his expedition. However, many other Europeans who initiated first-contact encounters also viewed themselves as agents of transformation, albeit sometimes with differing views of treasure, fame, and the course of history. Consider in this regard the journal entry of the Reverend George Brown as he approached the Duke of York Islands on August 14, 1875: "By 1PM we were well within the straits. The weather thick with rain squalls. ... New Ireland on our right and New Britain sketchy away on our left. What is before us? How long before these lands receive the Gospel? Not *will* they receive it! Faith repels such a question. But when? How long? How many will fail. ... [We] are sure but it may be that a soldier's grave awaits some of us here. Be it so the Victor's crown will follow" (Brown 1875a: n.p.).

Brown would probably have regarded adventurers like Michael Leahy as misguided in their search for worldly rewards and as irresponsible in their influence on future events.[1] Brown possessed a vision of a better society that Leahy, we suspect, lacked. Nonetheless, he shared with Leahy a sense of the portentous, a heroic sense of making history—of precipitating *events*.

It is this stance toward history and person—toward event—that had, we argue, been adopted by the contingent of Karavaran evangelicals with whom we are concerned such that they had come to see themselves as critical commentators on, and heroic transformers of, the social field. We see, in other words, the emergence of Papua New Guineans who more than a century after Brown's arrival had come to share in significant measure his sense of the portentous making of history.[2] Through a discussion of who these evangelicals were and why they emerged when they did, we explore the way that the intercultural conjunctures (cf. Sahlins 1985) during the colonial and postcolonial periods played out so as to affect and empower a specific kind of person: a Christian citizen, operating in the context of a nation-state, who envisioned a society of like-minded persons and a self capable of effecting that society. In this exploration, we extend and ethnographically embody Dipesh Chakrabarty's contention that the idea of "'history' [and its concomitant concept of anachronism] was absolutely central to the idea of 'progress' (later 'development') on which colonialism was based and to which nationalism aspired" (1992: 57). Along the way, we draw certain, perhaps surprising, comparisons among disparate characters and contexts in the contemporary nation-states of Papua New Guinea, the United States, and beyond.

In sum, our goal is to provide a social history (albeit partial) of the development of a particular sense of history: the acceptance by *certain* Duke of York Islanders, within the institutional context of the socially and economically differentiated Papua New Guinea state, of central aspects of the view of individualism and agency that brought George Brown (and Michael Leahy) to Papua New Guinea.

THE WORLD TURNED UPSIDE DOWN

Significantly, even though Europeans had been visiting the Duke of York Islands since the latter part of the eighteenth century, it was Brown whom Duke of York Islanders regarded as having initiated first contact, as having transfigured social life.[3] Indeed, as we said in our description of the Jubilee in Chapter 3, many credit Brown with having turned the world upside down and hence with having brought the people from darkness into light. Moreover, in the skit that accompanied the Jubilee, as well as in frequently told local accounts, the transforming effects of Brown's arrival were virtually instantaneous: So powerful was this first contact that savage hearts became Christian souls in the course of only three days.

The language of contemporary exegesis concerning first contact seen in this reenactment and in local accounts was well established early in the mission encounter with Duke of York Islanders. Thus by 1892, Aika Mitaralen, a local student in missionary training, had already learned the rhetorical dimensions of "then" and "now," a contrast still persisting today. In a letter written to the general secretary of the Mission Board of the Wesleyan Methodist Church of Australasia he testified as follows:

> This land was full of darkness, the people did not agree together, and they fought with one another every day, never resting, but continually carried their tomahawks, spears, slings and sling stones. When they fought and killed then they ate the bodies of the slain and there was no brotherly love at that time. The character of the chiefs was bad when they acted like that. When the "Lotu" [church] came to this land these things were not done away with at once, but now have ceased and the "Lotu" grows daily. (as quoted by William Brown 1892: n.p.)

There came to be, as we shall see, ongoing argument over what "things" were meant eventually to be "done away with" and what "things" properly belonged to the time of light. Nonetheless, George Brown and the missionaries who followed him were remarkably successful at converting Duke of York Islanders. So successful were they that it has become official history—part of a dominant discourse—to credit Brown with effecting first contact practically instantaneously.

The church succeeded for complex reasons. Among these, we believe, was an indigenous view of sociality. According to this view, powerful men, including missionaries, generated social order through their transactions. (See Chapter 2, Errington 1974a, and later in this chapter.) Another reason, as mentioned, was recognition that missionaries minimally supported social justice in a colonial world where officials favored labor practices serving plantation and other commercial interests. (See Threlfall 1975.) Certainly, by Fred's first field trip, the church had succeeded; all Islanders had long been converted. Most embraced George Brown's Methodist Church, subsequently the United Church, as the religion of tradition. On Karavar Island, where everyone was a United Church member, to be anything else would have been alienating and isolating; one in-marrying man had tried to maintain his allegiance to the Seventh-Day Adventist Church but was shunned into abandoning it for the United Church.

This unity had ceased, however, shortly before we came to Karavar in 1991.[4] During our first extended conversation there, we were told with considerable consternation that the matter of greatest importance occurring in the almost twenty years since Fred had last visited (in 1972) was the appearance of the New Church, an evangelical church that challenged the preeminence of the United Church. Our informant thought the New Church illegitimate because it was not the "mother" church. Indeed, with its emphasis upon guitar playing, hand clapping, praising, and providing spontaneous testimonies rather than upon hymn singing and formal preaching, it was inappropriate, almost disgusting.

But certainly not all people felt this way. A small but vocal minority claimed not only legitimacy for their evangelical teachings but primacy. They argued that local United Church members had strayed from George Brown's lessons. They had fallen, perhaps not quite into the darkness of paganism, but certainly into the twilight of serious apostasy; they spoke against sin but freely engaged in it nonetheless. These United Church members were in dire need of revival through a startling personal contact with God.

The evangelicals believed that it was the message of the early missionaries that had startled the benighted into enlightenment; it was the message that had in effect turned the world upside down. Several of them were therefore eager to help us when we undertook to translate one of the earliest sermons given in the Duke of York language.[5] This sermon had been delivered on November 15, 1881, by Isaac Rooney, Brown's immediate successor in the Duke of York Islands. They hoped, one told us, that the sermon would have the capacity to awaken their fellow Karavarans from their religious lethargy to the nature of their transgressions.

A few paragraphs from Rooney's text are sufficient to explain why the evangelicals were to be ultimately somewhat disappointed. Rooney drew his inspiration from Paul's second epistle to Timothy, verse 4, stanza 8, where—in our King James version of the Bible, at least—Paul told Timothy that "henceforth there is laid upon me a crown of righteousness, which the Lord, the righteous judge, shall give me at that day: and not to me only, but onto all them also that love his appearing." The fact Rooney referred to this passage suggests that (as with Paul) he saw his work to be one of heroic portent, work that might be rewarded—-to cite again Brown's thoughts upon approaching the Duke of York Islands—with the "Victor's crown." Yet Rooney's version of this passage from Timothy sounded as flat to our assistants as it did in translation to us: "The church is transcendent; it informs about things that are paramount in our life here and in the after life."

Rooney continued in language that had become largely commonplace:

> The church is mature. No person is the basis of the church. The church belongs to God. Jehovah is the basis of the church. God looks at us. We are lost; we go astray; we feel worried; we feel weak. God feels compassion for us and sends us a church so that we may live within it. ...
>
> The church teaches us that we believe in customs that are bad—we believe in fighting; we believe in sorcery, in theft, in lying; we believe in working destruction.
>
> A church unites us in love; a church unites our understandings. Fighting is finished; we live in the light. Sorcery, stealing, lying: all are finished. The working of destruction is finished. We are free; we rest; we go freely. We are afraid of nothing. Why? Because of the church.
>
> There is no more half light. No fighting. No shirking. No pubic leaf coverings. [This is not a statement favoring nudity!] No fear of death. We die here, but then later, no. Later, we live. We are entirely happy. We are entirely complete. We are complete without end, without end.
>
> The truth is with us now. The church has come to us. It has come to all people. It has come to all humans. It comes to everyone. (Found in Rooney 1888: n.p.)

Our assistants were disappointed with this sermon because they found it standard fare, not particularly revitalizing to their lives. True, they agreed, one should inveigh against continuing sorcery, theft, and lying, but attacks on these had long been the staples of weekly United Church preaching. However novel—portentous—in its time, the Good News, as Rooney presented it, was no longer "news." Though not fully anachronistic, the sermon was certainly passé.

THE PAST DISPLACED

The evangelicals were, it must be granted, a rather hard crowd to please. Most of the twenty-two adult New Church members on Karavar were in early middle age. Of the men, all but two had spent considerable time away from Karavar, working as, for example, heavy-vehicle mechanic, electrician, and teacher. Many of the men had a secondary education; a few, tertiary. All of the men were literate except for the elderly father of one. In all but two cases, the men had joined evangelical sects when living away from home. Their wives, for the most part, had converted after their husbands had. In addition, scattered relatives of the converts (a few widowed mothers and unmarried sisters) had been "reborn." In other words, they—certainly the men—were among the most sophisticated, most broadly traveled, most cosmopolitan of Karavarans.

All members of the Karavaran New Church saw evangelical sects as new, exciting, progressive—as the religion of the educated, contemporary Papua New Guinean. They would, for example, claim that most of the contemporary Papua New Guineans of influence were evangelicals, enumerating many instances. (In this regard, as we have implied, evangelicalism in Karavar and in the rest of East New Britain, and perhaps more broadly in Papua New Guinea, seemed to appeal to those in a higher-class position than it often did elsewhere.)

Several of the Karavaran evangelical men had been forced to return home when, with the closing of the Bougainville copper mine[6], they had lost their jobs. Others, working on resettlement (primarily oil-palm) blocks or in towns in other provinces in the country, had come back to Karavar because life away with increasing "law and order" problems had become too stressful and dangerous. A few had applied for new work but had been unable to find any given fierce competition for a declining number of jobs. (For instance, in East New Britain, one of the more prosperous areas of Papua New Guinea, employment had plummeted by 24% during 1989–1990 [*East New Britain Economic Newsletter* 1991b].) Although many still hoped to find new work eventually, they were, in the meantime, not depressed or demoralized. They were sustained by both a viable subsistence economy at home and their religious calling.

The Karavar these evangelicals returned to had been changing as well. The principal source of cash income for Duke of York villagers had been and still was copra production. However, copra prices, after peaking during the early 1970s, had fallen markedly (World Bank n.d.). (In 1991, all agricultural commodities produced in Papua New Guinea were trading at levels lower than ten years earlier: coffee at 74 percent; palm oil at 64 percent; copra at 60 percent; and cocoa at 59 percent [*East New Britain Economic Newsletter* 1991a].) Karavarans, although still well fed, thought themselves poorer than they had been at the time of Fred's first visit, and certainly, in obvious ways, they were. As one example, though many owned radios and flashlights, few had batteries for them. Most walked about at night by the light of burning palm fronds or glowing embers.

One of the most significant changes, a change often commented on by the Karavarans themselves, was the shift away from a social organization centered on the integrating activities of big men (cf. Epstein 1992: 52). This social organization had been at least partly created, certainly fostered, by a colonially imposed system of indirect rule based on the appointment of local headmen, the *luluai*. It also rested on an indigenous context of fluid land tenure and kinship (Errington 1974a). Under these circumstances, big men, many of whom were *luluai* and hence verified and sustained by colonial law, were able to control strategic resources, including labor (cf. Foster, 1988: 22–70). In particular, they had access to large numbers of coconuts, and they had from their kinship following sufficient labor to process them. The cash thus received could be readily converted into the locally more salient shell money, the basis, as we have seen, of transactions essential to forming groups and alliances. Indeed, to reiterate, Duke of York Islanders (and Tolai) viewed social life as generated by the use of shell money, especially—at least until recently—through the shell-money exchanges and other transactions of big men. These exchanges and transactions focused especially on ceremonies featuring the *dukduk* and *tubuan* ritual organization.

Members of this exclusively male organization engaged in the secret preparation of conically shaped *dukduk* and *tubuan* figures, which they publicly displayed on various ritual occasions. Any violation of the extensive rules and prohibitions of the organization, especially those of secrecy, were punished with heavy fines of shell money. Youths passed through a series of initiation grades whereby they paid fees in shell money so as to obtain knowledge about these figures and the rituals in which they appeared. Eventually, a few men of each generation became adepts with ritual prerogatives and skills necessary to sponsor and control the more important of these figures, the *tubuan*. The *tubuan* not only was the repository of a powerful and dangerous spirit but was central to the major mortuary ceremony (about which more will be said in the next chapter). This was the primary context in which big men, almost invariably adepts, displayed and dispersed their resources of shell money and mobilized their large followings. In fact, as we have said, the shell-money expenditures of big men for these and other activities constituted the politics of both self-aggrandizement and social reproduction.

By the time of our 1991 visit, the big men around whom Karavarans had organized themselves in the late 1960s and early 1970s had all died—the last in 1986. They had not been replaced largely because of the collapse of world copra prices on which their political power at least partly rested.

Such had been the fall of copra prices that few Karavarans regularly bothered to process coconuts at all, and the stands formerly controlled by big men were untended, open to anyone wishing to gather the nuts. Although contemporary mortuary ceremonies involving the creation of *dukduk* and *tubuan* figures were still staged with the previous frequency (about one every two years), they had come to be funded only minimally by their sponsors. Instead (as we shall see in more detail in Chapter 5), these sponsors often depended on modest contributions from nonresident Karavarans or from government officials seeking local support.

No longer as able as the big men of the past to muster impressive resources and extensive followings, increasingly dependent on outsiders for precarious and somewhat demeaning patronage, present sponsors were likely to derive only moderate prestige from what were often only adequate ceremonies. Indeed, many Karavarans noted with accurate nostalgia that the big men of the past had comported themselves more forcefully and had made more happen socially. In effect, social relations had become less focused on the persons and activities of big men: Individuals had become less controlled by big men who displayed their power in ceremonial contexts, and mortuary ceremonies in particular and male ritual in general, although still important, had become less compelling.

With these changes occurring in their social life, members of the New Church felt they could risk attacking beliefs and practices focusing on the *dukduk* and *tubuan*. They explicitly labeled the figures "satans," as among the "things" referred to earlier that George Brown and the early missionaries meant to do away with. (Brown and his immediate successors were, in fact, strongly opposed to the *dukduk* and *tubuan* complex but found it impossible to eradicate. They objected to it because it was not only pagan but also tyran- nical in its proclivity to levy fines [See Threlfall 1975: 58].) As one of our New Church informants put it, "Those who continue to worship these false gods are following the laws of the devil and not of God; they will burn in hell." (He continued by telling us that geologists, boring into the ground to explore for Papua New Guinea's mineral resources, had heard the cries of the damned emanating from the center of the earth.) Until recently such an attack would have been strongly condemned by very powerful men and visited with heavy fines by the *dukduk* and *tubuan* organization they controlled; until recently, such an attack would have been virtually suicidal. However, with the decline of the political economy focusing on copra and big men, such an attack, al- though still decidedly hazardous, was feasible. From the point of view of some it was admirable.

Significantly, none of the Karavaran evangelicals suggested revealing the ritual secrets, though there were fears that they might. (Such revelations had been made elsewhere in Papua New Guinea by Christian revivalists [Leavitt 1989; Tuzin 1989].) Instead, they spoke about religious freedom in a modern democracy, arguing that all people should be allowed to practice the religion of their choice without the constraint of *tubuan* fines. And when the New Church members discovered that other Karavarans would resort to violence to protect the religious homogeneity of their community, the evangelicals re- mained staunch, even cheerful. At least in talk, they were prepared to become heroic martyrs in defense of their faith (though they may well have hoped to receive at least some support and protection from the police). Although they had been rather disappointed with Isaac Rooney's speech, they insisted, with him, that "we are free. ... We are afraid of nothing."

THE CONVERSION OF THE METHODISTS

The anthropological literature on religious revivalism in Papua New Guinea is not extensive (see, however, Ryan 1969; Counts 1978; Schieffelin 1981; Barr 1983a, 1983b; Eyre 1988; Leavitt 1989; and Tuzin 1989). Most of these studies have followed from Lawrence's brilliant analysis of the Yali cargo cult. Lawrence (1964) held that the cult strongly reflected indigenous intellectual assumptions and concerns about knowledge, power, and material goods. Tuzin, examining a vision of the religious leader of the Ilahita Christian reviv- alists, stated that it was convincing to the community at large because it was a "blend of traditional ontological understandings concerning dreamlike states, images of local personages and settings, Christian cliches and messages, ideas derived from the immediate political scene, and a dash of cargo cultism" (1989: 199).

Much of this literature—emphasizing as it did continuities with a pre-Christian or early-Christian past—regarded revival movements as largely conservative, a perspective inclined to be (although it did not have to be) rather ahistorical. Leavitt, in a recent example focusing on psychosocial continuities, suggested that the Christian revival he studied in the East Sepik Province was based on long-term "cargo thinking," which helped resolve certain deep-seated existential "anxieties over establishing ties of intimacy and deep sensitivity to a perceived threat of being abandoned emotionally" (1989: 522).

Without contesting that revival movements might embody long-standing assumptions and concerns, the data we have so far presented suggest that Karavaran evangelicals were strongly influenced by important postcolonial transformations, including the appearance of the state as a source of support. These transformations both shaped their agenda and affected their capacity to pursue that agenda locally. Moreover, the brand of revivalism they were proposing was somewhat radical. They proposed a return not to their own past sensibilities at the time of contact but to those of George Brown, who had accepted the challenge of a soldier's grave and the "Victor's crown." In other words, we think that these evangelicals had accepted the challenge of becoming individualists of a specific kind. They had embarked on becoming persons of an altered sort, persons who would become intrepid historical agents.

It is, of course, difficult to know the extent to which Karavaran evangelicals actually had become different from other Karavarans, but certainly their perspectives about who they fundamentally were—their ideas of identity and agency—had importantly changed.[7] Whereas we will not here launch into a full analysis of the complexities of Karavaran views (both "traditional" and "transformed") of self and person, we will nonetheless suggest that the evangelicals were correct in thinking that a shift of considerable portent was under way.

Although we do not wish to exaggerate the extent of the shift such that the cultural and social contrasts appear essentialized, it seems to us that identity and agency as understood by the evangelicals can be accurately regarded as significantly *contrasting* with an indigenous background similar to that White described as widely reported throughout the Pacific: "In the tightly interwoven and constantly public arenas of village life where persons are conceptualized as enmeshed in interdependent relations of all sorts ... , social and moral thought frequently de-emphasize the individual as the primary locus of experience" (White 1991: 6). (For other Pacific examples of the burgeoning and varied literature about the "self," see Read 1955; Errington 1974a; Leenhardt 1979; Shore 1982; Kirkpatrick 1983; White and Kirkpatrick 1985; Clay 1986; Munn 1986; Wagner 1986; Strathern 1988; and Battaglia 1990.)

Geoffrey White's characterization should not, however, be taken to mean that communally oriented Pacific persons failed to assert themselves with respect to others or failed to resist being controlled by others. Certainly there was considerable self-assertion in indigenous Karavaran culture. The mark of a big man—the degree to which he had achieved personal eminence—was, in fact, his assertiveness, his forceful efforts to have his agenda accepted. Neither submerging himself in social life nor standing apart from it, he sought to shape sociality by having himself as its focus. As we have shown, self-aggrandizement and social reproduction came together in the big man.

It might be noted, as well, that this Melanesian big-man system only partly conformed to R. A. Shweder and E. J. Bourne's (1984) characterization of "sociocentric organic cultures." In accord with Shweder and Bourne's argument, the "traditional" (pre–New Church) Karavarans would have felt isolated and alienated if cut off from social relations; yet at the same time, we contend, they would have sought to control rather than acquiesce to various forms of social regulation. Such a circumstance of what might be called "socially embedded individuality" should, moreover, be understood as very different from that characteristic of the recent West wherein individuality was marked, at least ideologically, by the sense of self-sufficiency that allowed a person to remove himself or herself from social contexts (cf. Varenne 1977). In this regard, we agree with Gananath Obeyesekere's distinction between individualism as a social movement associated with the development of Western capitalism and ideas of the individual and individualism. For example, a "person who lives in a society that values collective responsibility can still have a sense of his own self-separateness and individuality. His sense of himself as an individual is, however, partially constituted out of his communal values" (Obeyesekere 1992: 204) and, we would add for Melanesia, his or her social transactions.

However, this having been said, we think that A. L. Epstein, writing about both the Karavarans and the Tolai, still did not adequately account for the *variety* of forms individuality might assume when he somewhat too broadly categorized the Tolai as "closer [on a continuum] to Homo Aequalis than they are to Homo Hierarchicus" (1992: 211). Our view is that Karavarans, as well as Tolai and members of Western society, might, to be sure, have recognized personal accomplishment and efficacy yet have done so in qualitatively different ways.

The Karavaran "traditional" rendering of this general view of identity and agency was further illuminated for us in a conversation we had with a local evangelical. The conversation was not directly about religion but, oddly, about fish traps. We had been told by several people that it was necessary to have the cut ends of the outer binding on a wicker fish trap all in the same plane. The fish trap, when placed in the sea, moreover, had to have these aligned ends down on the ocean floor. If this procedure was not followed, no fish would enter the trap. Our evangelical informant confirmed that such a technique was essential to the catching of fish. We then asked him what difference it would make to the fish where the cut ends were. He replied, stepping outside of his sociocultural context, that it did not make any difference to the fish per se but that if people *believed* that fish would not enter the trap under these circumstances, then fish would not do so.

One additional, clarifying story: During his first field trip, Fred asked a United Church member to help him gather a native edible green on Sunday. The man replied that he would be happy to do this for Fred except that if people saw him work on Sunday, they would gossip. And their gossip would "reach out and touch [him] like a string and make [him] sick."

These beliefs about the efficacy of (relatively) concerted thought and censure (an efficacy that did not, of course, presume a sort of collective identity, an absence of individual distinctiveness) made going against the social grain very difficult. Yet it was this willingness to oppose what was widely considered reasonable and moral conduct—to choose to set oneself in opposition to the rest of the community concerning the proper way to live—that characterized Karavaran evangelicals. Furthermore, these evangelicals sought to transform public opinion and practice. In so doing, they were very different from the traditional big men. Not only were the evangelicals attempting to alter centrally important Karavaran beliefs and practices concerning United Church practices as well as the *dukduk* and *tubuan* complex, but they were doing so from a very different social position. Whereas big men influenced through embodying the social grain, the evangelicals tried to affect by standing apart, by confronting public opinion as intrepid agents of transformation.

To be sure, we do think that evangelicals wanted to determine the social grain such that Karavaran life would eventually become, as it had been for big men, the manifestation of their influence. However, the social life they envisioned (perhaps the only one possible given the collapse of copra prices on which the big-man complex largely depended) was a transformed one. They envisioned a *society* in which freedom of religion (at least *their* religion) would be guaranteed, presumably by the state, rather than a *sociality* generated and constrained by the transactions of big men (cf. Strathern 1988). The evangelicals, at least in their rhetoric, explicitly repudiated a social life in which personal worth was a product and a manifestation of wealth, personal following, and coercive ritual authority.

Those Karavarans who were to become evangelicals had not, however, *initially* seen themselves either as dissidents or as agents of transformation, at least to judge by the conversion stories they related to us. Indeed, they described themselves in these stories as resisting the enlightenment of the Holy Spirit. Thus, Wilson Tovalaun (who eventually did convert) was approached by two members of his family who had converted: his brother, who had converted while working away from home on his oil-palm holding, and his daughter, who had converted while working as a seamstress in the nearby provincial capital of Rabaul. When questioned by his daughter, Tovalaun had had to admit that he did not experience strong religious feelings when attending United Church services, that neither was his "skin moved" nor was he compelled to "shed sin." Nonetheless, he forbade her to attend evangelical services. His argument was that it was important to "uphold the mother church."

Henry Landi conveyed to us the same initial resistance to conversion. While working in Bougainville as an electrician in the copper mine, he had become interested in, though not committed to, revivalism. However, on his return to Karavar after the mine closed, he attended United Church services as he had before his departure. But he became increasingly concerned that the pastors were poorly trained and that they and the members of the congregation were hypocritical; The sermons muted the revelation of Good News. They did not, for example, reveal that the water Jesus offered from the well to the woman of Samaria in John 4:9 was not primarily to sustain physical life but to give spiritual and everlasting life. Moreover, despite injunctions from the pulpit against such sins as theft, pastors and parishioners alike continued to steal from each other's gardens. Although increasingly disillusioned with the United Church on Karavar, Landi felt compelled to support his friends and relatives in their religious practices and for a long time said nothing.

Eventually—always after much misgiving and vacillation—Tovalaun, Landi, and the other New Church members to whom we talked made the hard choice to go against accepted beliefs by converting. Invariably, they described this choice as precipitated by especially troubling personal circumstances, circumstances that became comprehensible and bearable through visitation of the Holy Spirit. They experienced a revelation, a compelling enlightenment that changed their lives. In other words, they described their conversion in the same way that first contact was described: They suddenly encountered the Holy Spirit with a startling and transforming immediacy. Furthermore, the change in their lives had more than personal significance; it was portentous for them of other changes in the world. They would be the nucleus of a new and exemplary community of like-minded fellow believers who had also chosen to let the Holy Spirit into their lives. As such, they would become agents in a larger process of worldwide historical transformation.

Concerning the transformation Tovalaun experienced: Soon after he prohibited his daughter from attending the evangelical church, two of his younger children died. He began to think that perhaps his strong words to his daughter had caused their illnesses. In his words, "This thought stayed with me and eventually my thinking became clearer. Jesus was telling me that I had to change my life if I were to be saved. And then I talked to my brother and others who knew more about how to bring Jesus into their lives. They showed me the way, and now I must testify to show others the way as well."

In Landi's case, his wife and children became desperately ill. His description of conversion followed much the same pattern: "But I thought of Isaiah 53:4–5, where it speaks of how Jesus bore sorrows which weighed him down, how he was wounded and bruised for our sins, how he gave his flesh so that we could be healed; and I also thought of Matthew 8:17, where Jesus takes our sicknesses and bears our diseases; and Peter 2:24, where Jesus carries the load of our sins on his own body and then dies on the cross so that we can be finished with sin and lead a good life. And then I had a marvelous result. Once I based my faith on God's talk, once I built the word of God inside my consciousness, then my family was healed. And now, together with my family and friends, I praise His name."

As one last, perhaps synoptic, example, Bobby Alden, another Karavaran evangelical, told us about his life before Jesus entered it. While attending high school in Rabaul, he fell into bad company; he ignored his studies and led a dissolute and criminal life. Eventually he was arrested for theft, and Jesus came to him when he was in jail. As he put it, "Jesus changed my life, cleansed me of sin and made me whole. And now I have found others who wish to praise His name here on Karavar and who want to help others find the one, true way to salvation."

These Karavaran accounts of personal tribulation followed by the illuminating transformation of the Holy Spirit were typical—formulaic—among evangelicals more generally. And so was their reported discovery of the joyful coming together with like-minded others to give praise. (See, for example, Hollenweger 1972; Christianson 1979; Barr 1983a, 1983b; Calvert 1983;

Namunu 1983; Taruna 1983.) John Barr, in a volume about religious movements in Melanesia, characterized those movements emphasizing the Holy Spirit as providing a "new relevancy" to the participants. They placed "emphasis on experience rather than doctrine, on testimony rather than theology, on personal encounter rather than ideas about God. Faith is related more to a person's conscious life. God is discovered within one's immediate context" (1984: 171). And, Barr suggested, "those who experience a spirit baptism share a common experience while others may be kept outside because they have not received the Spirit" (p. 163).

That these Karavaran conversion narratives were similar to each other as well as to those told elsewhere is not surprising. From the evangelical perspective, their tellers had all been affected by the same transcultural phenomenon: the Holy Spirit. As Simeon Namunu explained, "The Holy Spirit ... cannot be programmed nor structured by men within time, tradition, theology or philosophy of any sort" (1983: 54). However, from our anthropological perspective, these narratives were similar because they employed what had become an established form. We would suggest that what distinguished these Karavaran evangelicals from their United Church neighbors was, therefore, not the tribulations they encountered (most Karavaran parents have had children become seriously ill) but that they responded to these experiences in a certain way, using an available *but not culturally obligatory* rhetoric.

To clarify the nature and extent of the shift in ideas about identity and agency—and by extension, about the basis of social life—revealed in these conversion narratives, consider what might at first seem a surprising analogy: The rhetoric of Karavaran evangelicals was strikingly similar to that Kath Weston found in the coming-out stories of American homosexuals. In both cases, the narratives conveyed a "personal struggle," an "odyssey of self-discovery," that put "established social ties to the test" so as "to lay claim to" a new kind of "community membership" (Weston 1991: 77–78). Narrators in both instances saw themselves as different from others and as "heroic figure[s] with definite task[s] to accomplish" (p. 78), including the task of creating communities of like-minded individuals.

In the case of American homosexuals, these communities were composed of persons who had often been rejected by kin and whose coming together was based on choice rather than on biologically based obligation. They were, as the title of Weston's book suggested, "the families we choose." In the case of Karavaran evangelicals, the communities envisioned were of Christians who had encountered resistance—in their view, persecution—from other Karavarans. (Shortly before our arrival in 1991, the police had been summoned to Karavar after United Church youths had stoned and damaged a house in which New Church services were being held.) Their coming together, therefore, was based on (often painful) choice rather than on social habit or compulsion.

We do recognize that this analogy is imperfect. The sociocultural context that compelled American homosexuals to come out differed in numerous and important respects from that enabling Karavarans to embrace the New Church. Most significantly, American homosexuals lived in a nation-state that, if it granted freedom of sexual preference at all, did so not because this freedom was generally regarded as desirable in itself but because it was the logical extension of other "freedoms" such as that of religion. Karavaran evangelicals, in contrast, could rely on considerable state support for their agenda.

Yet we do mean the analogy between these sets of lives to be more than provocative. As we have said, it is also instructive of what we see as a shift in the cultural grounding of Karavaran evangelicals. This shift, it seems to us, made the evangelicals in certain ways more akin to George Brown, Michael Leahy, and American homosexuals than to members of the Karavaran United Church.[8] They had become increasingly willing to differentiate themselves from and to confront their neighbors. Moreover, that George Brown, Michael Leahy, American homosexuals, and Karavaran evangelicals all shared important characteristics not only was a postmodern irony but suggests important processes of convergence. Specifically, what all these different persons shared—albeit in differing degrees and with different political effects—was a commitment to "Homo Aequalis" in the Western individualist sense: They all embraced choice, autonomy from ascribed social constraints, and the efficacy of personal agency in the historical process. And they all regarded the state as the context that would, or should, enable them to be (historically) effective actors.

HISTORICAL AGENTS MEET THE TUBUAN

On the evening of August 19, 1991, we were in our Karavaran house listening to the BBC World Service report of an attempted coup under way in the Soviet Union. As we contemplated what was presented as a historically reactionary effort to suppress newfound freedoms, we became caught up in events New Church members would regard as analogous. Suddenly, from the men's ground—a quarter-mile section of beach prohibited to women—came a late-night chorus of "wuk-wuk," indicating that the "forest had come alive"; the *tubuan* was afoot. (See Errington 1974a for an analysis of this ritual.) The ritual court had convened and the *tubuan,* escorted by a posse of young men, was going out into the community to collect a substantial shell-money fine for a ritual infraction. Fred immediately went to the men's ground, where he was told with some satisfaction that the *tubuan* was proceeding to the houses of New Church members. The women in these households had gone to the gardens that day despite a ritual prohibition on travel; if payment was not immediately forthcoming, their houses would be destroyed according to custom. Moreover, they would have no redress for the fine or damage in the government court or any other place because the *tubuan* was supreme on these occasions.

As the men talked to Fred and each other about these infractions and fines, the progress of the posse from one New Church house to another could be clearly heard and charted. The fines in most cases were quickly collected from the women, who happened to be alone in their houses at the time, and the posse returned to the men's ground. In one case, it was announced triumphantly that, since no payment was made, the *tubuan* and its supporters had been forced to destroy property. They had knocked down a cookhouse, overturned water tanks, and cut down banana trees. We later learned that there had also been talk of burning the house down.

Fred was also told that Kiapbong Mosley was in real trouble. Mosley was one of the most active—indeed militant—members of the New Church. There was thought to be strong evidence that he had revealed fundamental ritual secrets to some United Church women. In the past, Fred was told, he would have been killed. But he could still expect immense fines to be leveled against him not only by the Karavaran ritual court but by ritual courts throughout the sizable area in which the ritual was practiced. In addition, the copra drier he had recently established on communally owned property would be closed down.

A few minutes later, an event upsetting to virtually all took place. Although discord of any sort at the men's ground was a serious ritual infraction when a *tubuan* was present, a terrific ruckus began among those at one end of this area. As the other men rushed there, they discovered an altercation in progress. Mosley and his two brothers, all New Church members, had just learned of the *tubuan's* expedition. They were raging about the fines, the destruction of property, and what they claimed was the threat to life. They insisted that they and their wives were not bound by the laws of the *dukduk* and *tubuan* and therefore the fines and the damages were illegitimate. Moreover, there was talk of "murder" (English word used). Those threatening to burn the house had been aware that a terrified woman and her children were inside.

The tubuan *was afoot.*

No men had been home to protect this woman or the other women and to deal with the *tubuan* and the posse. They hotly denied that ritual secrets had been revealed but said that the *tubuan* was a false god.

Some of the United Church men began to shout back that the New Church should leave Karavar: The *tubuan* was not a satan; its laws were strong, important, and central to custom. If women knew the secrets, all the men would be ashamed. Mosley, spectacularly intransigent throughout, said that he had not brought the New Church, God had. His adversaries snorted derisively. Then an event perhaps unprecedented in Karavaran history took place. Tuembe Simel, a United Church member and an active participant in the *tubuan* organization, physically attacked Mosley, punching and kicking him. This was not only a serious breach of the ritual peace but a shocking violation of kinship. Simel was Mosley's close, junior matrilineal kinsman, his *actual* sister's son. Simel was younger and bigger, yet Mosley fought back with ferocity and was more than his assailant's match. Although Mosley's two brothers and coreligionists joined him and several others joined Simel, the fight did not escalate much or continue for long. After a few minutes Simel was winded and Mosley was restrained by his affines.

However, the matter was far from over. Later that night, Mosley's brother paddled to a neighboring island to use the Duke of York Islands community government radiophone to summon the police. The New Church members were convinced that the power of the state had to be invoked to ensure the protection of their property, lives, and freedom of worship. The next morning, two police arrived at a badly divided Karavar. They had come, they insisted several times, "not concerning any of the difficulties about custom, but to check the reports regarding damaged property and threats to life." They then inspected the damaged premises accompanied by the Karavaran magistrate, a *tubuan* adept and United Church member (one who had been quite inconspicuous the previous night), and by New Church members. The police said they would return in two days to hold a hearing. In the meantime, they wished those whose property had been damaged to itemize their losses. They warned that any more damage by the *tubuan* and its supporters prior to the hearing would result in arrest.

The same two police arrived on the appointed morning. Smartly uniformed, both carrying tear gas canisters and one carrying a shotgun, they were greeted with considerable respect, if not deference. To a group of assembled men—no women were present given that ritual matters might be discussed—the senior officer began by apologizing that the conversation would have to be in Pidgin English rather than in the local vernacular, since he was from

The police officer came, he said, to investigate the matter of the destroyed property.

Madang and his colleague, from the Sepik. He came, he said, to investigate the matter of the destroyed property and wanted to hear both sides of the story so that he could weigh them and try to find a solution. "I am on the side of the law," he said, "but here there are really two laws at work: one of custom and one of the government. We must try to coordinate these two. I don't know how, but we must try."[9]

A senior adept then responded to his invitation to present the side of custom. He explained why the women were not allowed to visit their gardens when the *tubuan* was active in the village, and concluded by saying: "When the Australians controlled the government, if someone protested a decision of the ritual court, the Australians would send the case back to us and tell us to straighten the trouble by our traditional means. The law of the *tubuan* and the law of the government have always been the same."

Mosley responded, explaining that as members of the New Church, the women were free to garden as they chose. Moreover, he argued, the ritual procedure had not been properly followed or equitably enforced. For women to go to the gardens under these circumstances was actually a very minor infraction of *tubuan* regulations, not one that warranted heavy fines and destruction of property. In addition, although United Church women had as well gone to the gardens, New Church women were the only ones fined. Furthermore, advance notice of the fines should have been given so that the men would be present to pay them: A "summons" (English word used) should have preceded the fines.

Considerable debate then ensued about proper procedure, which a policeman eventually interrupted, stating:

> The complaint which has come before the law is clear. There has been an attack on a house, on property. I have the report of the damages written out and I can take this report to court. ... I can't say that custom is wrong or that the law of the government is wrong. I come from a place of custom too. All of us in Papua New Guinea do. We two come here to represent the government, but we respect custom. We can take you to court but there will be ill feelings when you return from jail. ... But if I decide to support custom, then there will be ill feelings on the other side, from those who claim freedom to worship as they choose. These disagreements should stop. We want to reach a compromise. ... I can't force one. Papua New Guinea is a democratic government where people have freedom to do what they choose.

Discussion followed about the importance of a compromise. One man supported the police by saying: "Custom is very important, but so is property. Let us come up with a compromise we can agree on." Efforts to compromise failed, however, in part because no one seemed to have much idea of what a compromise would look like in this circumstance of polarization. Moreover, Mosley remained unmoved. After brief consultation with his brothers, he said that he wanted to take the matter to court, especially since this was the second time that the police had to be summoned. His adversaries, as well, were adamant. One said:

> As long as the New Church is inside Karavar, there is going to be trouble. On Saturday the Prime Minister came [for a phase of the ceremony, described in Chapter 5, for which the *tubuan* had appeared]. He said in his speech that we must hold on to custom and tradition. ... We must instruct our children in them. ... The teaching of the New Church deprecates custom. ... And I warn Mosley that he did not ask permission to build his copra drier on our land. I am talking about this because there is going to be trouble. Something is going to be burned down. The *tubuan* can't be flouted.

After almost three hours, the policeman closed the hearing. He said he was going to leave and give people time to think about how to reach a "balance between law and custom."

Those United Church members to whom we spoke found the whole episode, particularly the fight, extremely distressing. Many said that if Ambo, the last of the big men, were still alive, none of this would have happened. He would not have allowed the New Church to come to Karavar, much less have allowed neighbor to be turned against neighbor, kin against kin. United Church members who had affines in the New Church were especially upset; the breach between sides had become too great to mediate. They saw no compromise as feasible and feared that the New Church would have to leave Karavar and its members with it unless they rejoined the United Church.

The members of the New Church were far less distressed. They were, however, frightened at the possibility of further retribution, especially at the prospect of continuing heavy fines levied by those in the *tubuan* organization, both local and regional. But they also felt elated by their engagement in a portentous activity, one that might ultimately grant them the "Victor's crown." As an evangelical put it, "Nothing is strong enough to stop the church. The church moves ahead. Its members are sometimes persecuted, but it moves straight ahead. Its members are disciplined and have begun to resist. The Holy Spirit is within them. It will direct them."

They, too, saw no compromise as possible but were convinced that the present breach in kinship and community would eventually become resolved as a new community of believers was created by the Holy Spirit. Until that time, however, they had to remain vigilant: "People," one member said, "must fight for the freedom to worship as they choose."[10]

COLONIALISM, NATIONALISM, AND
INDIVIDUALISM REVISITED

As we described, the *tubuan* and the posse attacked New Church members at the same time the BBC reported that the leaders of a reactionary force in the Soviet Union were attempting to undermine the newfound personal, political, and economic freedoms of people there. In listening to this report, we wondered whether these new "freedoms" might themselves prove repressive; if so, it was unclear which faction would prove ultimately reactionary and which, truly liberating. We also were ambivalent in our response to the conflict erupting that night on Karavar between those of the New Church and the United Church.[11] On the one hand, our experience of evangelical Christians had made us wary of those who used a literal reading of the Bible to chart their life courses. Not only in America but in Karavar as well, we had seen that the insistence on religious freedom led to an intolerant spiritual elitism.[12] On the other, our sympathies, at least initially, were strongly with the New Church members. They were being attacked by a force that aroused for us images of vigilantes and nightriders. Under cover of darkness, our friends were being terrorized by the masked *tubuan* and its accompanying posse. (Coincidentally, the *tubuan* looks somewhat like a Ku Klux Klan figure.)

We also found ourselves sympathetic to the evangelicals because some of their rhetoric touched on important U.S. cultural values. In particular, some of it evoked an interrelated set of long-standing (though hardly unproblematic) liberal cultural themes focused on the value of a certain sort of individuality, an individuality regarded as relatively unfettered by social and cultural context or other forms of constraint. These themes encompassed the following: freedom of choice, including religious choice (and in the view of some, choice of sexual preference); the capacity of individuals to effect both personal and social change; the importance of individual rights and liberties; and, we must stress, a view of the state as guarantor of those rights and liberties.

These themes not only linked us as Americans with Karavaran evangelicals (indeed, much of their religious literature came from the United States) but linked us all (in certain regards) with Michael Leahy, George Brown, Isaac Rooney, and American homosexuals. All understood that it was possible and desirable to engage in personal, perhaps even heroic, odysseys so as to make history. All understood that to the extent these odysseys went forcefully against the social grain, they could shock in such a way as to generate and supplant anachronism. They were, in other words, first-contact encounters.

However, although Barr might be correct in saying that the "rediscovery of the Holy Spirit has liberated missionized Christians, enabling them to break with sincere but irrelevant ways of understanding faith and to assert new culturally appropriate ways" (1984: 171–172), it is important to understand that these new ways for Karavarans were old ones for many of us. In certain respects, the local evangelicals—who, it will be recalled, were among the best educated and most cosmopolitan of Karavarans—had become the proximate colonizers.

The process by which these Karavarans had, at least partially, replicated George Brown was, of course, a complex one. It had involved more than a century of multifocal conjunctures in Papua New Guinea: direct colonial rule; economic extraction of primary resources (such as Karavaran coconuts and Bougainville copper); a devastating world war; the imposition of a Western-style educational system (which, among other things, taught about individualism, history, and the importance of the nation-state [cf. Chakrabarty 1992]); and continued missionization, including the direct influence from U.S. evangelical and other churches.

In addition, since independence, Papua New Guinea politicians had adopted an especially portentous conjuncture from the last of their colonial predecessors: the articulation of local models of person and polity with those taken from modern nation-states. These adopted models posited the existence of "citizens," formally equal individuals (sharing, and recognizing that they shared, the same rights and responsibilities) who joined together to form the nation and to shape its trajectory. (See, among others, Anderson 1983; Handler 1988; Gewertz and Errington 1991; Foster 1992.)

In Papua New Guinea, this imported definition of the citizen as a particular sort of progressive individual was promulgated by politicians in state-sponsored campaigns, such as National Law Week, designed to produce and disseminate "in relatively self-conscious fashion, collective representations—images and ideals of the collectivity and of the persons who compose the collectivity" (Foster 1992: 33). These representations, however, were often in conflict with local, customary definitions of person and polity, which some saw as conservative and anachronistic. The state had to reconcile modernity with tradition through, as Foster argues, "producing and disseminating ideals and images of the nation. On the one hand, the state must produce representations in conformity with [imported] models of nation and citizen already in place; on the other, it must produce images and ideals that [build on tradition so as to] represent a distinct and unique identity for the nation and its citizens" (p. 44).

In the Karavaran case, this collision between imported and modern and local and traditional models formed an important aspect of the contention between the members of the New Church and the United Church.[13] Significantly, in the police inquiry this conflict was represented as one between law and custom and between property and custom. As we have seen, the efforts to achieve reconciliation proved ineffective; the balance remained elusive.

It is clear that contemporary Karavaran United Church members were no longer willing to have their world turned upside down by those we might call George Brown look-alikes. Despite the early years of strong mission disapproval, they had been able to articulate Christianity with their men's ritual organization. Grace, indeed, was routinely said before ritual feasts at the men's ground.[14] Likewise, members of the New Church did not wish to change their position. In their embrace of what were, in fact, many of the values of Western individualism, local evangelicals were striving for change rather than compromise. They saw themselves as the wave of the future. One told us that "revivalism is sweeping Papua New Guinea; when the older generation at Karavar dies, it will become strong there as well."

It is important to note that this problematic conjuncture whereby Western liberal models of person and polity were superimposed on existing models implied other transformations, especially in the economy, in Papua New Guinea (and, we might add, in the Soviet Union). For example, in recent decades as Papua New Guinea "developed" as a free-market economy, there had been growing class differentiation to such an extent that many villagers increasingly found themselves disadvantaged and peripheral. Thus, for instance, at least in the perception of many local people, sale of Papua New Guinea's considerable mineral and timber resources to both Western and Asian firms by those well positioned within the state seemed to have contributed to ecosystemic degradation and economic inequality without significantly raising the local standard of living. (Recently, in this regard, there have been reports that the East New Britain Forestry Department has predicted that, due to operations of such enterprises as the Malaysian company Rimbunan Hijau [which reputedly does over US$1 billion annual business in Papua New Guinea], East New Britain will have no forests left by 2005 [Apakabar net, August 30,1993].)

Given this direction of change in Papua New Guinea, Karavaran evangelicals might not be served all that well by the economic and political system into which they were indirectly buying. Although they were the most sophisticated of Karavarans, they were not in national (much less, international) terms that well placed (particularly relative to the Tolai). It will be recalled, for example, that many had returned home because they had lost their jobs in a recession economy. For people so placed—peripheral in what was itself a peripheral country within a world system—local models and local resources might in the long run prove more reliable. In sympathizing with the personal dilemmas of these evangelicals, we have also come to view their transformative project as far from an unambiguously liberating one. Indeed, soon after the attempted coup in the former Soviet Union, many there were having second thoughts about the cost of their (most recent) first contact with free markets.

EPILOGUE: NOSTALGIA FOR THE FIRST CONTACT

It is not surprising that at the time a postcolonial Papua New Guinea was attempting to establish itself as a viable nation-state based on a free-market economy, some of its citizens had begun to see themselves as heroic transformers of the social field, as the makers of history. Correspondingly, it is not surprising, to us at least, that at a time when the postmodern United States was attempting to reestablish itself in the face of economic decline and social fragmentation,[15] some of its citizens experienced nostalgia for the heroic transformers of yesteryear. Thus, more than half a century after the already somewhat anachronistic Michael Leahy (remember, Papua New Guinea was described as the *last* unknown) carried his Mauser and Leica into the Highlands, Americans were seriously considering Ross Perot, a man widely esteemed for his entrepreneurial success in pursuit of treasure and fame, for president. Despite a purported postmodern distrust in the capacity of metanarratives (both personal and social) to convince and compel and despite proclamations that with the triumph of capitalism the end of history had arrived, Americans appeared to admire—in fact, yearn for—someone who in his (not, as yet, her) efficacy could act as personal exemplar and collective leader. Might this be why evangelical Christianity was sweeping America as well?[16]

*   *   *

One of the objectives of this book has been to reduce conceptual distance between Karavarans and ourselves by presenting their lives, especially their interests and aspirations, as intelligible. What we have seen in this chapter is that these interests and aspirations have been neither unchanging nor uniform, that conflicts of colonial and postcolonial interaction have generated new interests, new aspirations—indeed, new conflicts—such that some have recently emerged as more willing than others to accept Western visions of personal identity and worth as their own.

In the next chapter, we explore the emergence and the nature of yet other, often sharply contrasting, images of personal identity that Papua New Guineans have adopted to describe their relationships and responsibilities to their particular communities as well as to the nation-state. Our ethnographic concern is in how these images were rhetorically employed during the recent national elections in Papua New Guinea both to link the present to the past and to envision and shape the future.

NOTES

1. Early missionaries in the Duke of York Islands strenuously objected to the unscrupulous practices of, for example, labor recruiters.

2. This circumstance was perhaps analogous to the Highlanders producing their own Michael Leahys (such as Joe Leahy?—see Connolly and Anderson 1988) or the Hawaiians producing their own (non-Lono) Captain Cooks (see Sahlins 1985).

3. Klaus Neumann, who worked among the neighboring Tolai, likewise reported that he "was not told any story about explorers, whalers, or early traders that described their visits from a Tolai point of view ... [while there] are detailed accounts of the arrival of Methodist and Catholic missionaries" (1992: 50).

4. The denominational split more created than followed lines of cleavage on Karavar. As will be seen, it often divided families.

5. Although in a dialect of the Duke of York language different from that spoken by Karavarans and containing archaic words, our informants had little trouble understanding the sermon.

6. The copper mine at Bougainville, one of the world's largest, was closed by sabotage in May 1989; this came after years of protest by locals who claimed the compensation they had received for yielding their lands to the mine had been inadequate. The conflict subsequently spread such that Bougainville became a war zone with the Bougainville Revolutionary Army locked in secessionist combat with the Papua New Guinea Defense Force.

7. Since ideas about identity constituted aspects of identity, a change in those ideas was, perforce, a change in identity. In a whole spectrum of ways, Karavaran New Church members insisted that they were significantly different from United Church members. Thus, the New Church members said they were unafraid of sorcery, in part because God would protect them from evil. They also eschewed matters of competition and display because these fostered personal vanity and the disparagement of others. But many areas of Karavaran life remained acceptable to them. Kin ties were still regarded as important because these could be valued as constituting "family." However, New Church members also talked about (and sometimes engaged in) "backsliding" and in so doing recognized the extent to which "traditional" concerns such as those focusing on male prestige still exerted power over them.

8. For an interesting analysis of the association of evangelism with broader U.S. values, see Hvalkof and Aaby (1981). In fact, the Karavaran evangelical discourse was heavily influenced by U.S. sources; many of the religious pamphlets Karavaran evangelicals consulted were published in the United States.

9. Throughout East New Britain at this time, policemen were intervening in conflicts between members of evangelical churches and those claiming to be followers of "custom." These conflicts had become sufficiently chronic and acute that one government official characterized them to us as "the holy wars." For a fascinating analysis of the complex relationship more generally between law and custom in Papua New Guinea, see Aleck (n.d.).

10. An anonymous reviewer of this chapter suggested that it "seems not improbable that these men have an agenda far beyond 'freedom of religion.' Religion may be important here because it has become marketable and relatively safe discourse which can be applied to help unhinge current power structures among the islanders." It may well be that the New Church agenda was an effort to replace the influence of big men with that of the evangelicals. However, despite the (qualified) support of the state, the

New Church challenge to custom, especially as it focused on the *dukduk* and *tubuan* rituals, did, in the perception of both the evangelicals and the others, incur very significant risks.

11. Our responses to these Karavaran evangelicals were considerably different, therefore, from Harding's (1991) reaction to the U.S. fundamentalists she studied.

12. Even those well disposed to evangelical Christianity noted this possibility. Barr, for example, wrote: "People who experience a spirit-baptism may see themselves as being above the cares and needs of this world. They may perceive of themselves as being specially favoured by God, as being an elite or an elect people who have passed through a second (and more superior) conversion experience" (1984: 172–173).

13. An anonymous reviewer of this chapter raised the interesting question of whether the United Church members' resistance to New Church members was comparable to the Karavarans' response to George Brown at the time of his arrival. The accounts by Karavarans and other Duke of York Islanders about this first contact soon became heavily affected and distorted by missionization, as the letter written in 1892 by the recent convert, Aika Mitaralen, indicates (Brown 1892). Yet it is also evident that most Karavarans and other Duke of York Islanders remained largely unmoved by mission teaching concerning the *dukduk* and *tubuan* rituals. Moreover, as we have to some extent seen, the missionaries themselves often commented on the initial obdurance of their prospective flock.

14. As Burke made clear, "The fact that an activity is capable of reduction to intrinsic, autonomous principles does not argue that it is free of identification with other forms of motivation extrinsic to it. ... Any specialized activity participates in a larger unit of action" (1969: 27).

15. At the time of this writing, the United States was in an economic recession; it was also still reeling from the shock of riots in Los Angeles precipitated by the acquittal of police officers who were videotaped beating a black motorist, Rodney King.

16. It is, to be sure, a matter of ongoing debate whether metanarratives can ever produce liberation.

5

The Triumph of Capitalism in East New Britain?

A Contemporary Papua New Guinean Rhetoric of Motives

Aₛ HAS BEEN clear throughout our book, change has not only happened *to* Karavarans and their neighbors since the European intrusion, it has also been precipitated *by* them. They have been active participants in the construction of their presents and have been energetically debating the shape of their futures. In this chapter, we examine another aspect of this debate. We extend our discussion in the last chapter about what sorts of persons contemporary Papua New Guineans wished to be and focus on their concerns about the kinds of leaders they should have and about the sorts of commitments to local people these leaders should fulfill. What, for instance, should be the nature of social and political life in the modern state with its developing class system? Should local social and political structures become increasingly permeated and transformed by unentailed, capitalistic economic relations?

That this debate was well advanced in East New Britain should not have been a surprise to us. Duke of York Islanders and Tolai have, after all, been described as preadapted to capitalism by virtue of their long experience in employing an indigenous, universal, and divisible currency. (See Epstein 1968.) Moreover, as we have seen, these East New Britains—the Tolai, in particular—have come to be known as among the best educated and most prosperous of Papua New Guineans.

An earlier version of this chapter appeared in *Oceania* 64, 1 (September 1993): 1–17. Reprinted by permission.

Nonetheless, as we walked down the streets of the provincial capital of Rabaul shortly after first arriving there in 1991, viewing the sights with relatively fresh eyes, we were startled by the extreme position taken by a schoolboy in an essay on money. Posted in a window of the United Church's Memorial Hall among selected compositions on various topics by other Tolai teenagers, Martin's essay struck us, in its unalloyed celebration of economic individualism, as a remarkably condensed (if somewhat adolescent) expression of a fully (and frighteningly) developed—no longer preadapted—spirit of capitalism. We reproduce it below as written:

Money makes me smile.
   Money means beer.
   Money digs up the skul [Pidgin English for school].
   I love money more than anything else.
   When I lose even one toea [about US$.01] I almost beat myself to a pulp.
   Hey girls money can find you a lover, make you comfortable and bring harmony to your life.
   Money is the dream of every teen-ager.
   To hell with love. With money you can have refrigerators and stereos.
   The age-old fairy-tale of love is fast being replaced by the hard reality of money.
   If I'm a rich man I can get to marry the prettiest woman.
   Somebody who doesn't have money cannot make love.
   People work, people sweat, people suffer, people die, all for money.
   When I have money, I'll live in a high quality house, eat good food and be recognized by other people as someone to respect.
   It will lead to girls quarreling over IAU [Tolai for "I/me"].
   YOU'VE GOT TO HAVE MONEY
   BEFORE YOU CAN DO
   ANYTHING YOU WANT!

What startled us about this essay was that (minor details aside) we could well believe it had been written by a young Donald Trump. To be sure, Tolai and Duke of York Islanders were often preoccupied with accumulating shell money. Yet shell money served as the basis of personal prestige and efficacy primarily to the extent that it was used to generate the relations of mutual entailment that constituted sociality. Although we realized that teenagers might often be more self-centered and self-consciously iconoclastic than adults, we were, even so, struck by the degree to which Martin focused almost entirely on the short-term and instrumental uses of money in contrast to those uses that were long-term and socially (or cosmologically) regenerative. Whereas

Martin did want to be admired and respected by others, he made no obvious acknowledgment that he accepted any social obligations or entailments or that he recognized his views as having social consequences. In these respects, it seemed to us (returning to Bloch and Parry's [1989] argument discussed in Chapter 2) that he had internalized crucial elements of capitalist ideology, ones that saw short-term instrumental and long-term regenerative goals not only as thoroughly distinct but as, ordinarily, not requiring coordination.[1] (This is not to describe capitalism as entirely monolithic [see Kelly 1992] or to deny that under circumstances of perceived crisis, there might be pressure to think explicitly about long-term social goals.)

We do not know precisely how Martin came to value so exclusively these private and instrumental short-term goals. In fact, we know no more about Martin as an individual than he revealed in his essay. Nor do we know the criteria by which his essay was chosen for display. Yet he became for us a persona, an "ideal type" (Weber 1949). Martin, we realized, might turn out to be somewhat atypical of modern East New Britain youth. He was, though, certainly one possible outcome of a complex history. His statement of aspiration, we suspected, might illuminate contemporary social, political, and economic processes in East New Britain as well as in the changing nation of Papua New Guinea more generally. We came to regard "Martin" not only as an ideal type for us but for many East New Britains as well.[2]

As we pursued our subsequent research on Karavar in the Duke of York Islands, "Martin" remained at least on the periphery of our thoughts and, we discovered, the thoughts of virtually everyone we met. Certainly when our Karavaran friends commented on the sorry state of regional and national politics they seemed to have "Martin" on the mind. Politicians, for instance, were frequently disparaged in phrases suggestive of "Martin," such as, "come in a politician, go out a [very wealthy] businessman." We were to hear such disparaging sentiments often during our research as politicians engaged in a flurry of local campaigning in anticipation of the 1992 national parliamentary elections.

Indeed, many East New Britains (and, we think, many other Papua New Guineans) used "Martin" as a point of rhetorical reference to appraise, shape, justify, and contest their political alternatives. As such a reference, Martin's essay had mythic aspects. Less a *charter* for existing social, political, and economic relationships (Malinowski 1926) than a pole on a *chart* of possible relationships, his essay nevertheless indicated certain existing preoccupations.[3] "Martin," thus, was both good to think about and with (Levi-Strauss 1963).

"Martin" did not, however, stand alone. In the East New Britain appraisal of politicians, for instance, "Martin" was frequently contrasted to other ideal types, the contrast thereby giving each persona rhetorical sharpness and clarity. (As Kenneth Burke noted, "rhetoric, according to Aristotle 'proves opposites'" [1969: 25].) In this chapter we first discuss "Martin" in relationship to a diametrically opposed pole on the chart of possible political relations in contemporary East New Britain. This contrasting pole was invoked, at least on Karavar, as the basis of a sociality both local and beyond that was composed not of atomized citizens but of entailed kin.

Our primary ethnographic focus again concerns the appearance of the then–prime minister of Papua New Guinea, Rabbie Namaliu. The occasion this time was the staging on Karavar of a major ceremony, a *matamatam*. It may have been partly to dispel any possible association between himself and a "Martin" that Namaliu asserted both his local grounding and his social entailment to his audience by comparing himself to the persona of a mythologized leader named Tovetura. Tovetura was the most illustrious of the ancestors commemorated at the *matamatam* Namaliu was attending. In being at the ceremony, Namaliu was claiming that his interests and those of the Karavarans were entirely as inseparable and conjoined as Tovetura's had been with his supporters. He thereby argued that he not only understood but also met the local standard for the evaluation of leaders.

We will maintain, however, that the "Tovetura" standard of particularistic connection, though locally compelling, was likely to prove unworkable in the context of regional and national politics. Under these circumstances, national and regional politicians had great difficulty achieving reelection to office.[4] This difficulty, in turn, we suspect, encouraged them to make the most of their opportunities so that they would be able to leave office as wealthy businessmen. (We stress here that we are not accusing any particular politician, certainly not Prime Minister Namaliu, of lacking probity. Yet as we shall elaborate further, there was throughout Papua New Guinea the probably accurate perception that politicians often used their offices for personal profit. This perception, coupled with images coming from the Western media about the good life, most likely had affected the "historical" Martin.) Hence, the invocation of "Tovetura" by Namaliu and other politicians—rather than countering "Martin"—had, in certain regards, the unintended consequences of supporting him.

In response, to this oppositional deadlock, some have proposed a new pole on the chart of political possibilities, one seen as appropriate if Papua New Guinea was to become a progressive nation. This persona, that of the "statesman," appeared to temper the self-interest of "Martin" and broaden the sociality of "Tovetura." But the promise of this new persona, we shall show, would probably be misleading. The "statesman" would likely discredit the pole of sociality through which local people tried to make their politicians accountable and leave the pole of self-interest relatively strong, to the extent that the "Martins" would remain essentially unscathed. In other words, with the invocation of the "statesman," the triumph of capitalism was being enjoined, although many, we suspect, would find the argument unconvincing. Our suggestion, thus, is that the triumph of capitalism was by no means predetermined, even among the shell-money users of East New Britain.

Throughout the analysis of what is essentially a contemporary Papua New Guinea rhetoric of motives (Burke 1969), we will be more suggestive than definitive. We do not, for instance, wish to claim that the political personae we consider as ideal types exhaust those current in East New Britain, much less in Papua New Guinea. Nonetheless, we did find that they figured significantly in the discourse concerning national and local political interests during this election period.

TOVETURA AS IDEAL TYPE

The following is one of the accounts we collected about what had become the rather standardized, almost codified (cf. Neumann 1992: 84), mythic persona of Tovetura:

> Tovetura was from Utuan [Karavar's closest neighboring community in the Duke of York Islands]. He was a bad man who seduced many women, including those of his own matriline. He alienated even members of his own family who wanted to kill him. He alienated Karavarans too, but not as thoroughly. He was a flying fox [large fruit bat] who flitted from one place to another.
>
> Soon he fled to Ulu [another nearby Duke of York island] which was then just like bush. At Mauke [a particularly wild area on Ulu], he came in contact with a *turangan* [a powerful and dangerous spirit]. As he was living there, he became hairy. His beard grew; his hair grew. When thirsty, he drank the water which collected at the forks of trees. He lived below the ground, in a burrow.
>
> The *turangan* asked him what he was doing at Mauke. He told it that he had run away because everyone wanted to kill him, and asked it how he could go back without being killed. The *turangan* told him to tell his mother to weave many baskets, and then to get one of them and put it in his underground dwelling. He did so and when he returned one day, he found it filled with shell money. He did this with each of the baskets his mother had woven.

Then he went to Karavar and gave Tombar's ancestors five fathoms of shell money to gain access to part of the men's ground. He said he was going to hold a mortuary ceremony at which much shell money would be distributed. All of the men of Karavar wondered how this flying fox was going to accomplish this. He had some of his Karavaran cousins and brothers clear for his ceremony the area that came to be called *Tamanawa.* The meaning of *"Tamanawa"* is "what sort of place is this?" It got this name because people wondered how such a man could make anything of significance happen there. They did not know about the *turangan* and the shell money.

Tovetura pulled it off. Moreover, he did so with a *liu* [a dance which is the most expensive form of mortuary ceremony because each of the many dancers must be generously paid in shell money]. He had women string all the shell money the *turangan* had given him. People thought he would never manage to succeed at a *liu,* because one has to be extremely wealthy to sponsor one.

Tovetura was a big man because he moved so quickly from a poor to a rich one. He became a leader of the Germans because of his power. No one could defy him. Tovetura became the paramount *luluai* [to recall, an administration-appointed headman] of the area. It was he who appointed subsidiary *luluais.* First he appointed Militay of Karavar. He gave Militay a hat and a staff [symbols of office] and said, "You must watch, you must be ready. I am putting this hat on you so that you will watch your territory and look out for all your people. I am giving you this staff to settle all problems and wrongs."

After he gave the hat and staff to Militay, he gave them to Tuba of Matupit; then to Pero of Yelakur, then to Bramtovovo of Vunamami [the latter three are all Tolai]. Then, he himself took the white cap [marking the highest government appointment, that of paramount *luluai*] and became the boss of them all. It was he who wrote the "constitution" and created the "rules" [these were the English words used]. For example, if someone committed incest, he must either pay one hundred fathoms of shell money or be killed. If someone slept with the wife of another man, he must pay thirty fathoms to the offended wife and thirty fathoms to the offended husband.

Tovetura was a man who would kill you if you did not listen to him. The German government observed his rules and followed them. It is true that the Germans flogged men, but we did this before they came. We said that if a man cannot pay for his wrongs with shell money, then he should be flogged. Some people back then wanted to practice cannibalism. But Tovetura thought they were crazy. If they tried to do this, he had them pay or be flogged. It was Tovetura who heard the courts; he was the first magistrate.

Familiarity with cross-cultural mythology would suggest that the Tovetura story was once a classic example of what might be called the "emergence of society" genre. (For many examples, see Lévi-Strauss 1969.) In such stories, human sociality began when a precultural, animalistic being was either transformed or transformed himself through the imposition or assumption of cultural rules (cf. Gewertz and Errington 1991: 33–37). However, the story as we collected it—in almost codified form—may well have been modified in response to the changes brought by colonialism: It concerned not the birth of society so much as the birth of a new society.

In the account, society already existed in clearly recognizable form. It was Tovetura who initially flouted its established rules, especially those pertaining to sexuality, such that he came to live outside of society. Ostracized, unkempt, unshorn, he sheltered and foraged as a solitary animal. Significantly, with the acquisition of shell money Tovetura moved from feral fugitive to socializing magistrate.[5] He changed from one who broke the prohibitions against incest and adultery to one who not only upheld but substantially strengthened these prohibitions. Indeed, he put such teeth in the rules he had himself broken that Karavaran society became for the German colonists a model for the well-ordered polity.

But how could Tovetura's acquisition of large amounts of shell money be plausibly described as "civilizing" not only himself but his society? How, in contrast to money, which provided Martin with the means to pursue unencumbered self-interest, could shell money provide Tovetura with the basis of (enhanced) sociality?

To recall our earlier discussions (especially in Chapter 2) of shell money and its relationship to money, like money, shell money was a major standard by which everything as well as everyone was evaluated. The differences in the amount of shell money that individuals owned and used in public ceremonies distinguished persons of importance from those of mere respectability and the latter from those of no consequence. Yet unlike money, regarded by many in the West as either "devilish acid" or "guarantor of [personal] liberty" (Bloch and Parry 1989: 30), shell money was understood by its East New Britain users as neither dissolving social ties nor freeing persons from obligations to each other. Shell money was not only fundamental to the prestige system but fundamental to social ordering.

For both Tolai and Duke of York Islanders, big men—those wealthiest in shell money—generated social order in several respects. For instance, they had an important part in ensuring that compensation for social and ritual offenses was paid. Moreover, big men were the principal organizers of mortuary ceremonies. These ceremonies were not only to commemorate but also to replace the dead, especially those who had been big men during their lifetimes. As such, these ceremonies were crucial contexts for aspiring or established big men to demonstrate their own contemporary leadership and eminence, to show that they could adequately supersede their predecessors. This demonstration consisted of meeting heavy ceremonial expenses and showing that they had sufficient resources to control a large following. To once again cite Salisbury's statement concerning the Tolai, a big man "creates a name, not for himself alone, but in terms of which other people can organize themselves" (n.d.: 30). In these respects, big men *were* society. Their shell-money expenditures for these and other activities constituted the politics of both self-aggrandizement and social reproduction. Unlike the capitalist circumstances described by Bloch and Parry, short-term personal and long-term social interest were perceived by East New Britain shell-money users as, in their essence, conjoined.

It is important to note that in the speeches and harangues with which such mortuary ceremonies culminated, really big men such as Tovetura would proclaim, *"iau, iau, iau"* (I, I, I). They then embellish by saying that they alone were weighty on the island, that they were the only ones sufficient to make things happen. It is, almost certainly, Martin's familiarity with a big man's rhetoric that led him to insert this Tolai–Duke of York Island word into his English essay.

But we can now see more clearly the difference in Martin's and (e.g.) Tovetura's usages. In effect, the *"iau"* Martin wished to be was more akin to the asocial, fugitive Tovetura than to the victorious big man and magistrate. Whereas Martin's *"iau"* was an assertion of the sufficiency of his instrumental and self-focused agenda, Tovetura's ceremonial triumph was the basis of a renewed, indeed accentuated and momentarily unified, social order, one that included not only indigenous but early colonial society. Contrasting personae in the same (somewhat broadly conceived) social field, Martin and Tovetura together provided the range of political possibilities imagined when Prime Minister Namaliu visited Karavar.[6]

THE MORTUARY CEREMONY AND
THE INVOCATION OF TOVETURA

The *matamatam* Namaliu attended commemorating Tovetura (and others) was widely regarded by Karavarans as less well financed than it might have been. The principal sponsors were Toliplipnawa Daki and Eric Alden, members of separate but related matrilineages. As the first portion of their ritual work, they had arranged for the construction of an *aim,* a cement commemorative marker (comparable to the one unveiled on Mioko during the Jubilee) much like a large and elaborate gravestone. Inscribed on their *aim* were the names of both sets of their matrilineal dead, including the name of Tovetura.

However, some members of Daki's matrilineage were reluctant to help him cover the expenses of this *aim* and those of the *matamatam* to follow. (Such a marker and its concomitant ceremonies, if lavishly celebrated, might cost sponsors and their matrilines a thousand kina [about US$1,100] and hundreds of fathoms of shell money.) Daki became so angry at their foot-dragging that he said he would pay for the *aim* and the ensuing ceremony without their help. Moreover, he decided to have his own name inscribed on the *aim*. In this way he indicated to them and to everyone else that he did not regard them to be truly his relatives at all. He was asserting that he would commemorate his own death, even before he died, since he could not count on them to do so later. Despite Daki's assertion that he would manage his portion of the ceremony essentially on his own, many doubted that he had the resources to do so. (As it turned out, we helped Daki because he and Fred were "brothers," Daki's father having adopted Fred years before.)

Alden, too, was evidently underfinanced. But more cosmopolitan than Daki (in part by virtue of more extensive work experience), he had the skill to use the forthcoming national election to augment his resources. He knew that at such a time politicians often rewarded the local leaders who they felt could deliver the votes. Thus, Alden invited major national and regional politicians from competing political parties to his *matamatam*. In this way, he sought not only to impress them and play them off against each other but to gain local respect as one with important outside connections.

It is important to remember that most contemporary Karavarans such as Daki and Alden had become dependent on outside help for their ceremonial performances. As we noted in Chapter 4, in even the relatively recent past, control over large stands of coconuts and the followers necessary to process them provided big men with much of the wealth—money was readily converted into shell money—upon which their political power rested. Yet by 1991, there had been such a fall in copra prices that few Karavarans regularly bothered to process coconuts at all. Consequently, sponsors of contemporary mortuary ceremonies frequently were forced to depend not on their own resources but on modest remittances from employed Karavarans (cf. Carrier and Carrier 1989) and on gifts from government officials (non-Karavaran, often even non–Duke of York Island) sporadically trying to please their constituents (cf. Bradley 1982).

Both Prime Minister Rabbie Namaliu, of the Pangu Party, and East New Britain Provincial Premier Sinai Brown, of the Melanesian Alliance Party, accepted Alden's invitation and provided economic support for his *matamatam.* However, as it happened, only Namaliu assumed an important public role. Brown arrived with an entourage the evening before the major events of the ceremony began and spent the night in private conversation with Alden and others he was cultivating as political allies. He then left early the next morning before Namaliu came. Brown clearly did not wish to engage Namaliu directly on this occasion. The reason, our friends suggested, was that Namaliu was visiting Karavar not primarily as a politician but as a kinsman mourning and commemorating local dead. Under such a circumstance, Brown, who lacked such close connections to Karavar, would, in contrast to Namaliu, have appeared unseemly—as unduly instrumental in his pursuit of political self-interest.

Namaliu arrived by helicopter around 8:30 AM. He and his entourage, including one who videotaped the prime minister and his interactions, were greeted primarily by Alden and his kin. Namaliu was dressed informally in a *laplap* (to recall, a piece of cloth wrapped around the waist), a brightly colored shirt, and moccasins without socks. After Alden's niece had presented him with a necklace of flowers and Alden had said a few words of welcome, Namaliu was escorted to the men's ground. There he removed his shirt and changed into thongs. His assistants also handed him an elaborate, commercially prepared wreath and a basket containing shell money. Namaliu was also adorned with the powders and charms that all initiated men wore to protect themselves from the danger of the ritually powerful *dukduk* and *tubuan* figures active throughout the *matamatam.* The party then emerged from the men's ground and proceeded to the marker commemorating the dead, the *aim.*

At the *aim,* Alden introduced Namaliu to the throng of assembled men, women, and children, some 300 in all. Then after placing the wreath and ten fathoms of shell money on the *aim,* Namaliu delivered the following speech in Pidgin English, which we present in its entirety:

> Eric [Alden] and all fathers and all brothers and all cousins, I want to give just a little speech. I think Eric explained already the story of the *aim;* this is not new to us; it is an old custom of ours. I am happy to be with you at this time, at the village of my father. I cannot stay long, but I am happy that I was able to come for a short time to be with Eric and to put some flowers on the *aim*—a wreath—as is customary.
>
> The big man commemorated here was the first paramount *luluai.* He was appointed long ago, when the German administration first came here to our land.

After placing a wreath and then shell money on the aim, *Namaliu delivered a speech.*

I am very happy about this because I think it was he who opened the road of the government at this place of ours. And I understand that if he had not opened the road and gone first in providing leadership, then I would not be able to engage in this kind of work. He came first and I follow in his path. So I am very happy to be with you here but am very sorry that I am unable to stay the whole day. My father is also unable to come today because his leg is bothering him. He must remain in the house. But Tombing [a Tolai with close kinship connection with Karavar and one of Namaliu's employees and strongest supporters] and all of our other brothers will be coming to be with you during this time when you finish all the work according to the custom of the village.

What we are engaged in here is a very important custom of course: It involves finishing all of the obligations we have incurred. Eric and his matriline will make this ritual work and all the people here will understand that, yes, the work has been completed according to custom. Now it is finished and the work can go to another line.[7] And I am extremely happy about this because such work of completing our customs is important to strengthening our life here in the community.

If we do not uphold our customs, then our village will not be strong. And it is the same for the country. Our country will not be strong unless we keep the cultures of our communities strong. And here, concerning we who live in the Duke of Yorks, this particular custom is important. We can die, yet the custom remains and is strong. And I say thank you to all the members of the family and to the matrikin for organizing today's work. I hope that everything will run smoothly during the rest of the day, according to plan.

I must go to Kabalo Teachers College. That is why I cannot stay with you. I must visit there where they are celebrating their twenty-fifth anniversary. I am very sorry about this, but I wish Eric and his line the best for the rest of today. And next time I come here, I will know that everything was finished well according to the custom of the community. And the next mortuary ceremony will be held by another line whose turn it will be. But, concerning us, everything will be finished well which has now been started. Later [today], important things will come forth. They are things for which you have worked and I say thank you for them as well. I mean the *tubuan* and the *dukduk*. They mark this event; they do not appear for trivial matters. And we are additionally strengthened by this good custom. Before all the work is finished, these things will be concluded in the men's ground according to the custom of this place.

And I am extremely sorry because many of our fathers died and I was not here. It was not because I did not want to be here. It was work which prevented me from spending much time here. Tuembe died, and I was not here. Before that, when I was young, Tonga was alive, and then he died, and I was not here. Many of our fathers, our brothers, they died and my father was able to come with all of the mothers and all of the brothers and all of my other fathers too. They were able to come and stay with you here at the village.

Frequently my father used to tell me stories. I understand a great deal because he did so: about how he grew up here; about the time he was small; about how he lived with his cousins here. I understand all of this well, and I also know about the time after I was born when I lived for three years at Watnabara [the Methodist hospital and school complex on the neighboring island of Ulu]. I lived there for the first three years of my life and they brought me here to Karavar where I stayed with my grandparents and fathers.

So I have "family roots" [English terms used] that go back here and are strong. And that is why, every time something comes up, I am sorry that I am unable to be with you. And that is why I am happy, very happy, to be here today. And I wish to thank Eric because he came with Tombing to remind me when this work was to be. And last week, the two of them came with Harry [Eric's in-married brother-in-law who was a candidate for office in the national capital of Port Moresby] to remind me. And I am very happy because they helped me come together with all of my brothers, and Eric, and all of my cousins to mark this day, this day commemorating our fathers and our ancestors who have died.

So I think that this is all there is to my little speech. And I wish you the best for the rest of the day and I am sure that everything will run well. I think that is all. My little talk is finished.

Several onlookers were themselves moved when Namaliu and Elit were seen sobbing together in memory of their close kinsman.

The connections to Karavar that Namaliu stressed in his speech convinced most of our friends that he came to the *matamatam* more than simply as a politician breezing through at election time. He was, people recognized, rooted to Karavar in a number of important ways. Not only did he have close and well-maintained kinship links with an important matriline—that of Tonga and Tuembe— but, as he emphasized, he and his family had a long-term involvement in Karavaran affairs. (Namaliu's kinship ties with Karavar had been maintained, in part, by decades of mutual ritual assistance and participation;[8] these ties were particularly strong with Tuembe, to whom Namaliu was linked both patrilaterally and matrilineally.)

Namaliu did, indeed, have "family roots" at Karavar, roots the Karavarans accepted as mattering to him very much. Several onlookers were themselves clearly moved when, for example, directly after Namaliu spoke, he and Elit, the sister of the deceased Tuembe, were seen sobbing together in memory of their close kinsman. Certainly, most were willing to accept his statement that work had kept him away from other important ritual occasions in the past. They were willing to grant that, although a Tolai, his local connections to Karavar were in good order.

Namaliu also presented himself plausibly as a supporter of custom. He was, as everyone knew, not only an initiated male but a ritual adept in the *dukduk* and *tubuan* society. In his speech, he stressed the importance of following long-established ritual procedures and sequences exactly and completely.

Of more significance even than Namaliu's emphasis on the durability of his local connections to Karavar and on the importance of maintaining continuity in custom was his decision to focus on Tovetura (only one of a number being commemorated). He did this, we think, to stress Tovetura's greatness in the past and to link that greatness to the viability, to the strength, of the present and future Papua New Guinea. Tovetura, it may be recalled, both reinforced Karavaran law and extended it to the Germans. By operating as a particularly effective big man, as "boss of them all," he had opened the road to the government. Consequently, Tovetura, though long dead, was far from an anachronism; he was a model for emulation in the present. Namaliu, as prime minister, was claiming to be his analogue and his political descendant and, perhaps in a broad sense, his genealogical descendant.

Namaliu's statement of political continuity had some similarity to the Solomon Island speeches White (1991) analyzed. These speeches, White argued, gave local people a sense of who they were in a changing world by providing an ideology of indigenous agency in the face of the profound social and political upheavals of the colonial era. Typical of such speeches was a denial of anachronism so as to contend that old ways remained feasible and desirable models for contemporary life.

It seems to us, however, that Namaliu's speech did this and more. His denial of anachronism also operated to conflate the role of a traditional local leader with that of a modern one (e.g., a prime minister). We think that in so doing Namaliu was actively conjoining short- and long-term personal and public interests through extending the limits of a kin-based polity. These were the claims he made: I am your big man in the way that Tovetura was; you should support me because I am his analogue. My successful self-aggrandizement—my continued eminence as prime minister or, at least, as member of Parliament—will be to our common benefit because we are bound in mutual sociability. Just as Tovetura was both big man and paramount *luluai,* I am both Karavaran big man and prime minister. Just as Tovetura made the broader world accord with Karavaran custom, so will I. Hence, as long as our custom remains strong, so too will the nation remain strong. Because I am here honoring Tovetura—showing that I am one with you, that we are united in kinship, custom, and sentiment—you should vote for me. (In what proved a very close election, it was the Duke of York Islands vote that provided the margin sufficient to return Namaliu as member of Parliament.) Namaliu was, in other words, assuring his Karavaran audience he was not a "Martin."

Those to whom Namaliu spoke recognized, as we have said, that they had become increasingly dependent on outsiders, including politicians, for outside resources if they were to enact their customary ceremonies in more than basic form. They were, in consequence, receptive to his message. But they were also cautious about accepting his protestations of solidarity and kinship: To what extent was he entailed to them? To what extent could they elicit from him?

Namaliu, as it turned out, provided at least two semipublic demonstrations proving his good faith. In advance of his visit he sent word to Papala, the widow of Tuembe (with whom, it will be recalled, his primary Karavaran ties focused), that she should present a gift of food to him. She did so as he and the accompanying throng passed her house after his address. He responded to her gift in a way both intimate and public: by whispering words of comfort about Tuembe into her ear and by, within sight of others, pressing a roll of kina notes—K100 (US$110) in all—into her hand. In addition, he had let it be seen that he gave a similar amount to Tuembe's sister, Elit, when the two of them wept for Tuembe.

Karavarans had also set their own tests of his entailed kinship. For example, in anticipation of his visit, a woman asked us to type and send the following letter to Namaliu. We translate it from the (Pidgin English) dictation she provided with names changed:

Dear Prime Minister Namaliu,

Rabbie, I of your matriline, would like to ask you for your help. I wish to make you look at my problem. In this regard I would like you to help me with K1,000 [US$1,100] so that I can buy a boat. I of your matriline, my husband, Benny Peng, died. Isaac took his place to watch over his children. Now I would like you to help me and all of us—Isaac and Marawut [Isaac's father]. We are trying you out with this letter. We want to borrow money from you. Later, after we put the boat to work, we will repay you.

That is it: that is the worry of me of your matriline and of Isaac and Marawut. All three of us, including me of your matriline, want your help.

Thank you.

The author of this letter was arguing that her claims upon Namaliu's resources were particularly strong and that they were reciprocal: She was a reasonably close kinswoman of his—related through Tuembe—and, moreover, promised to pay him back. However, Karavar was a small, substantially endogamous community in which kinship was sufficiently fluid that ties could be readily established (as through adoption or ritual cooperation, for instance). Namaliu, thus, could have—and probably had at one time or another—received requests from virtually everyone on Karavar, all based on kinship ties.

It also followed from the existence of an overlapping, interpenetrating kinship nexus that Namaliu would as a "Karavaran" receive requests for community projects. Indeed, we were asked by the members of the local school board to type a letter (which we omit!) petitioning him for funds to construct a two-story permanent-materials school. According to letters we received after leaving the field, he eventually complied with this appeal.

Karavarans did realize that Namaliu would not, could not, comply with every request they directed to him. No Karavaran, not even the big men of the past, had done so. After all, not even their own children working elsewhere granted all of their requests for money. (We were also asked to type many letters requesting money from these migrants.) Though great, Namaliu's resources were also recognized as limited. Nonetheless, if he was to maintain his entailment to them, he would have to come through at least some of the time.

Although it was possible for Namaliu to come through sufficiently to keep Karavarans reasonably happy, it was extraordinarily difficult for him (or anyone) to extend "kinship" throughout an entire electorate, and this was not only because his resources were finite. Simply put, his constituency was too large to be easily treated as a kinship unit. Hence, from the Karavaran (or other particular) perspective, any substantial gifts Namaliu gave to those elsewhere whom Karavarans themselves did not recognize as close kin might well suggest one of two things: Either he was claiming primary kinship grounding at too many places to be plausible or, even if he could make a case for such multiple groundings, his gift to one group bespoke his relative lack of entailment to the other. In the former case, his implausibility would cast him as a self-serving "Martin"; in the latter case, he would appear to be another group's "Tovetura."

THE "STATESMAN" AS
COMPROMISED ALTERNATIVE

We have in this chapter described "Martin" and "Tovetura" as personae who constituted two poles on the chart of political possibilities envisioned by at least some of East New Britain's contemporary shell-money users. As reference points for local people, these personae conveyed sharply contrasting models of person and polity: Martin concluded his essay with an unentailed *"iau,"* reflecting a socially disconnected preoccupation with private interests; Tovetura concluded his *liu* with (we surmise) a *"iau"* reflecting a triumph that was not only personally gratifying but regarded as socially constituting.

We have argued that, at least in generalized form, these personae figured quite explicitly in the claims made by and against elected officials at Karavar. For officials to prove that they were not "Martins," not exclusively out for themselves, they had to subscribe convincingly to the standards of (locally defined variants of) "Tovetura." Yet in so doing, they embraced, at least in rhetoric, an unworkable model of translocal constituency, one based on the construction and maintenance of interpersonal entailment. National (much less regional) politicians could not plausibly sustain the networks of kinship through which they claimed connection with their constituencies.

We suggest as well that comparable personae were on the minds of people not only elsewhere in East New Britain but more broadly throughout contemporary Papua New Guinea. For instance, newspapers cited widespread popular skepticism about who would profit from the various development schemes (timber projects, gold mines, oil fields) advocated by politicians. It is no wonder that at a time when many Papua New Guineans suspected their politicians of making empty promises in order to obscure self-interested concerns, another pole on the chart of political possibilities was called for. In a recent edition of the *Times of Papua New Guinea*—the issue reporting the final results of the national election of 1992—the following editorial appeared:

> It is ironic that at a time when nationalism should be put before anything else, our elected leaders are already divided into their little regions vying for whatever position they can get in the new government.
>
> Already some names that make the person on the street shudder have been announced as candidates for the position of prime minister. It is obvious that some of these self-interested groups are not concerned in getting the best person into the country's top position. Their main concern seems to be to get the best deal for themselves. Any thoughts about the people who have elected them into parliament have already been pushed to the back of their minds and no doubt this will be the trend for the next five years.
>
> With intense lobbying going on now among the political parties and independent members, we hope some of them still have enough integrity to vote with a clear conscience. The people of this country want to see a strong leader at the helm of a government that is going to do the right thing by the people.
>
> The life of the last government ended on a very bad note with ministers resigning before they could answer charges for breach of the Leadership Code or even outright criminal offenses. Do we want these people back in government?

What happened to all the anti-corruption talk that was spilling out from the Opposition's camp a month ago? …

The province or region where the prime minister comes from is a very minor concern to the people of this country. A strong stable government led by the right person with the right qualities is what should be the major concern to the members of parliament and the people on the street. (1992b: 7)

Significantly, this editorial attacked the self-interest of politicians because it led them to ignore not only the concerns of their constituencies but also the welfare of the nation. It described them, in other words, as "Martins," as those who made no attempt to join short-term private with long-term public interests. Interestingly, the primary countermodel suggested for "Martin" was not a "Tovetura" but a new persona who might be termed the "statesman."

Such a persona, an image perhaps borrowed from the West (as was the idea of the nation itself), referred to a politician who, neither unduly self-interested nor parochial, had primarily the interests of the nation in mind. The "statesman," by focusing on long-term public goals, was able to establish a vision of the general good that provided the context in which individuals would be able to pursue their private interests. He, or at least his persona, had been useful in the capitalist West at times of systemic and exceptional crises such as those of war or economic depression. It was then when his vision was likely to be called upon to articulate (to refer again to Bloch and Parry's discussion [1989]) that usually unexplicated in capitalism: the relationship between short-term private and long-term public goals.

The image of the "statesman" came, therefore, from the same system of "fully developed" capitalism in which "Martin" was at home. It is significant that the editorial invoking the "statesman" appeared in the national English-language newspaper regarded as appealing to only the best educated. Moreover, the editorial was printed directly above an advertisement sponsored by an association of capitalist developers, the PNG Chamber of Mines and Petroleum. This ad queried the elite readers thus: "Did you know that more than one third of the tax that Government collects each year comes from the Mining and Petroleum Industry?" (*Times of Papua New Guinea* 1992c: 7).

Given the socioeconomic context in which the persona of the "statesman" appeared, we wonder about the ideological implications of its invocation in the rhetoric of motives characteristic of contemporary Papua New Guinea politics. Following Burke's example of the shepherd who "acts for the good of the sheep, to protect them from discomfiture and harm" but who "may be 'identified' with the project that is raising the sheep for market" (Burke 1969: 27), we do not wish to impugn the objectives of the editorialist advocating the persona of the "statesman." We do wonder, however, about this persona's "identification with other orders of motivation extrinsic to it," about the "larger unit of action" (p. 27) in which it participates. In particular, we suspect that the "statesman" might, in fact, operate within the chart of political possibilities less to offset the "Martins" than to discredit—to supplant—the "Toveturas." The "statesman" would make the "Toveturas" appear obsolete and anachronistic in a progressive, developing country, one in which the mining and petroleum industry provided such substantial public, and private, revenues (cf. Chakrabarty 1992).

There was, as well, the implication in the editorial that those who supported "Tovetura" were themselves anachronistic. They were not—to refer to what was another, though implicit, persona in the editorial—the generalized "good citizen." Preoccupied with particularist ties that led them to search for their local "Tovetura," they were not "the people on the street" or "the people of this country" to which the editorial alluded. They were not, for instance, among those who were unconcerned about the region from which the prime minister came; they were not among those who shuddered at some of the names suggested for this office.

Although the editorial purported to be an attack on the "Martin"-like behavior of politicians, it would, in effect, serve to remove the principal alternative. By defining (either directly or indirectly) the indigenous models of person and polity—which we have been glossing as "Tovetura" and his local followers—as anachronistic in modern Papua New Guinea, the editorial appears to reduce the chart of acceptable political possibilities to the (linked) persona of "citizen" and "statesman." In our view, though, the context in which the mining and petroleum industry contributed so heavily to public (and private) revenues might well be one in which "citizens" and "statesmen" existed primarily in rhetoric to obscure the prevalence of "Martins." We worry, in other words, that those who abandoned a "Tovetura" in hope of getting a "statesman" might well simply end up with a "Martin." (This is not to say that "statesmen" did not or could not exist in parliamentary or other democracies but that they were certainly rare.)

Whatever its limitations (and these, we have indicated, were substantial), the "Tovetura" standard by which politicians were found so frequently wanting was the primary one through which local interests could be asserted (sometimes to the bedevilment of multinational corporations who thought "the deal was done"). "Tovetura," after all, represented a system (whether preadapted to capitalism or not) in which the connection between leaders and followers and between short-term private and long-term public interests was understood as intimate, if not indissoluble. In contemporary Papua New Guinea, this model might continue to prove the most impressive and effective standard of accountability available.

*   *   *

The preceding chapters have all been about the articulations that have been a part of and that have generated complex changes in what once was regarded as the "last unknown." In the concluding chapter, we consider one last articulation, one we consider rather paradigmatic of many of the struggles and the transformations thus far described whereby local people tried to achieve identity and worth—tried to negotiate successfully the relationships of reciprocity that marked equality. This paradigmatic articulation, in addition, reveals some of the errors that can be made when simplistic models of change are applied to complex processes.

Our ethnographic focus is on the destruction of a tourist facility designed, it was claimed, to help Karavarans "develop" so that they might receive more of the benefits of the modern world. In explaining why Karavarans sabotaged the facility, why they exhibited such contentious obstinacy in asserting their local interests, we are, moreover, led to consider further their future and that of the nation as a whole.

NOTES

1. We realize that most Tolai and Duke of York Islanders usually struck a course focusing somewhere between self-interest and social commitment. Perhaps they navigated closer to either alternative depending on particular and sometimes changing life circumstances such as age, education, gender, and position—whether villager, local big man, urban wage earner, government bureaucrat, or politician. Nonetheless, those like Martin did, we argue, present, especially for village people, a relatively novel and troubling alternative.

2. These ideal types were far more general than those Young described operating among Goodenough Islanders, where clan leaders actually modeled their lives on the careers of their particular mythical predecessors (Young 1983).

3. We refer here, of course, to Malinowski's view of myth as charter (Malinowski 1926) and to the fact that the connection between particular myths and existing social organizations may be much less direct than he believed (Bourdieu 1977; Sahlins 1981; Gewertz 1988).

4. In the national election of 1968, 23 out of 46 members of Parliament were returned to their seats; in 1972, 38 out of 73; in 1977, 35 out of 91; in 1982, 48 out of

92; 1987, 56 out of 104; and in 1992, 48 out of 108. We thank Ron May for providing these statistics.

5. In 1991, many Karavarans thought that those who had acquired great wealth, including some still alive, were likely to have done so with the help of *turangan,* who gave them access to caves filled with shell money.

6. The contrast between these ideal types might, of course, be sharper in the rhetoric of claims than in enactment of conduct, particularly in everyday life. In this regard we found instructive a recent photo-essay in the English-language *Times of Papua New Guinea* that appeared in a section designed to address the problems and concerns of "youth." A young, educated Papua New Guinea woman was shown taking a job in a provincial town so that she could be near her family. Soon, she found their demands for money overwhelming. A girlfriend advised her to find work far from her family in the national capital of Port Moresby. She accepted this advice and, with assurance that her friend would visit, departed. As far as readers knew, she found her relocation and her separation from her kin and their claims entirely satisfactory (July 2, 1992a: 17). Yet in our experience, it would still be the exceptional young migrant who would wish to spend his or her entire life separated from natal home and from the claims of family. Indeed, many we have known who left home in similar circumstances did eventually remit and did periodically return. These migrants reported to us, sometimes with wry ambivalence, that even after living away for years, they still regarded the approval of their kin as a major determinant of personal worth. (See Carrier and Carrier 1989; Gewertz and Errington 1991: 111–125.)

7. Karavaran mortuary exchanges moved not only between matrilines but between matrimoieties.

8. Indeed, the first *matamatam* Fred attended with Karavarans in 1968 was held by Namaliu's Tolai kin in East New Britain.

Conclusion

Bloody-Mindedness in the Duke of York Islands— Toward Seeing Ourselves in the Other

W E HAVE INTENDED these chapters to make grounded sense of how those living in a rather small place have engaged with some of the rather large and widely compelling issues of our time. In particular, we have been concerned with understanding the efforts of local people to establish identity and worth in complex contexts of disparate power. We have struggled, moreover, to get this story relatively "right" as it has unfolded, and not simply in the interests of scholarly accuracy. We believe that getting the story "wrong" would likely serve to discount the aspirations of local people; it would, in addition, serve to discount the consequences of the actions of those such as ourselves with disproportionate power and lead to misdirecting the responsibility for those consequences. (We remind our readers that in the unfolding of history we have described, this category of the disproportionately powerful has come to include not only Europeans but Asians and, in increasing numbers, Papua New Guineans.) To these ends, we have mustered the strengths of anthropology: We have sought to present ethnographic analysis that both in its fine grain and in its scope does some justice to the complexity and significance of change in a colonial and postcolonial world—a world that has caught all of us up in ongoing processes of cultural construction, historical contingency, and mutual determination.

In our conclusion, we present as parable a contemporary encounter that both summarizes and, in its striking immediacy, brings this argument "home." We suggest that as paradigmatic of over a century of continuities and changes in the relations between locals and others, this parable may prove a useful point of departure for thinking about the Karavaran future. Importantly, we see the parable as balancing the initial one we told of the mutually unsatisfactory confrontation between the Reverend Rickard and a local leader in which the former did not reciprocate the presentation of betel nut by the latter. This early colonial interaction, we suggested, encapsulated and embodied much of the ensuing history of unsatisfactory transactions, a history in which locals often felt ill used and Europeans, frequently frustrated. The final story we tell here provides a context to think both about what has been learned and what has happened since the introduction, when "we"—both as reader and as colonial emissary—made initial contact with the Duke of York Islanders.

We trust that one thing learned about Karavarans and other Duke of York Islanders as they have determined, negotiated, and pursued their aspirations and interests in long-term engagement with powerful others is that they are comprehensible as people, *like ourselves,* with the ambition and capacity to shape their own lives. In describing this engagement, we have sought to clarify areas of misunderstanding between those such as Rickard and the chief such that both locals and those powerful others would become more nearly comparable in intelligibility—that is, so that we might imagine ourselves as either. However, struggling to imagine ourselves acting as either might have is not enough. To see these encounters from both sides should be to recognize the existing disparities in power. And hence we must also recognize that the responsibility for the often mutually unsatisfactory nature of the encounters was and is likely for some time to remain as unequally distributed as the power underwriting it.

A CONTEMPORARY PARABLE

Near the end of our fieldwork we visited a curious ruin on the island of Kambakon. (As mentioned, the loss of this island reputedly began when a Karavaran ancestor killed the dog of a missionary living there.) In an overgrown clearing about fifty yards from shore, we glimpsed the remains of an obviously modern construction. As we approached the small (about eight by twelve feet) cinder-block structure, we were dazzled by the reflection of the noonday sun as it streamed through the open roof and out again through the doorless entrances. Drawing nearer, we could see that the reflection came from expanses of white tile that lined the interior. This was the "state-of-the-art ablution block, as nice as at the Travel Lodge," previously described to us

This was the "state-of-the-art ablution block, as nice as at the Travel Lodge."

by its European owner, a man we will call Jones. Jones was a Rabaul shipping magnate and naturalized Papua New Guinea citizen married to an Australian-educated indigenous woman from the Milne Bay Province.

We entered to confirm what we had already been told. Toilets had been smashed; showers and piping had been ripped out of the walls and left on the floor in twisted heaps; everything that could be scavenged for local use, such as the corrugated metal roofing, had been taken. We were looking at the remains of a carefully planned but, nonetheless, failed business venture. The ablution block was part of the facility Jones had organized and financed on Kambakon in the late 1980s to attract well-paying tourists. It was a place where they could swim, snorkel, and soak up the sun.

We had asked Karavarans to show us the ruin, in part so as to complete a task set for us by the Tolai research officer of the East New Britain provincial government. All foreign researchers in the province were obliged to accomplish an applied study the government deemed essential. Our assignment had been to investigate the possibilities of developing tourism as an industry in the Duke of York Islands (a project given to us because we had studied tourism in the East Sepik Province [see Errington and Gewertz, 1989]). One of the written "terms of reference" with which we were charged by the Tolai re-

Toilets had been smashed; showers and piping had been ripped out of the walls and left on the floor in twisted heaps; everything that could be scavenged for local use, such as corrugated metal roofing, had been taken.

search officer was to "identify constraints on any such development including potential opposition groups." The story of what had happened at Kambakon seemed relevant to this charge.

Having earlier interviewed Jones, we knew something of the circumstances that had led to the failure of his business venture, at least from his point of view. The venture had failed, he claimed, because the Karavarans with whom he had been dealing had been so "bloody-minded" (a British-Australian term meaning unreasonably obstinate). Jones explained: After giving many gifts, he had acquired from Karavaran village elders, or so he thought, a lease on a small portion of Kambakon, a point of land, for five years. In return for this lease, at the end of five years the Karavarans would own and assume control of what by then would be a well-established business. Pursuant to this agreement, he constructed five native-material houses, a cooking facility, and a barbecue area in addition to the aforementioned "state-of-the-art ablution block."

While developing this tourist facility, Jones continued to make presents to Karavarans, especially of much-needed medicine. He also offered employment to them. He had proposed that they earn money by providing materials and labor for the construction of these houses. A few local people would also be hired to maintain the enterprise by cutting the grass and cleaning the houses. In addition, money would enter the local economy through the sale of food, shells, and handicrafts to the visitors. At designated times, a few Karavarans would, for instance, be invited to sell fruits to the tourists, or some little children would be encouraged to bring shells. Perhaps a list would be drawn up so that each Karavaran would have a chance to sell things. However, it was important, Jones explained, that the tourists be protected from too much contact with Karavarans; the tourists would not want to be overwhelmed by the native presence.

As it turned out, the Karavarans did not avail themselves of his offer to employ them in constructing the houses. And so it was necessary for him to engage Tolai youth groups to gather the materials and build them. This appreciably increased the costs of construction insofar as he had to provision the workers and transport them and the materials. Moreover, he claimed that Karavarans pilfered large quantities of building supplies. (He said he had to bring in quantities sufficient to build ten houses.)

Despite these difficulties and expenses, Jones was initially quite pleased with the enterprise. Among the first tourists Jones brought in one of his boats to use the facilities were some 100 Korean cadet sailors whose training ship was docked in Rabaul harbor. He told us that they thoroughly enjoyed the day of swimming, relaxing, and barbecuing that he provided.

Karavarans began to object to these arrangements almost immediately, for reasons we will describe shortly. They expressed their objections to Jones, but he thought them ill conceived, if not irrational. Eventually, they took matters into their own hands and destroyed the facility. Jones thought them ungrateful and their actions self-defeating. He had been extremely generous to them and had, moreover, given them a chance to earn the money they needed now that they lived in the modern world. Through "bloody-mindedness" they blew it.

*   *   *

In many ways, this contemporary encounter between Jones and the Karavarans was no more satisfactory than that between Rickard and the chief: After over a century of interaction, locals continued to feel ill used and Europeans, frustrated. Yet much of importance had happened and the principal actors had changed in significant ways. What, then, can we conclude about the course of change over this period and the continuity of mutual disgruntlement?

One thing should be clear: The models of the fragile Eden and the inflexible tradition do not adequately account for these Karavaran actions. The Karavarans were not demoralized and disoriented with the shattering of their formerly beautiful customs by modernity and thereby plunged into anomie, lacking any sense of a greater good. They were not resistant to the benefits of change, remaining forever primitive and waging a benighted war against progress. Nor had they been transformed into moderns. And Jones's interpretation of the "bloody-minded" native, which appears to be derived from or at least related to both the fragile Eden and the inflexible tradition models does not account adequately for the Karavaran actions either.

The "bloody-minded," Jones told us, were especially likely to be the natives in between, half-transfigured, sometimes half-educated. Their Eden had been shattered, their tradition broken, but their transformation into modernity remained incomplete.[1] They were dislocated from traditional customs without having become fully developed. (Recall, in this regard, "The Educated Native" poem presented in Chapter 3.) Such individuals, Jones believed, were discontented because they lacked the assurance of a secure grounding in either the traditional or the modern life; they frustrated and aggravated even those who were trying to help them by making insistent and unreasonable demands. Importantly, Jones's ideas about the consequences of dislocation and being in between, like the models of change from which they were derived or related, served to render illegitimate indigenous demands that inconvenienced or otherwise thwarted the plans of those seeking control.

As we have insisted, these models of change, including, as we shall show more fully, such applied derivatives as that of "bloody-mindedness," are best confounded by the kind of evidence we have provided about Karavarans confronting, negotiating, and contending with powerful intrusive forces during the changing world of the past century. During this time, they have looked to the future as well as to the past, looked outward as well as inward. We have, in other words, shown Karavarans shaping and pursuing their objectives in order to enhance identity and worth in a manner they would regard as insistent but *not* as unreasonable. In this light, let us focus somewhat more on the events, both long and short-term, that led to the destruction of the Kambakon "ablution block."

Certainly, by the time of Jones's project, Kambakon had acquired much of the weight of colonial and postcolonial history. According to land records, it was entirely alienated for plantation use in 1879, early in the colonial period. Its people were evidently then displaced to Karavar, where they merged with the local population. Kambakon was subsequently operated as a plantation by a sequence of owners or managers, some of whom were distinctly "colorful." For example, in 1903 it was acquired and managed by a German nudist vegetarian, August Engelhardt, who regarded the island as a potential Eden. Advocating a philosophy based on the worship of the sun (the source of all life) and on the consumption of coconuts (the substance most completely embodying the sun's beneficent powers), Engelhardt and, at times, a small band of often seriously ill disciples lived on Kambakon for about ten years.[2] Shortly thereafter, the plantation was acquired by Burns Philp, a vast Australian-based firm. In 1977, following independence and after years of struggle and agitation, Karavarans (with substantial governmental intervention and a large loan) bought the island back from Burns Philp. The Karavarans felt triumphant, vindicated in their long-term perseverance. Moreover, they expected that the plantation would bring them substantial prosperity, certainly enough readily to retire their loan from the government.

However, under Karavaran management and with Karavaran labor, the enterprise did not flourish. The plantation closed after a few years because of inefficiency, falling coconut prices, and (probably) misappropriation of funds. (In consequence, most of the government loan remained outstanding, although it seems, in effect, to have been forgiven; Karavarans, for their part, have said that they should not have had to pay anything for land they already rightfully owned.) The island is now used for gardens. Indeed, it has become the primary source of garden land for a rapidly increasing population.

It was under these circumstances that Jones approached Karavarans with his project. Since Kambakon was no longer a source of income and since the point of land Jones wished to develop was sandy and therefore unsuitable for gardening, he thought it would clearly be in Karavaran interests to cooperate with him.

As Karavarans explained to us, although they certainly wanted a source of income, they disapproved of Jones's proposal for various reasons. First, many complained that they had never given *their* permission to Jones. They contended that since Kambakon had come to be owned by Karavarans collectively, all should have been consulted. Although Jones had met on several occasions with Karavarans, it was claimed that he consulted primarily with a relatively few old men who had neither the authorization nor the understanding necessary to appraise Jones's offer. Some Karavarans went even further and charged that Jones dealt almost exclusively with one senior man whose family received most of the benefits, including most of Jones's gifts. And several younger men had argued forcefully that after the five-year lease period, there might be little of the business left for the Karavarans to manage given the likely deterioration of the native materials used in building the houses. They had insisted that if Jones was not going to share out profits immediately, he should at least construct permanent-material houses. (In his turn, Jones reiterated that the charm of the Duke of York Islands as a tourist site virtually necessitated the use of native materials.) Finally, these young men wished a more clearly specified contract. They wanted obligations delineated in writing and a guarantee that no permanent alienation of land would take place.

Several Karavarans also told us that Karavaran dissatisfaction had been exacerbated by a local leader whose in-married brother-in-law was promoting his own scheme for developing tourism on Kambakon. This local leader played on Karavaran fears that the land, for which they had so long struggled, might again be tricked away from them, this time by Jones.

There were other problems as well in the operation of the business. Karavarans said that they did not know when to clean up the houses for the arrival of guests. Those who did clean the houses when guests did not arrive were not paid and felt cheated. And many Karavarans resented being restricted in their access to these premises, both when the guests were there and were not there. In fact, Karavarans fishing at night from the point of land where the houses stood began to use them for shelter. For a variety of reasons, the houses began to deteriorate. As they became run down, they were vandalized, and materials, especially metal roofing, were appropriated for use in both public and private Karavaran projects.

What Jones in his frustration blamed on the "bloody-minded" Karavarans, they largely blamed on Jones. They distrusted Jones's ultimate intentions; were exasperated over poor communication, lack of immediate and broadly shared remuneration, and degrading exclusion from their own hard-redeemed Kambakon; and resented that other Karavarans had unduly bene-fited. Overall, they regarded their responses as more reasonable and legitimate than his.

Yet Karavarans did not contend that they were easy to deal with. They viewed their role in these events as predictably Karavaran: contentious and obstinate.[3] They admitted with a mixture of pride and wry deprecation that they were contentious: They were resolutely competitive and fiercely jealous toward the ascendancy of others, likely to misappropriate in efforts to gain as-cendancy, ready to accuse each other of misappropriation, and frequently at cross-purposes in their work with each other. And they viewed their obstinacy more as a source of strength and protection than as a liability. Certainly, on the whole they felt they were justified in blocking Jones in his project, espe-cially so because they sensed from him, as from many of his predecessors, con-descension in his attitude.

*   *   *

Though the encounter between Jones and the Karavarans was in many re-gards as unsatisfactory as that between Rickard and the Duke of York chief, it took place under what were significantly altered circumstances. Not only had Jones become a citizen of the country he wanted to "develop," he needed broad-based Karavaran approval of his plans; not only had Karavarans come to realize that indigenous identity brought indigenous rights in law, they could envision doing the tourist project without Jones. Whereas Jones, like Rickard, wished Karavarans to stop being so "bloody-minded," he also knew he could not command either their attention or compliance. Although Karavarans, like the Duke of York chief, came to recognize that Jones was un-willing to engage with them on equal terms, they also recognized that they could prevent him from engaging with them at all.

But the changes went beyond these general postcolonial ones. Simply put, Jones (and, we imagine, "Martin") knew better than Rickard: Jones would not only have picked up the betel nut but would also have eaten it and recip-rocated. For their part, the Karavarans also knew better than the Duke of York chief: They would not only have thought a return gift appropriate but, if it came, would have been quick to recognize any manipulating condescension behind its apparent promise of commitment. Yet there was, of course, certain continuity: Both sets of encounters led to an impasse. That one standoff suc-ceeded another speaks, it seems to us, to importantly enduring disparities of power, disparities that would likely continue.

WHAT OF THE FUTURE?

We do not know what might prove an appropriate parable for a Karavaran future. However, we suspect that the same contentiousness and obstinacy Karavarans have shown in both their past and more contemporary encounters might serve them in Papua New Guinea for some considerable time. Certainly these qualities have proven their usefulness over time, sustaining them in their struggle for identity and worth against colonial powers that deprecated and often ill-used them. In addition, these qualities have sustained them in refusing to accept their inequality as ontological—as other than the product of immediate and alterable social circumstances.

To be sure, their contentiousness and obstinacy has also limited their engagement in the activities through which they might enhance identity and worth. Indeed (and this would be a portion of our answer to the charge given to us by the East New Britain provincial government concerning "the constraints" on the implementation of a tourist industry in the Duke of York Islands), we doubt that any "development" project requiring long-term Karavaran cooperation would likely run at all smoothly and effectively unless the activities themselves were mutually entailing (as, for example, in the *dukduk* and *tubuan* ceremonies). Thus, despite initial high hopes, their plantation at Kambakon floundered in part because Karavarans became convinced that it was being poorly run and that its revenues were being stolen. Likewise (as we saw in Chapter 1) Karavarans eventually lost faith in the Kaun in part because they concluded (probably accurately) that its resources were being seriously mismanaged and misappropriated.

Nor can it be denied that this same contentiousness and obstinacy might make it difficult for many Karavarans living at home to embrace more than temporarily a nationalist agenda demanding responsibility to those such as fellow "citizens" with whom they were not immediately entailed, with whom they had no direct and regulating social relationship.[4] Yet we suspect that such contentiousness and obstinacy toward those who might advocate shifting allegiance from local self-interest to a broader "common good" should not necessarily be decried. We were somewhat relieved in this regard when the dramatically compelling representations in the Jubilee skit of shared, national experience came to an end and—while the prime minister flew off in his helicopter—members of the audience dispersed to their separate villages. Once home, we imagined, they would be less willing to be carried away by nationalist visions, less willing to cede their autonomy to the state as the source and guarantor of common identity and benefit. And we would be equally relieved to learn that shell money had been rejected as a symbol of national unity, that these East New Britains had *not* come to represent all Papua New Guineans. We also eventually came to sympathize more with the traditional Methodists than with the modern evangelicals, fearing that the latter's transforming embrace of God might open the way to a transforming embrace of a regulating, if not repressive, state.

Indeed, we suspect that such a contentious and obstinate stance of insisting on the tangible benefits and markers of social entailment in return for political allegiance has, on balance, been advantageous to Papua New Guinea villagers and would continue to be. As we have seen throughout the book, class was operating in this world of nationalist agendas much as caste had in the world of colonial domination. And it would be as much in the interests of those with nationalist agendas (with their rhetoric of decontextualized "citizens" and "statesmen") as it was in the interests of those with colonialist agendas (with their rhetoric of "children" and "parents") to define the self assertive and protective responses of villagers—their contentiousness and obstinacy— as illegitimate, as bloody-minded. In fact, we think that contentiousness and obstinacy not only have been but would continue to remain essential so long as those interacting with local people remain unentailed to them in the manner of colonists—including many of the missionaries—as well as the more contemporary "Joneses" and "Martins."

However, it must be recognized that although this contentious and obstinate stance might well have prevented an undue consolidation of power, it has also limited the positive effects the state might have, including its capacity to control serious conflict between (contentious and obstinate) local groups. Such conflict has become frequent in Papua New Guinea. In some areas, especially in the Highlands, groups have engaged in outright warfare despite attempts by the national police and the army to curtail the violence.[5] Many of the efforts by which local groups have asserted their identity and worth might appear reasonable and rational within their particular circumstances, but these activities could in their cumulative effect be quite destructive (cf. Meggitt 1991).

Fortunately for Papua New Guinea, the same cultural pluralism that has limited the power of the state to impose its order also would make it doubtful that any particular group could completely dominate its neighbors. The persistence of a precolonial structure whereby neighboring groups were both relatively small and evenly matched in strength suggests that one group would find it difficult to obliterate another. Papua New Guinea would, therefore, not likely become either a Nigeria or a Bosnia. In short, we suspect that Papua

New Guinea would remain neither the best nor the worst of all possible (or even existing) worlds, that it would continue to be a rather weak, rather corrupt, and rather inefficient state. And for those reasons, it would be, under most circumstances (those short of attempted secession) rather benign.[6]

We think that the probable course for the immediate future would be a continuation of guarded attempts to negotiate what would remain an unequal balance between local and national interests. Such negotiation, it will be recalled, was sought by the police brought to Karavar to settle the dispute between evangelicals and United Church members (when local contention and obstinacy had got out of hand). As a policeman put it then (in what proved an inconclusive effort at mediation), "I can't say that custom is wrong or that the law of the government is wrong. I come from a place of custom too. All of us in Papua New Guinea do." Such an uneasy standoff would at least leave room for the continued negotiation of local identity and worth.

NOTES

1. Interestingly, Jones wanted his guests to experience the physical Eden from which locals had been largely displaced—and to which they would be periodically readmitted when bearing portions of nature's bounty.

2. For an exposition of Engelhardt's philosophy, see the book he wrote with one of his Kambakon disciples, August Bethmann (Bethmann and Engelhardt, 1913). In it, they justify in poetry and prose their particular form of vegetarianism, arguing, for example, "Mankind differs from the monkey, the animal resembling him most, by the shape of the head. The skull of the monkey is like a roof with concave hollow surface, while the human skulls are arched as the sky. And therefore we can expect from God that he created our food in the shape of our heads. There are no animals with human-like shaped heads; are there plants of such a form? The head is the most vital and substantial part of men, and so is the fruit the most vital part of the plant. Are there plants with human-like heads? God would not be the finished artist if he had not created them—but he did create them in giving us the cocoanut tree. These nuts are vegetal human heads, and they alone are the proper human nourishment" (p. 14).

3. In this regard, it will be recalled from Chapter 1 that Karavarans refused for years to pay government taxes even when government services were withheld from them.

4. The experience of those living in the towns and cities of Papua New Guinea was, of course, often significantly different from those in the villages. These urban dwellers might have responded somewhat positively (although perhaps transitorily) to such nationalist presentations as the 1991 staging of the South Pacific Games in the national capital of Port Moresby. Compare Feinberg (1990), Hirsch (1990), Rosi

(1991), and Foster (1992) for discussions of other largely urban efforts to create nationalist sensibilities.

5. For a recent film that portrayed the upsurgence of violence in the Highlands, see Connolly and Anderson 1991. Lamentable as such violence might well be, the film, in our view, did not provide adequate explanation of it. Thus viewers were encouraged to see the combatants as motivated primarily by "bloody-mindedness." For a more extensive review of the film, see Gewertz and Errington 1992.

6. The Papua New Guinea state did seem to be using virtually all of its resources to prevent the secession of Bougainville. The Papua New Guinea military had been trying to quell an insurrection there since 1989 (Chapter 4, note 6), most recently through a blockade of food and medical supplies, which many commentators both inside and outside Papua New Guinea have found in violation of basic human rights. The Papua New Guinea state certainly has the potential for repression. Yet it has also demonstrated itself relatively ineffectual, even in Bougainville.

The extent to which Papua New Guineans might find their country livable in the future would be affected not only by governmental repression but by governmental management of natural resources. Certainly, there have been very disquieting reports of considerable ecosystemic destruction throughout the country (see Chapter 4) due to either governmental collusion with or incapacity to control expatriate companies exploiting timber and mineral resources.

References

Abu-Lughod, Lila. 1990. "The Romance of Resistance: Tracing the Transformations of Power Through Bedouin Women." *American Ethnologist* 17:41–55.

Ackroyd, John. 1925. "Impressions of New Britain Missions." *Missionary Review* 35:5–7.

Aleck, Jonathan. n.d. "Traditional Law and Legal Traditions in Papua New Guinea: A Reappraisal of the Relationship Between Law and Custom." Unpublished manuscript.

Anderson, Benedict. 1983. *Imagined Communities*. London: Verso.

Asad, Talal, ed. 1973. *Anthropology and the Colonial Encounter*. London: Ithaca Press.

Babadzan, Alain. 1988. "Kastom and Nation Building in the South Pacific." *In Ethnicities and Nations*. R. Guidieri, F. Pellizi, and S. J. Tambiah, eds., pp. 199–228. Austin: University of Texas Press.

Barr, John. 1983a. "Spiritistic Tendencies in Melanesia." In *Religious Movements in Melanesia Today*," vol. 2. Wendy Flannery, ed., pp. 1–34. Goroka: Melanesian Institute.

———. 1983b. "A Survey of Ecstatic Phenomena and 'Holy Spirit' Movements in Melanesia." *Oceania* 54:109–132.

———. 1984. "The Age of the Spirit." In *Religious Movements in Melanesia Today*, vol. 3. Wendy Flannery, ed., pp. 158–185. Goroka: Melanesian Institute.

Battaglia, Debbora. 1990. *On the Bones of the Serpent*. Chicago: University of Chicago Press.

Bauman, Richard. 1975. "Verbal Art as Performance." *American Anthropologist* 77:290–311.

Beckett, Jeremy. 1987. *Torres Strait Islanders: Custom and Colonialism*. Cambridge: Cambridge University Press.

Bethmann, August, and August Engelhardt. 1913. *A Carefree Future*. Butler, N.J.: Benedict Lust.

Biersack, Aletta. 1991. "Introduction: History and Theory in Anthropology." In *Clio in Oceania*. Aletta Biersack, ed., pp. 1–36. Washington, D.C.: Smithsonian.

Bloch, Maurice. 1986. *From Blessing to Violence: History and Ideology in the Circumcision Ritual of the Merina of Madagascar*. Cambridge: Cambridge University Press.

Bloch, Maurice, and Jonathan Parry. 1989. "Introduction: Money and the Morality of Exchange." In *Money and the Morality of Exchange*. Jonathan Parry and Maurice Bloch, eds., pp. 1–32. Cambridge: Cambridge University Press.

Bourdieu, Pierre. 1977. *Outline of a Theory of Practice.* Cambridge: Cambridge University Press.

Bradley, Christine. 1982. "Tolai Women and Development." Unpublished Ph.D. diss., University College of London.

Bradley, William. 1969. *A Voyage to the South Seas, 1786–1792.* Sydney: Public Library of New South Wales.

Bray, Mark. 1985a. "An Overview of Issues." In *Education and Social Stratification in Papua New Guinea.* Mark Bray and Peter Smith, eds., pp. 1–30. Melbourne: Longman Cheshire.

———. 1985b. "Social Stratification and Disparities in Access to Education in East New Britain." In *Education and Social Stratification in Papua New Guinea.* Mark Bray and Peter Smith, eds., pp. 182–193. Melbourne: Longman Cheshire.

Brown, George. 1875a. Letter Books of the Reverend George Brown. Mitchell Library, Sydney.

———. 1875b. The Journals of the Reverend George Brown. Mitchell Library, Sydney.

———. 1887. *Vocabulary of the Dialect Spoken in the Duke of York Islands with Additions and Corrections Made by Benjamin Danks.* Mitchell Library, Sydney.

———. 1972 [1910]. *Melanesians and Polynesians.* New York: Benjamin Bloom.

Brown, William. 1892. *Habits and Customs of the Natives of Duke of York and New Ireland.* Mitchell Library, Sydney.

Burke, Kenneth. 1969. *A Rhetoric of Motives.* Berkeley: University of California Press.

Burridge, Kenelm. 1969. *New Heaven, New Earth.* New York: Schocken Books.

Burton, John W. 1925. "Notes of J. W. Burton's New Britain Visit." Methodist Overseas Mission Papers, no. 330, Mitchell Library, Sydney.

———. 1929. "Notes of J.W. Burton's New Britain Visit." Methodist Overseas Mission Papers, no. 330, Mitchell Library, Sydney.

Calkowski, Marcia. 1991. "A Day at the Tibetan Opera: Actualized Performance and Spectacular Discourse." *American Ethnologist* 18:643–657.

Calvert, Lin. 1983. "A Renewal Movement in the United Church, Kapuna, Gulf Province." In *Religious Movements in Melanesia,* vol. 1. Wendy Flannery, ed., pp. 189–194. Goroka: Melanesian Institute.

Carrier, James. 1992. "Occidentalism." *American Ethnologist* 18:195–212.

Carrier, James, ed. 1992. *History, Tradition and Articulation in Melanesian Anthropology.* Berkeley: University of California Press.

Carrier, James, and Achsah Carrier. 1989. *Wage, Trade and Exchange in Melanesia.* Berkeley: University of California Press.

Chakrabarty, Dipesh. 1992. "The Death of History? Historical Consciousness and the Culture of Late Capitalism." *Public Culture* 4:47–65.

Christianson, L. 1979. *The Church Is Charismatic: The World Council of Churches and the Charismatic Revival.* Geneva: World Council of Churches.

Clay, Brenda. 1977. *Pinikindu.* Chicago: University of Chicago Press.

————. 1986. *Mandak Realities.* New Brunswick: Rutgers University Press.

Clifford, James, ed. 1988a. *The Predicament of Culture.* Cambridge: Harvard University Press.

————. 1988b. "Identity in Mashpee." In *The Predicament of Culture.* James Clifford, ed., pp. 277–346. Cambridge: Harvard University Press.

Clifford, James, and George Marcus, eds. 1986. *Writing Culture.* Berkeley: University of California Press.

Comaroff, Jean. 1985. *Body of Power, Spirit of Resistance.* Chicago: University of Chicago Press.

Comaroff Jean, and John Comaroff. 1991. *Of Revelation and Revolution.* Chicago: University of Chicago Press.

Comaroff, John. 1989. "Images of Empire, Contests of Conscience: Models of Colonial Domination in South Africa." *American Ethnologist* 16:661–685.

Comaroff, John, and Jean Comaroff. 1992. *Ethnography and the Historical Imagination.* Boulder: Westview Press.

"Confidential Report Submitted to the Methodist Board of Governors in Australia." Methodist Overseas Mission Papers, no. 194, Mitchell Library, Sydney.

Connolly, Bob, and Robin Anderson. 1987. *First Contact.* New York: Penguin.

————. 1988. *Joe Leahy's Neighbours.* Cambridge: Documentary Educational Resources.

————. 1991. *Black Harvest.* Santa Monica: Direct Cinema.

Cooper, Frederick, and Ann Stoler. 1989. "Tensions of Empire: Colonial Control and Visions of Rule." *American Ethnologist* 16:609–621.

Counts, David, and Dorothy Counts. 1970. "The Vula of Kaliai: A Primitive Currency with Commercial Use." *Oceania* 41:90–105.

————. 1992. "Exaggeration and Reversal: Clowning Among the Lusi-Kaliai." In *Clowning as Critical Practice.* William Mitchell, ed., pp. 88–103. Pittsburgh: Pittsburgh University Press.

Counts, Dorothy. 1971. "Cargo or Council." *Oceania* 41:288–297.

————. 1978. "Christianity in Kaliai: Response to Missionization in Northwest New Britain." In *Mission, Church and Sect in Oceania.* James Boutilier et al., ed., pp. 355–394. Ann Arbor: University of Michigan Press.

Cowlishaw, Gillian. 1988. *Black, White or Brindle: Race in Rural Australia.* Cambridge: Cambridge University Press.

Danks, Benjamin. 1888. "On the Shell Money of New Britain." *Journal of the Royal Anthropological Institute of Great Britain and Ireland* 17:305–317.

di Leonardo, Micaela. 1989. "Malinowski's Nephews." *Nation,* March 13: 350–352.

Dirks, Nicholas. 1992. "From Little King to Landlord: Colonial Discourse and Colonial Rule." In *Colonialism and Culture.* Nicholas Dirks, ed., pp. 175–208. Ann Arbor: University of Michigan Press.

Dominguez, Virginia. 1986. "The Marketing of Heritage." *American Ethnologist* 13:546–555.

———. 1990. "Representing Value and the Value of Representation: A Different Look at Money." *Cultural Anthropology* 5:16–44.

Douglas, Mary. 1967. "Primitive Rationing." In *Themes in Economic Anthropology.* Raymond Firth, ed., pp. 119–147. London: Tavistock.

Durkheim, Emile. 1964. *Rules of the Sociological Method.* New York: Free Press.

East New Britain Economic Newsletter. 1991a. Vol. 2, No. 1. Planning and Technical Services, Rabaul.

———. 1991b. Vol. 2, No. 2. Planning and Technical Services, Rabaul.

Einzig, Paul. 1949. *Primitive Money in Its Ethnological, Historical and Economic Aspects.* London: Eyre and Spottiswoode.

Epstein, A. L. 1963. "Tambu: A Primitive Shell Money." *Discovery* 24:28–32.

———. 1969. *Matupit.* Berkeley: University of California Press.

———. 1979. "Tambu: The Shell Money of the Tolai." In *Fantasy and Symbol.* R. H. Hook, ed., pp. 149–205. New York: Academic Press.

———. 1992. *In the Midst of Life.* Berkeley: University of California Press.

Epstein, T. S. 1968. *Capitalism, Primitive and Modern.* Canberra: Australian National University Press.

Errington, Frederick. 1974a. *Karavar.* Ithaca: Cornell University Press.

———. 1974b. "Indigenous Ideas of Order, Time and Transition in a New Guinea Cargo Movement." *American Ethnologist* 1:255–267.

———. 1987. "Reflexivity Deflected: The Festival of Nations as an American Cultural Performance." *American Ethnologist* 14:654–667.

———. 1990. "The Rock Creek Rodeo: Excess and Constraint in Men's Lives." *American Ethnologist* 17:628–645.

Errington, Frederick, and Deborah Gewertz. 1986. "The Confluence of Powers: Entropy and Importation Among the Chambri." *Oceania* 57:99–113.

———. 1987a. *Cultural Alternatives and a Feminist Anthropology.* Cambridge: Cambridge University Press.

———. 1987b. "Myths of Matriarchy Reexamined: The Ideological Components of Social Order." In *Myths of Matriarchy Reconsidered.* Deborah Gewertz, ed., pp. 195–212. Sydney: Oceania Publications.

———. 1989. "Tourism and Anthropology in a Post-Modern World." *Oceania* 60:37–54.

Eyre, Stephen. 1988. "Revival Christianity Among the Urat of Papua New Guinea: Some Possible Motivational and Perceptual Antecedents." Ph.D. diss., University of California, San Diego.

Fanon, Frantz. 1968a. *Black Skins, White Masks.* London: MacGibbon and Kee.

———. 1968b. *The Wretched of the Earth.* New York: Grove Press.

Feinberg, Richard. 1990. "The Solomon Islands' Tenth Anniversary of Independence: Problems of National Symbolism and National Integration." *Pacific Studies* 13:19–40.

Fischer, Michael. 1989. "Museums and Festivals; Notes on the Poetics and Politics of Representation Conference." *Cultural Anthropology* 4:204–221.

Foster, Robert. n.d. "Studying National Culture in Papua New Guinea." Unpublished manuscript.

———. 1987. "Komine and Tanga: A Note on Writing the History of German New Guinea." *Journal of Pacific History* 22:56–64.

———. 1988. "Social Reproduction and Value in a New Ireland Society." Unpublished Ph.D. diss., University of Chicago.

———. 1990. "Commoditization and the Emergence of Kastam as a Cultural Category." Unpublished manuscript.

———. 1991. "Making National Cultures in the Global Ecumene." *Annual Reviews in Anthropology* 20:235–260.

———. 1992. "Take Care of Public Telephones: Moral Education and Nation-State Formation in Papua New Guinea." *Public Culture* 4:31–45.

Foucault, Michel. 1979. *Discipline and Punish: The Birth of a Prison.* New York: Vintage.

———. 1982. "Afterword: The Subject and Power." In *Beyond Structuralism and Hermeneutics.* Hubert Dreyfus and Paul Rabinow, eds., pp. 208–226. Chicago: University of Chicago Press.

Geertz, Clifford. 1973. "Religion as a Cultural System." In *The Interpretation of Cultures.* Clifford Geertz, ed., pp. 87–125. New York: Basic Books.

Genovese, E. D. 1975. "Class, Culture and Historical Process." *Dialectical Anthropology* 1:71–79.

Gewertz, Deborah. 1983. *Sepik River Societies.* New Haven: Yale University Press.

Gewertz, Deborah, ed. 1988. *Myths of Matriarchy Reconsidered.* Sydney: Oceania Publications.

Gewertz, Deborah, and Frederick Errington. 1991. *Twisted Histories, Altered Contexts: Representing the Chambri in a World System.* Cambridge: Cambridge University Press.

———. 1992. "Review of Black Harvest." *American Anthropologist* 94:1026–1027.

Gewertz, Deborah, and Edward Schieffelin, eds. 1985. *History and Ethnohistory in New Guinea.* Sydney: Oceania Monographs.

Gordon, Robert. 1992. *The Bushman Myth.* Boulder: Westview Press.

Gramsci, Antonio. 1977. *Selections from the Prison Notebooks.* London: Lawrence and Wishart.

Gregory, Christopher. 1982. *Gifts and Commodities.* New York: Academic Press.

Grosart, Ian. 1982. "Nationalism and Micronationalism: The Tolai Case." In *Micronationalist Movements in Papua New Guinea.* Robert May, ed., pp. 139–175. Canberra: Australian National University.

Gwaltney, John. 1981. *Drylongso.* New York: Vintage.

Handelman, Don. 1990. *Models and Mirrors.* Cambridge: Cambridge University Press.

Handler, Richard. 1985. "'On Having a Culture." In *Objects and Others: Essays on Museums and Material Culture.* George Stocking, ed., pp. 192–217. Madison: University of Wisconsin Press.

_____. 1988. *Nationalism and the Politics of Culture in Quebec.* Madison: University of Wisconsin Press.

Hanson, Allan. 1989. "The Making of the Maori." *American Anthropologist* 91:890–902.

Harding, Susan. 1991. "Representing Fundamentalism: The Problem of the Repugnant Cultural Other." *Social Research* 58:273–293.

Hart, Keith. 1986. "Heads or Tails? Two Sides of the Coin." *Man* 21:637–656.

Hillerman, Tony. 1989. *Talking God.* New York: Harper and Row.

Hirsch, Eric. 1990. "From Bones to Betelnuts: Processes of Ritual Transformation and the Development of National Culture in Papua New Guinea." *Man* 25:18–34.

Hobsbawm, Eric, and Terence Ranger, eds. 1983. *The Invention of Tradition.* Cambridge: Cambridge University Press.

Hollenweger, W. J. 1972. *The Pentecostals.* Minneapolis: Augsburg Publishing House.

Hooper, Anthony, et al., eds. 1987. *Class and Culture in the South Pacific.* Auckland and Suva: Center for Pacific Studies and Institute of Pacific Studies.

Hvalkof, Soren, and Peter Aaby, eds. 1981. *Is God an American?* London: Survival International.

Jameson, Fredric. 1981. *The Political Unconscious: Narrative as a Socially Symbolic Act.* Ithaca: Cornell University Press.

Jenkin, N. J., and Burton, J. W. 1925. "Report of the Delegation to the New Britian District." Methodist overseas Mission Papers, no. 194, Mitchell Library, Sydney.

Kapferer, Bruce. 1983. *A Celebration of Demons.* Bloomington: Indiana University Press.

_____. 1988. *Legends of People, Myths of State.* Washington, D.C.: Smithsonian.

_____. 1989. "Nationalist Ideology and a Comparative Ideology." *Ethnos* 54:161–199.

Kaplan, Martha. 1990. "Meaning, Agency and Colonial History." *American Ethnologist* 17:3–22.

Kaplan, Susan. 1976. "Ethnological and Biogeographical Significance of Pottery Sherds from Nissan Island." *Fieldiana* 66:35–89.

Karp, Ivan, and Steven Lavine. 1991. *Exhibiting Cultures.* Washington, D.C.: Smithsonian.

Keesing, Roger. 1989. "Creating the Past: Custom and Identity in the Pacific." *Contemporary Pacific* 1:19–42.

Keesing, Roger, and Robert Tonkinson, eds. 1982. "Reinventing Traditional Culture." *Mankind,* Special Issue 13.

Kelly, John. 1992. "Fiji Indians and 'Commoditization of Labor.'" *American Ethnologist* 19:97–120.

Kirkpatrick, John. 1983. *The Marquesan Notion of the Person*. Ann Arbor: University of Michigan Research Press.

Kokopo Patrol Reports no. 6, 1956–1957; no. 3, 1968–1969.

Kopytoff, Igor. 1986. "The Cultural Biography of Things." In *In the Social Life of Things*. Arjun Appadurai, ed., pp. 64–94. Cambridge: Cambridge University Press.

Kulick, Don, and Margaret Willson. 1992. "Echoing Images: The Construction of Savagery Among Papua New Guinean Villagers." *Visual Anthropology* 5:143–152.

Larmour, Peter. 1992. "The Politics of Race and Ethnicity: Theoretical Perspectives on Papua New Guinea." *Pacific Studies* 15:87–108.

Lass, Andrew. 1988. "Romantic Documents and Political Monuments: The Meaning-Fulfillment of History in Nineteenth Century Czech Nationalism." *American Ethnologist* 15:456–471.

Lattas, Andrew. 1991. "Sexuality and Cargo Cults: The Politics of Gender and Procreation in West New Britain." *Cultural Anthropology* 6:230–256.

———. 1992. "Skin, Personhood and Redemption: The Doubled Self in West New Britain Cargo Cults." *Oceania* 63:27–54.

Lawrence, Peter. 1964. *Road Belong Cargo*. Melbourne: Melbourne University Press.

Leavitt, Stephen. 1989. "Cargo, Christ and Nostalgia for the Dead: Themes of Intimacy and Abandonment in Bumbita Arapesh Social Experience." Ph.D. diss., University of California, San Diego.

Leenhardt, Maurice. 1979. *Do Kamo: Person and Myth in the Melanesian World*. Chicago: University of Chicago Press.

Lévi-Strauss, Claude. 1963. *Totemism*. Boston: Beacon Press.

———. 1969. *The Raw and the Cooked*. New York: Harper and Row.

Lindstrom, Lamont. 1990. *Knowledge and Power in a South Pacific Society*. Washington, D.C.: Smithsonian.

———. 1993. *Cargo Cult! Strange Stories of Desire from New Guinea and Beyond*. Honolulu: University of Hawaii Press.

Linnekin, Joceyln. 1983. "Defining Tradition: Variations on the Hawaiian Identity." *American Ethnologist* 10:241–252.

———. 1990. "The Politics of Culture in the Pacific." In *Cultural Identity and Ethnicity in the Pacific*. Jocelyn Linnekin and Linette Poyer, eds., pp. 149–173. Honolulu: University of Hawaii Press.

Linnekin, Joceyln, and Linnette Poyer, eds. 1990. *Cultural Identity and Ethnicity in the Pacific*. Honolulu: University of Hawaii Press.

LiPuma, Edward, and Sara Meltzoff. 1990. "Ceremonies of Independence and Public Culture in the Solomon Islands." *Public Culture* 3:77–92.

Macfarlane, Alan. 1985. "The Root of All Evil." In *In the Anthropology of Evil*. David Parkin, ed., pp. 57–76. Oxford: Basil Blackwell.

Malinowski, Bronislaw. 1921. "The Primitive Economics of the Trobriand Islands." *Economic Journal* 31:1–16.

————. 1926. "Myth in Primitive Psychology." In *Magic, Science and Religion.* Bronislaw Malinowski, ed., pp. 93–148. New York: Anchor Books.

————. 1954. "Magic, Science and Religion." In *Magic Science and Religion.* B. Malinowski, ed., pp. 17–92. Garden City, N.Y.: Doubleday-Anchor.

Mangi, Jo. 1989. "The Role of Archaeology in Nation Building." In *Conflict in the Archaeology of Living Traditions.* R. Layton, ed., pp. 217–227. London: Unwin Hyman.

McBryde, I., ed. 1985. *Who Owns the Past?* Oxford: Oxford University Press.

McDowell, Nancy. 1985. "Past and Future: The Mature of Episodic Time in Bun." In *History and Ethnohistory in New Guinea.* Deborah Gewertz and Edward Schieffelin, eds., pp. 26–39. Sydney: Oceania Monographs.

————. 1988. "A Note on Cargo Cults and the Cultural Construction of Change." *Pacific Studies* 11:121–134.

Meggitt, Mervyn. 1991. "The Ambiguities of Advocacy: Fieldwork in the New Guinea Highlands." In *Man and a Half: Essays in Anthropology and Ethnobiology in Honour of Ralph Bulmer.* Andrew Pawley, ed., pp. 593–599. Auckland: Polynesian Society.

Memmi, Albert. 1965. *The Colonizer and the Colonized.* Boston: Beacon.

"Minutes of the New Britain District Synod." 1923. Methodist Overseas Mission Papers, no. 191, Mitchell Library, Sydney.

Mitchell, Timothy. 1990. "Everyday Metaphors as Power." *Theory and Society* 19: 545–577.

Mitchell, William. 1992. "Introduction: Mother Folly in the Islands." In *Clowning as Critical Practice.* William Mitchell, ed., pp. 31–57. Pittsburgh: University of Pittsburgh Press.

Molot Patrol Report no. 1, 1971–1972.

Morphy, Howard. 1983. "'Now You Understand'—An Analysis of the Way Yolngu Have Used Sacred Knowledge to Retain Their Autonomy." In *Aborigines, Land and Land Rights.* N. Peterson and M. Langton, eds., pp. 110–133. Canberra: Institute of Aboriginal Studies.

Mosko, Mark. 1992. "Clowning with Food: Mortuary Humor and Social Reproduction Among the North Mekeo." In *Clowning as Critical Practice.* William Mitchell, ed., pp. 104–129. Pittsburgh: Pittsburgh University Press.

————. 1993. "Other Messages, Other Missions; Or, Sahlins Among the Melanesians." *Oceania* 63:97–113.

Mouton, Jean Baptiste Octave. 1936. Personal and Business Papers. Pacific Manuscripts Bureau, no. 603, Canberra, Australia.

Munn, Nancy. 1986. *The Fame of the Gawa.* Cambridge: Cambridge University Press.

Myers, Fred. 1988. "Locating Ethnographic Practice: Romance, Reality and Politics in the Outback." *American Ethnologist* 15:609–624.

————. 1991. "Representing Culture: The Production of Discourse(s) for Aboriginal Acrylic Paintings." *Cultural Anthropology* 6:26–62.

Nadel-Klein, Jane. 1991a. "Picturing Aborigines: A Review Essay on *After Two Hundred Years.*" *Cultural Anthropology* 6:414–423.

————. 1991b. "Reweaving the Fringe: Localism, Tradition and Representation in British Ethnography." *American Ethnologist* 18:500–517.

Namunu, Simeon. 1983. "Charismatic Renewal on the Gazelle Peninsula." In *Religious Movements in Melanesia Today,* vol. 2. Wendy Flannery, ed., pp. 54–71. Goroka: Melanesian Institute.

Nelson, Hank. 1982. *Taim Bilong Masta.* Sydney: Australian Broadcasting Commission.

Neumann, Klaus. 1989. "Not the Way it Really Was." *Journal of Pacific History* 22: 209–220.

————. 1992. *Not the Way It Really Was.* Honolulu: University of Hawaii Press.

Obeyesekere, Gananath. 1992. *The Apotheosis of Captain Cook.* Princeton: Princeton University Press.

Ohnuki-Tierney, Emiko. 1990. "The Ambivalent Self of the Contemporary Japanese." *Cultural Anthropology* 5:197–216.

O'Rourke, Dennis. 1987. *Cannibal Tours.* Santa Monica: Direct Cinema.

Ortner, Sherry. 1984. "Theory in Anthropology Since the Sixties." *Comparative Studies in Society and History* 26:126–166.

Packard, Randall. 1989. "The 'Healthy Reserve' and the 'Dressed Native': Discourses on Black Health and the Language of Legitimation in South Africa." *American Ethnologist* 16:686–703.

Parry, Jonathan. 1989. "On the Moral Perils of Exchange." In *In Money and the Morality of Exchange.* Jonathan Parry and Maurice Bloch, eds., pp. 64–93. Cambridge: Cambridge University Press.

Ploeg, Anton. 1991. "Citizenship in Papua New Guinea." In *Man and a Half: Essays in Anthropology and Ethnobiology in Honour of Ralph Bulmer.* Andrew Pawley, ed., pp. 606–612. Auckland: Polynesian Society.

Pomponio, Alice. 1992. *Seagulls Don't Fly into the Bush: Cultural Identity and Development in Melanesia.* Belmont, Calif.: Wadsworth.

Post Courier. 1991. "Cultural Shipment Confiscated." October 17:3.

Rabaul Patrol Report (RPR) no. 2, 1950–1951.

Rabaul Times. 1925a. "The Educated Native." May 15:n.p.

————. 1925b. "Letter to the Editor: Corporal Punishment." August 7:n.p.

————. 1935. "Welcome, 'Oronsay.'" August 8:n.p.

————. 1941a. "Where the Cultures Meet." August 8:n.p.

————. 1941b. Advertisement for the Commonwealth Savings Bank. March 28:n.p.

————. 1957. "Native Clients Attend Bank Opening." March 29:n.p.

Raymond, Chris. 1989. "Some Scholars Upset by Stanford's Decision to Return

American Indian Remains for Re-Burial by Tribe." *Chronicle of Higher Education,* July 5:A5, 7.

———. 1990. "Dispute Between Scholar, Tribe Leaders over Book on Hopi Ritual Raises concerns About Censorship of Studies of American Indians." *Chronicle of Higher Education,* October 17:A6, 8–9.

Read, Kenneth. 1955. "Morality and the Concept of the Person Among the Gahuku-Gama." *Oceania* 25:233–282.

Rebel, Henry. 1989. "Cultural Hegemony and Class Experience." *American Ethnologist* 16:117–136.

Rickard, R. H. 1882. Letter Books. Mitchell Library, Sydney.

Roheim, Geza. 1923. "Heiliges Geld in Melanesien." *Internationale Zeitschrift für Psychoanalyse* 9:384–401.

Rooney, Isaac. 1888. The Letter Books and Journal of the Reverend Isaac Rooney. Mitchell Library, Sydney.

Roseberry, William. 1992. "Multiculturalism and the Challenge of Anthropology." *Social Research* 59:841–858.

Rosi, Pamela. 1991. "Papua New Guinea's Parliament House: A Contested National Symbol." *Contemporary Pacific* 3:289–324.

Rostow, W. W. 1971. *The Stages of Economic Growth.* Cambridge: Cambridge University Press.

Rubel, Paula, and Abraham Rosman. n.d. "Aliens on Our Shores: A History of New Ireland-European Contact." Unpublished Manuscript.

Ryan, Dawn. 1969. "Christianity, Cargo Cults and Politics Among the Toaripi of Papua." *Oceania* 40:99–118.

Sack, Peter. 1985. "'Bobotoi' and 'Pulu'— Melanesian Law: Normative Order or Way of Life?" *Journal de la Societe des Oceanistes* 41:15–23.

Sack, Peter, and Dymphna Clark. 1979. *German New Guinea: The Annual Reports.* Canberra: Australian National University Press.

Sahlins, Marshall. 1981. *Historical Metaphors and Mythical Realities.* Ann Arbor: University of Michigan Press.

———. 1985. *Islands of History.* Chicago: University of Chicago Press.

———. 1991. "The Return of the Event, Again." In *Clio in Oceania.* Aletta Biersack, ed., pp. 37–100. Washington, D.C.: Smithsonian.

Said, Edward. 1978. *Orientalism.* New York: Pantheon.

Salisbury, Richard. n.d. "DukDuks, Dualism and Descent Groups." Unpublished Manuscript.

———. 1966. "Politics and Shell-Money Finance in New Britain." In *Political Anthropology.* Marc Swartz, Victor Turner, and Arthur Tuden, eds., pp. 114–128. Chicago: Aldine.

———. 1970. *Vunamami.* Berkeley: University of California Press.

Schieffelin, Edward. 1981. "Evangelical Rhetoric and the Transformation of Traditional Culture in Papua New Guinea." *Comparative Studies in Society and History* 23:150–156.

———. 1985. "Performance and the Cultural Construction of Reality." *American Ethnologist* 12:707–724.

Schieffelin, Edward, and Robert Crittenden. 1991. *Like People You See in a Dream.* Stanford: Stanford University Press.

Schneider, Oskar. 1905. *Muschelgeld-Studien.* Dresden: Ernst Engelmann's Nachfg.

Schwartz, Theodore. 1962. The Paliau Movement in the Admiralty Islands. New York: American Museum of Natural History.

Scott, James. 1985. *Weapons of the Weak.* New Haven: Yale University Press.

Seneka, Konio. 1991. "The Cost of Urban Drift." *Times of Papua New Guinea,* July 4: 12.

Seremetakis, C. Nadia. 1991. *The Last Word.* Chicago: University of Chicago Press.

Shore, Bradd. 1982. *Sala'ilua: A Samoan Mystery.* New York: Columbia University Press.

Shweder, R. A., and Bourne, E. J. 1984. "Does the Concept of the Person Vary Cross-Culturally?" In *Culture Theory: Essays on Mind, Self and Emotion.* R. A. Shweder and R. A. Levine eds., pp. 158–199. Cambridge: Cambridge University Press.

Sider, Gerald. 1986. *Culture and Class in Anthropology and History.* Cambridge: Cambridge University Press.

———. 1987. "Why Parrots Learn to Talk and Why They Can't: Domination, Deception and Self-Deception in Indian-White Relations." *Comparative Studies in Society and History* 29:3–23.

Silverman, Martin. 1977. "Making Sense: A Study of a Banaban Meeting." In *Symbolic Anthropology.* Janet Dolgin et al., eds., pp. 451–479. New York: Columbia University Press.

Simet, Jacob. 1976. "From a Letter by Jacob Simet." *Gigibori* 3:1–2.

———. 1992. "Tabu." Unpublished Ph.D. diss., Australian National University.

Souter, Gavin. 1963. *New Guinea: The Last Unknown.* Sydney: Angus and Robertson.

South Pacific Post. 1968. "Villagers Are Hostile Say 2 Americans." January 12:4.

Stoler, Ann. 1989. "Making Empire Respectable: The Politics of Race and Sexual Morality in Twentieth Century Colonial Cultures." *American Ethnologist* 16:634–660.

Strathern, Marilyn. 1980. "No Nature, No Culture: The Hagen Case." In *Nature, Culture and Gender.* Carol MacCormack and Marilyn Strathern, eds., pp. 174–219. Cambridge: Cambridge University Press.

———. 1988. *The Gender of the Gift.* Berkeley: University of California Press.

———. 1992. "The Decomposition of an Event." *Cultural Anthropology* 7:244–254.

Taruna, Joseph. 1983. "Revival in the Kieta Circuit of the United Church, North Solomons Region." In *Religious Movements in Melanesia,* vol. 1. Wendy Flannery, ed., pp. 175–188. Goroka: Melanesian Institute.

Taussig, Michael. 1987. *Shamanism, Colonialism and the Wild Man.* Chicago: University of Chicago Press.

Terrell, John. 1991. "Disneyland and the Future of Museum Anthropology." *American Anthropologist* 93:149–152.

Thomas, Nicholas. 1989. "The Force of Ethnology." *Current Anthropology* 30:27–41.

———. 1990. "Sanitation and Seeing: The Creation of State Power in Early Colonial Fiji." *Comparative Studies in Society and History* 32:149–170.

———. 1991. *Entangled Objects.* Cambridge: Harvard University Press.

———. 1992a. "Colonial Conversions: Difference, Hierarchy and History in Early Twentieth Century Evangelical Propaganda." *Comparative Studies in Society and History* 34:366–389.

———. 1992b. "Substantivization and Anthropological Discourse." In *History and Tradition in Melanesian Anthropology.* James Carrier, ed., pp. 1–19. Berkeley: University of California Press.

Threlfall, Neville. 1975. *One Hundred Years in the Islands.* Rabaul, Papua New Guinea: United Church, New Guinea Islands Region.

Times of Papua New Guinea. 1992a. "Youth Times." July 2:17.

———. 1992b. "The Times Opinion." July 9:7.

———. 1992c. Advertisement for PNG Chamber of Mines and Petroleum. July 9:7.

———. 1993. "The Times Review of the Week." July 15:9.

Trigger, David. 1992. *Whitefella Comin'.* Cambridge: Cambridge University Press.

Tuzin, Donald. 1989. "Visions, Prophesies and the Rise of Christian Consciousness." In *The Religious Imagination in New Guinea.* Gilbert Herdt and Michelle Stephen, eds., pp. 187–208. New Brunswick: Rutgers University Press.

Uys, Jamie. 1980. *The Gods Must Be Crazy.* Botswana: C.A.T. Films.

Varenne, Hervé. 1977. *Americans Together.* New York: Teachers College Press.

Wagner, Roy. 1986. *Asiwinarong.* Princeton: Princeton University Press.

Wals, P. 1961. *Confidential Report on the Account Movement.* Rabaul: District Headquarters.

Weber, Max. 1949. *The Methodology of the Social Sciences.* New York: Free Press.

Weston, Kath. 1991. *Families We Choose.* New York: Columbia University Press.

What Is Wealth. n.d. Reserve Bank of Australia.

Whisnant, David. 1983. *All That Is Native and Fine.* Chapel Hill: University of North Carolina Press.

White, Geoffrey. 1991. *Identity Through History.* Cambridge: Cambridge University Press.

White, Geoffrey, and John Kirkpatrick, eds. 1985. *Person, Self and Experience: Exploring Pacific Ethnopsychologies.* Berkeley: University of California Press.

Wilford, John. 1990. "Anthropology Seen as Father of Maori Lore." *New York Times,* February 20:C1, 12.

World Bank. n.d. *Prices.* International Economics Department.

Worsley, Peter. 1968. *The Trumpet Shall Sound.* New York: Schocken.

Young, Michael. 1977. "Doctor Bromilow and the Bwaidoka Wars." *Journal of Pacific History* 12:130–153.

––––––. 1983. *Magicians of Manumanua.* Berkeley: University of California Press.

Your Money. n.d. Reserve Bank of Australia.

About the Book and Authors

This remarkable book explores questions of identity and value posed by people living on (or near) the small Pacific island of Karavar in Papua New Guinea. The complex social and cultural changes that occurred during the century after Europeans first arrived in the area have led Karavarans to wonder about—and to assert—who they are and who they might become as citizens of a developing country that is striving to create national coherence across some seven hundred linguistic and cultural groups.

Focusing on how the Karavarans' long-term preoccupation with identity and worth has played out in various social contexts, Errington and Gewertz convey a grounded sense of how these people have actually lived and dealt with such widely significant issues as ethnic diversity and the development of national unity. The authors present a historical and ethnographic analysis that, in its scope and mastery of detail, does justice to the complexity and significance of change in a colonial and postcolonial world.

Errington and Gewertz's discussions convey a perspective that simultaneously makes both "other" and "ourselves" more understandable and readily comparable as culturally constructed, historically contingent, and mutually determinative. This book will be of interest to anthropologists, sociologists, Oceanists, and all scholars concerned with questions of national identity.

Frederick K. Errington is Charles A. Dana Professor of Anthropology at Trinity College. **Deborah B. Gewertz** is G. Henry Whitcomb Professor of Anthropology at Amherst College.

Index